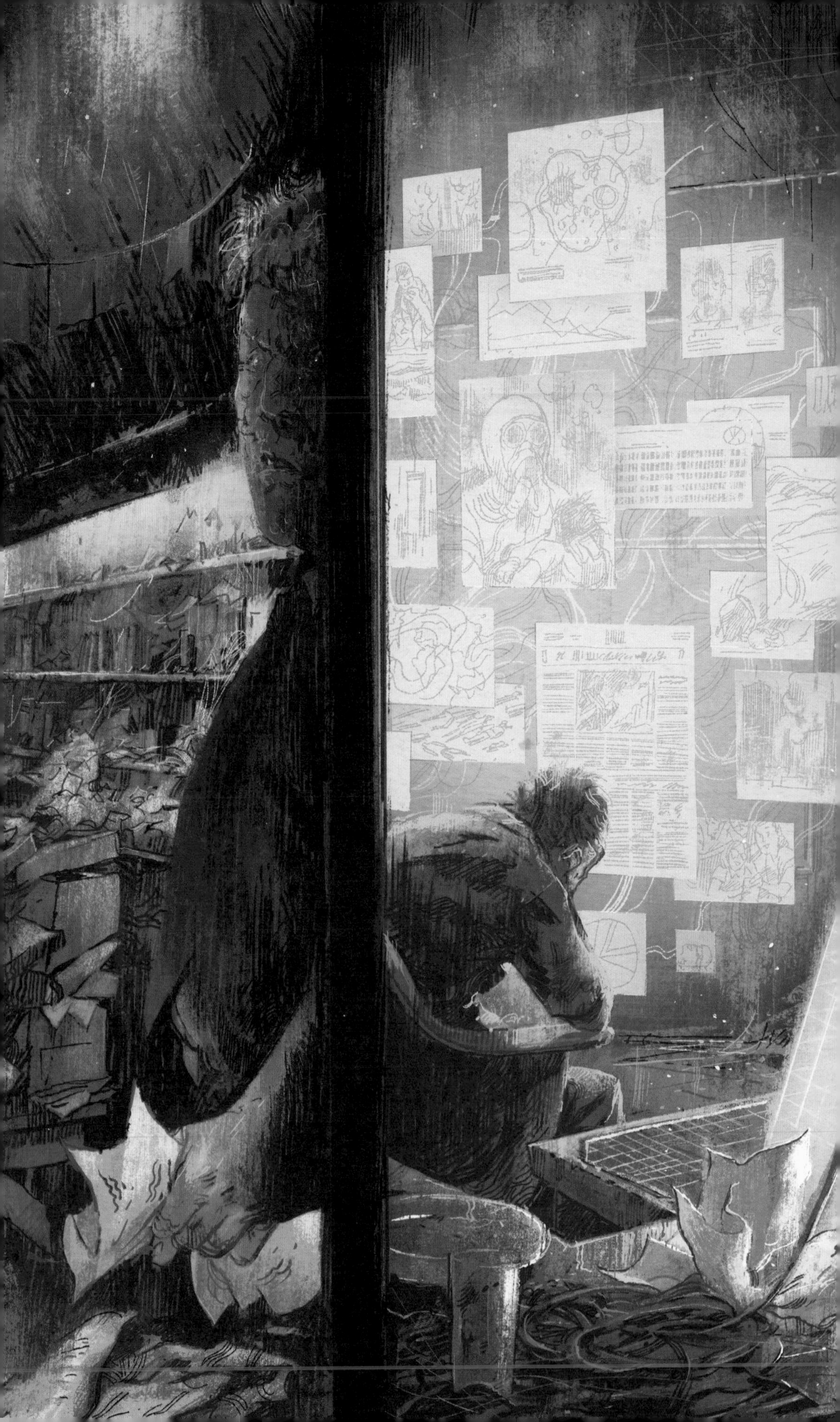

THE BUNKER

VOLUME 2

Written by
Joshua Hale Fialkov

Illustrated, Colored, and Lettered by
Joe Infurnari

Flatted by
Jason Fischer

Edited by
James Lucas Jones and Robin Herrera

Designed by
Jason Storey

PUBLISHED BY ONI PRESS, INC.

Publisher, Joe Nozemack
Editor In Chief, James Lucas Jones
VP of Business Development, Tim Wiesch
Director of Sales, Cheyenne Allott
Director of Publicity, Fred Reckling
Production Manager, Troy Look
Graphic Designer, Hilary Thompson
Production Assistant, Jared Jones
Senior Editor, Charlie Chu
Editor, Robin Herrera
Associate Editor, Ari Yarwood
Inventory Coordinator, Brad Rooks
Office Assistant, Jung Lee

VOLUME 2

**This volume collects issues 5-9 of the
Oni Press series *The Bunker***

ONIPRESS.COM
FACEBOOK.COM/ONIPRESS • TWITTER.COM/ONIPRESS
ONIPRESS.TUMBLR.COM • INSTAGRAM.COM/ONIPRESS
THEFIALKOV.COM/@JOSHFIALKOV • JOEINFURNARI.COM/@INFURNARI

FIRST EDITION: LIBRARY OF CONGRESS CONTROL NUMBER: ISBN 978-1-62010-210-7
APRIL 2015   2014953741   eISBN 978-1-62010-211-4

10 8 6 4 2 1 3 5 7 9

PRINTED IN CHINA

CHAPTER
05

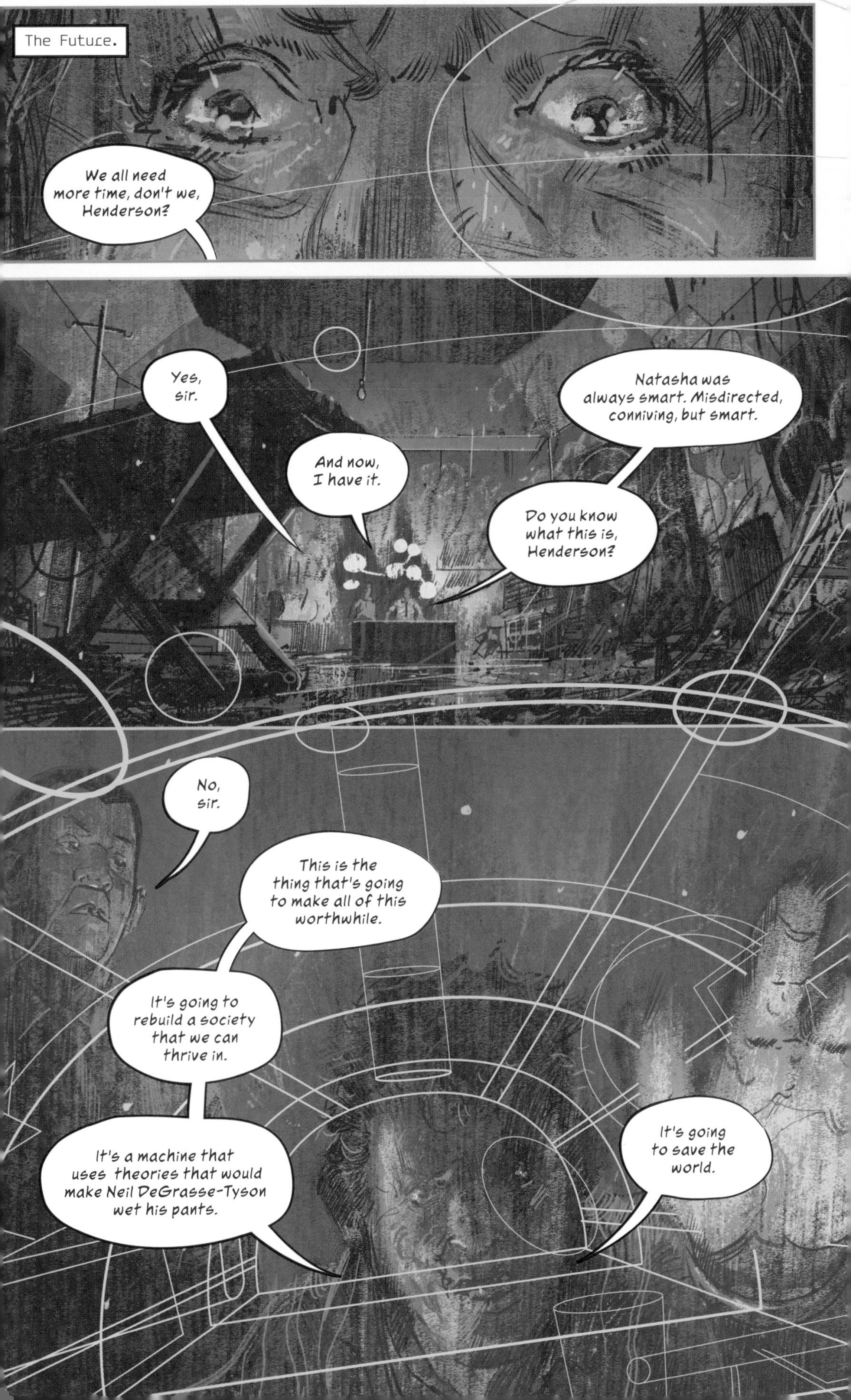
The Future.
We all need more time, don't we, Henderson?
Yes, sir.
Natasha was always smart. Misdirected, conniving, but smart.
And now, I have it.
Do you know what this is, Henderson?
No, sir.
This is the thing that's going to make all of this worthwhile.
It's going to rebuild a society that we can thrive in.
It's a machine that uses theories that would make Neil DeGrasse-Tyson wet his pants.
It's going to save the world.

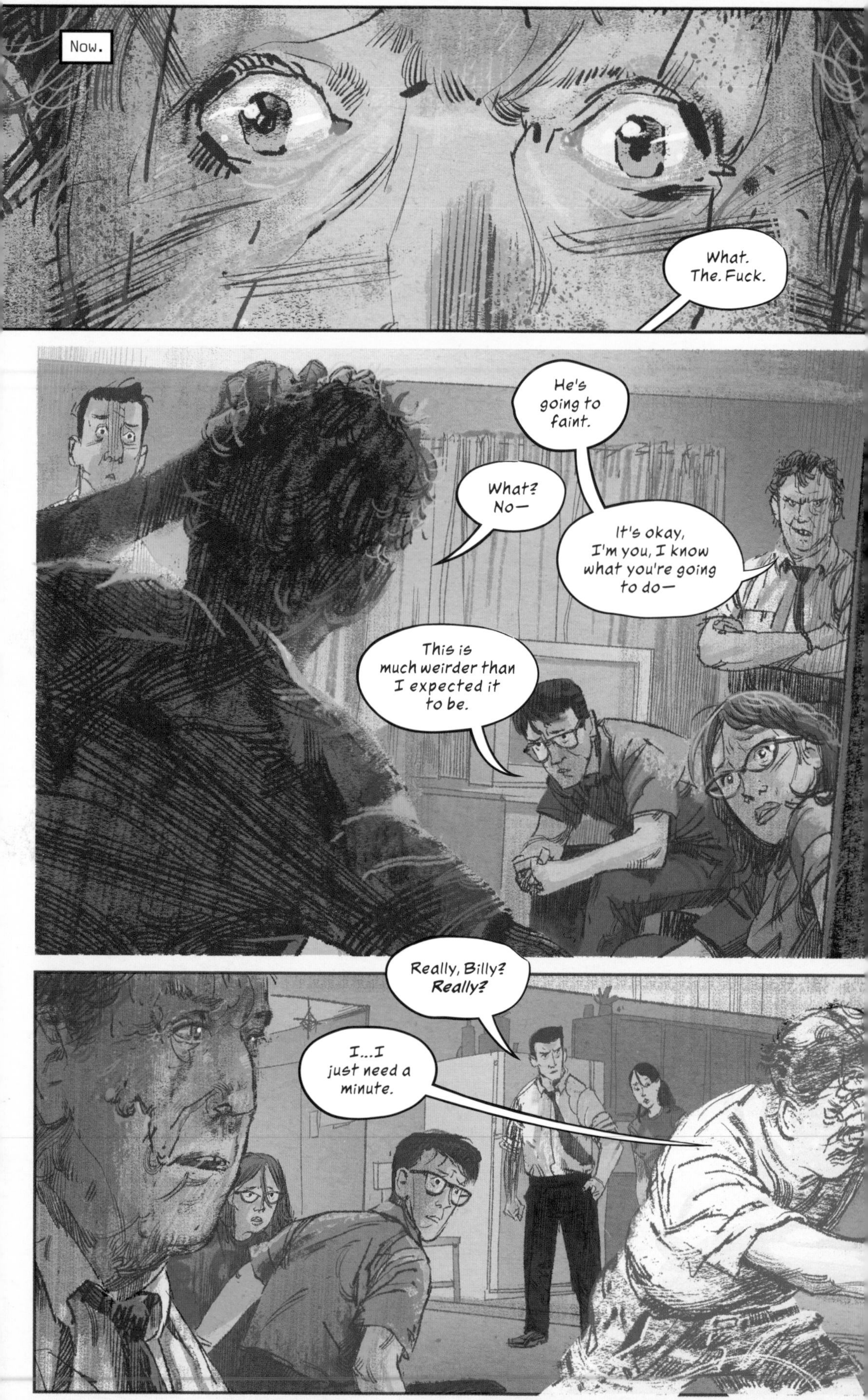
Now.
What. The. Fuck.
He's going to faint.
What? No—
It's okay, I'm you, I know what you're going to do—
This is much weirder than I expected it to be.
Really, Billy? *Really?*
I... I just need a minute.

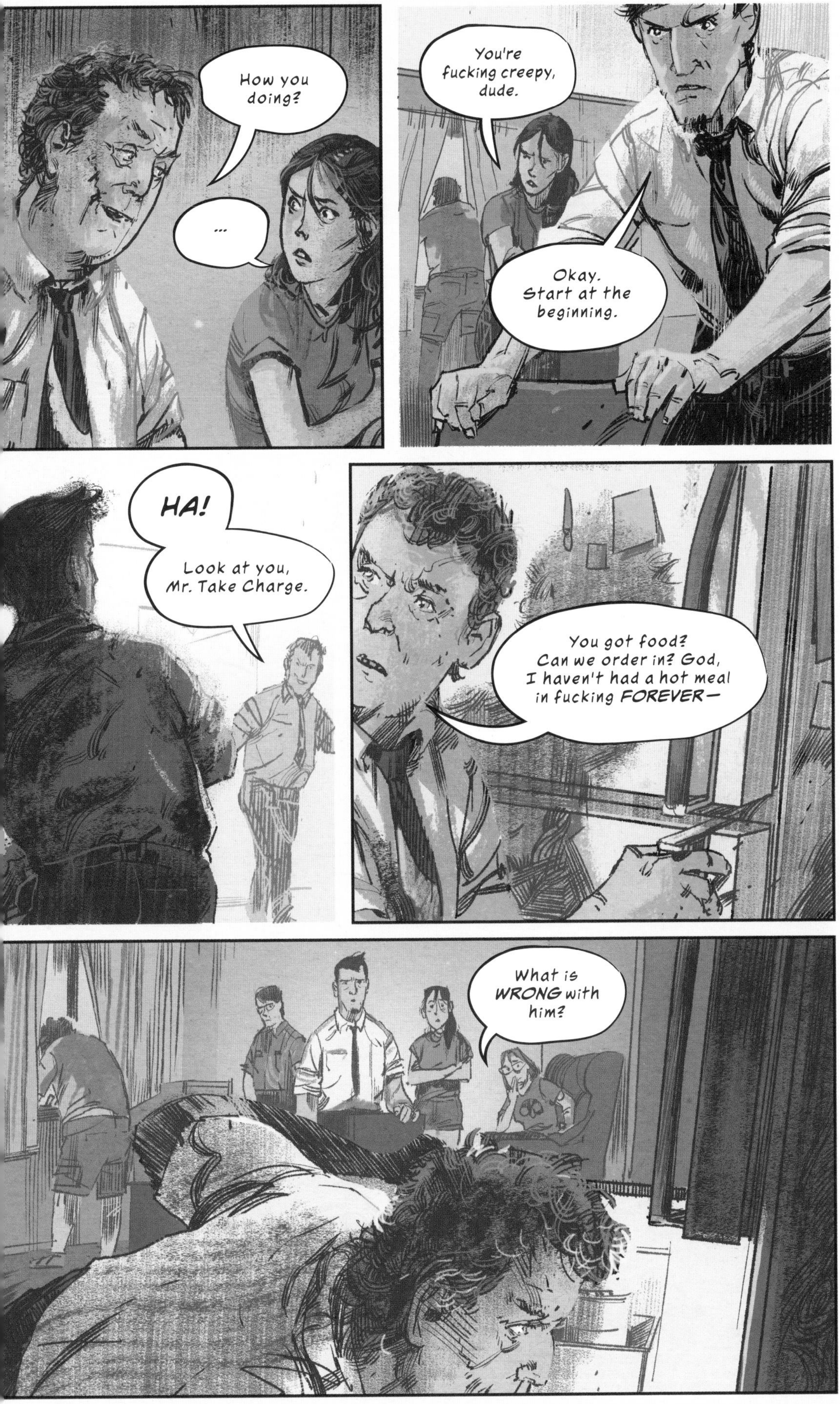
How you doing?
...
You're fucking creepy, dude.
Okay. Start at the beginning.
HA!
Look at you, Mr. Take Charge.
You got food? Can we order in? God, I haven't had a hot meal in fucking FOREVER—
What is WRONG with him?

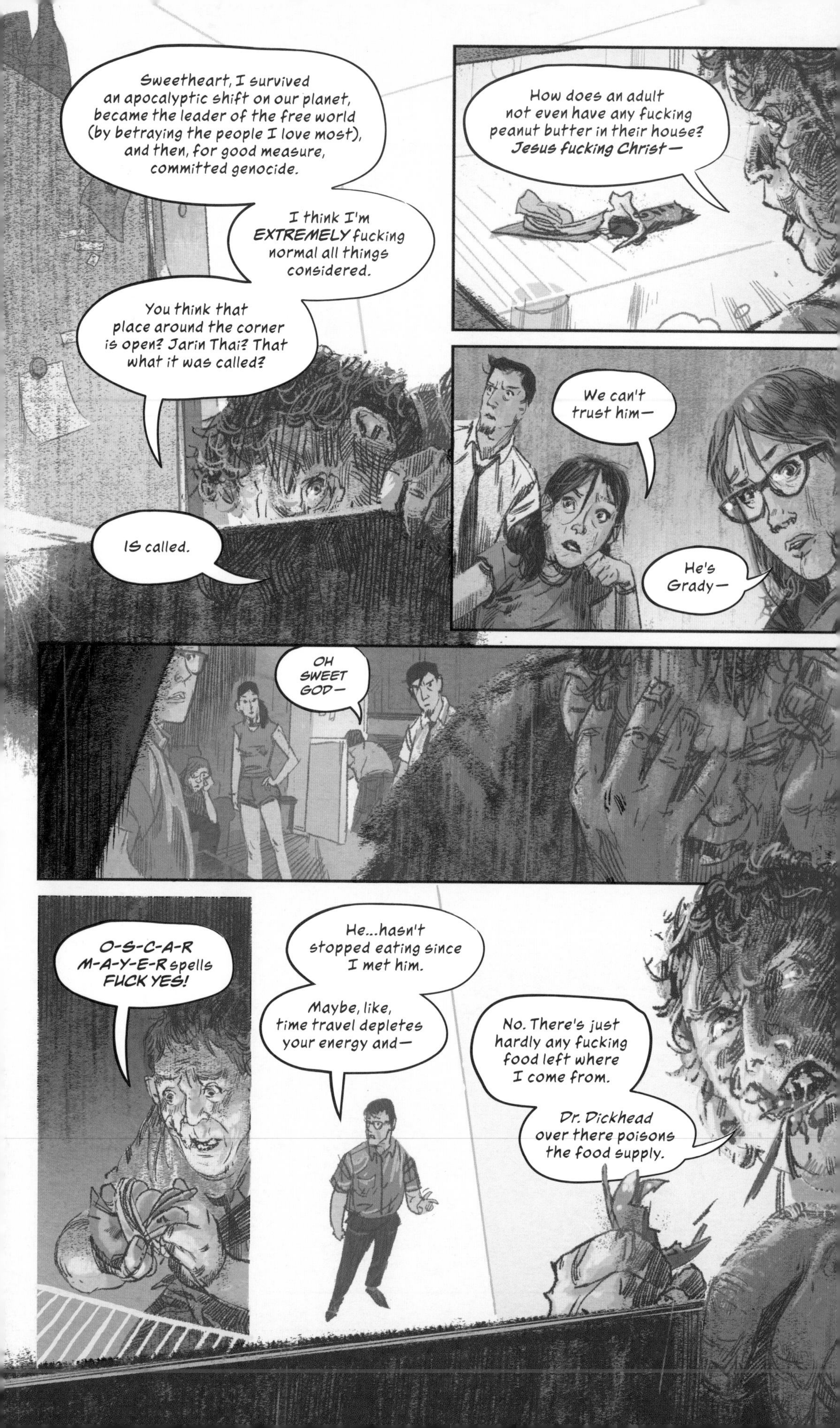
Sweetheart, I survived an apocalyptic shift on our planet, became the leader of the free world (by betraying the people I love most), and then, for good measure, committed genocide.
I think I'm EXTREMELY fucking normal all things considered.
How does an adult not even have any fucking peanut butter in their house? Jesus fucking Christ—
You think that place around the corner is open? Jarin Thai? That what it was called?
IS called.
We can't trust him—
He's Grady—
OH SWEET GOD—
O-S-C-A-R M-A-Y-E-R spells FUCK YES!
He...hasn't stopped eating since I met him.
Maybe, like, time travel depletes your energy and—
No. There's just hardly any fucking food left where I come from.
Dr. Dickhead over there poisons the food supply.

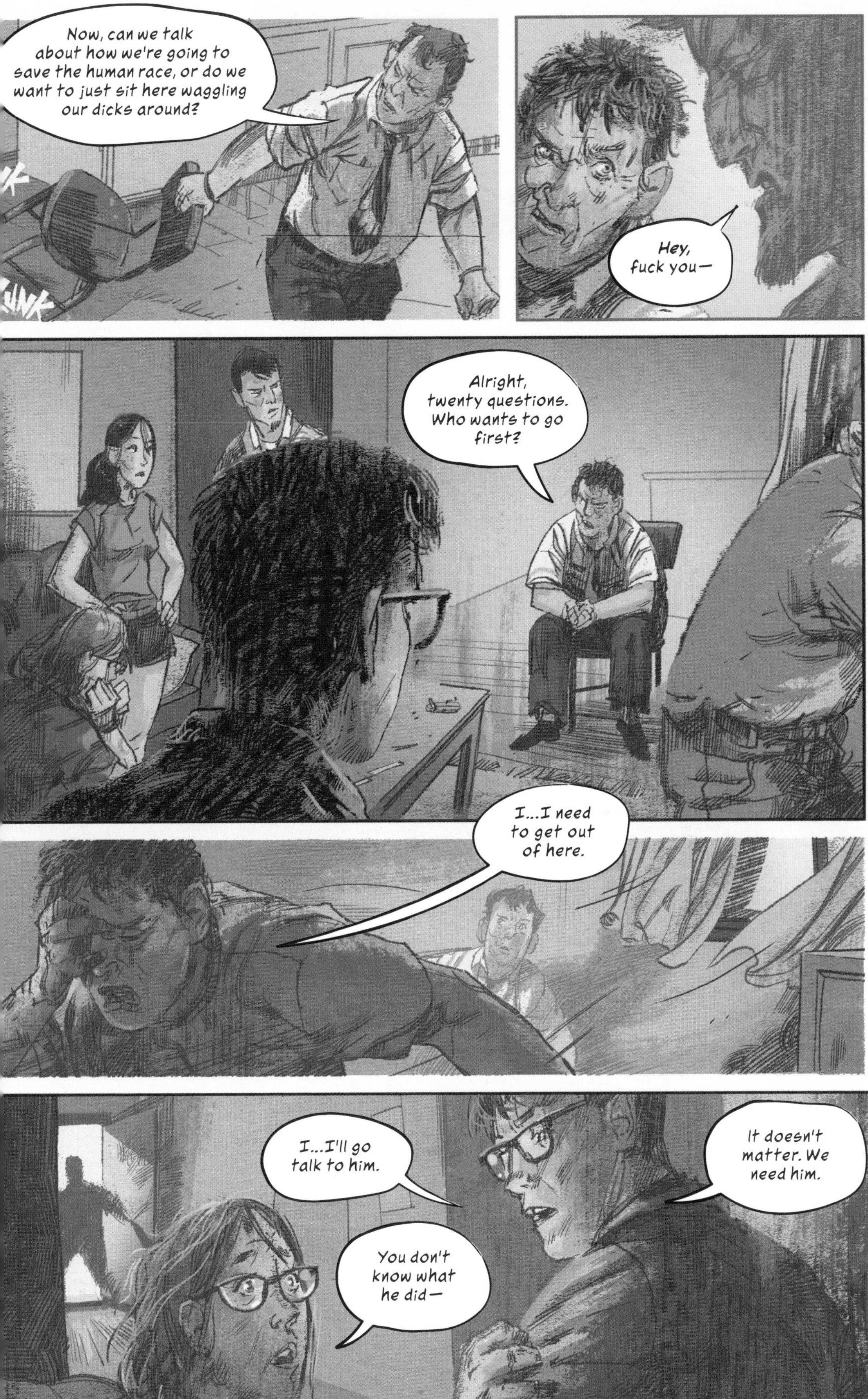
Now, can we talk about how we're going to save the human race, or do we want to just sit here waggling our dicks around?
Hey, fuck you—
Alright, twenty questions. Who wants to go first?
I...I need to get out of here.
I...I'll go talk to him.
You don't know what he did—
It doesn't matter. We need him.

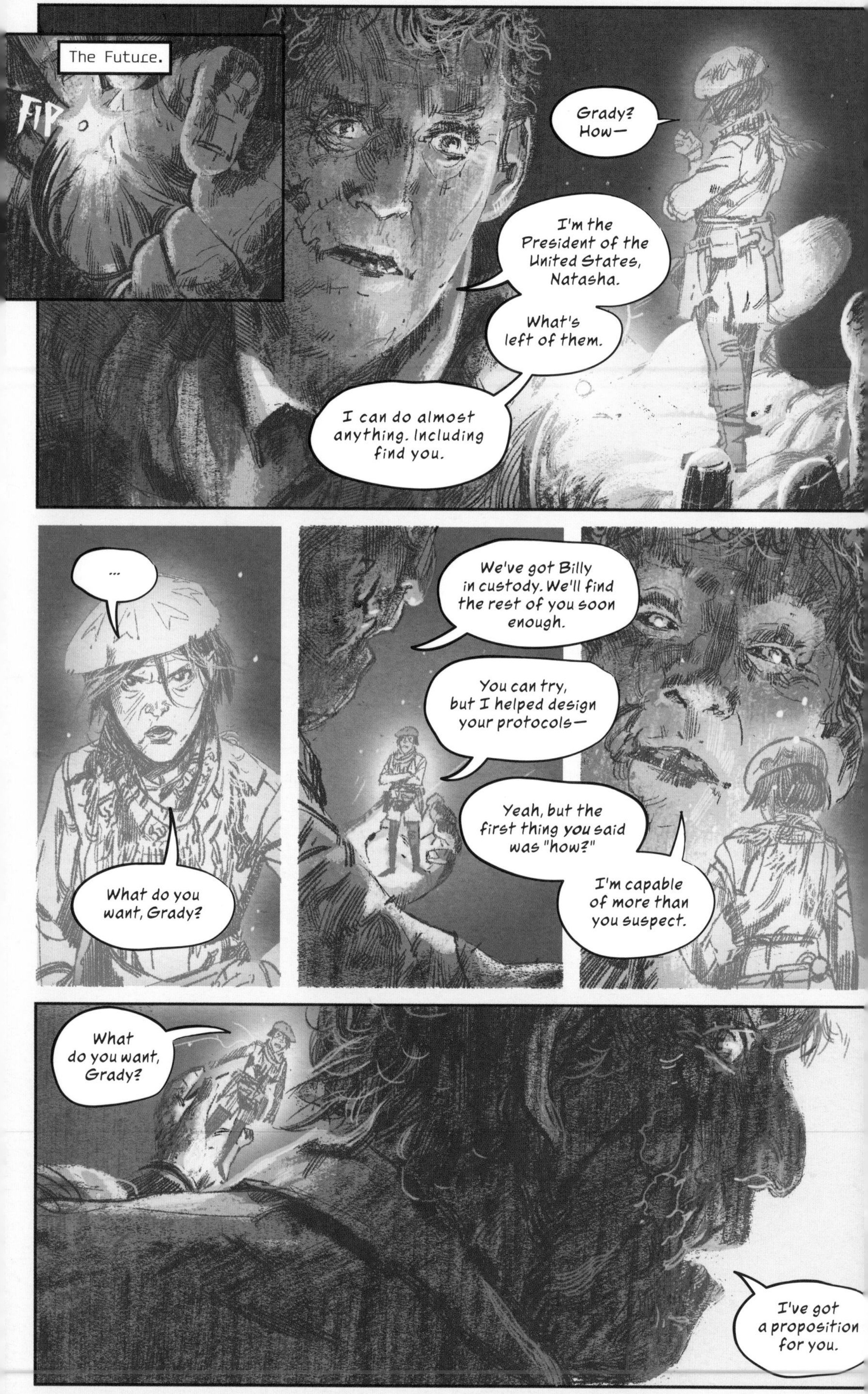
The Future.
FIP
Grady? How—
I'm the President of the United States, Natasha.
What's left of them.
I can do almost anything. Including find you.
...
What do you want, Grady?
We've got Billy in custody. We'll find the rest of you soon enough.
You can try, but I helped design your protocols—
Yeah, but the first thing you said was "how?"
I'm capable of more than you suspect.
What do you want, Grady?
I've got a proposition for you.

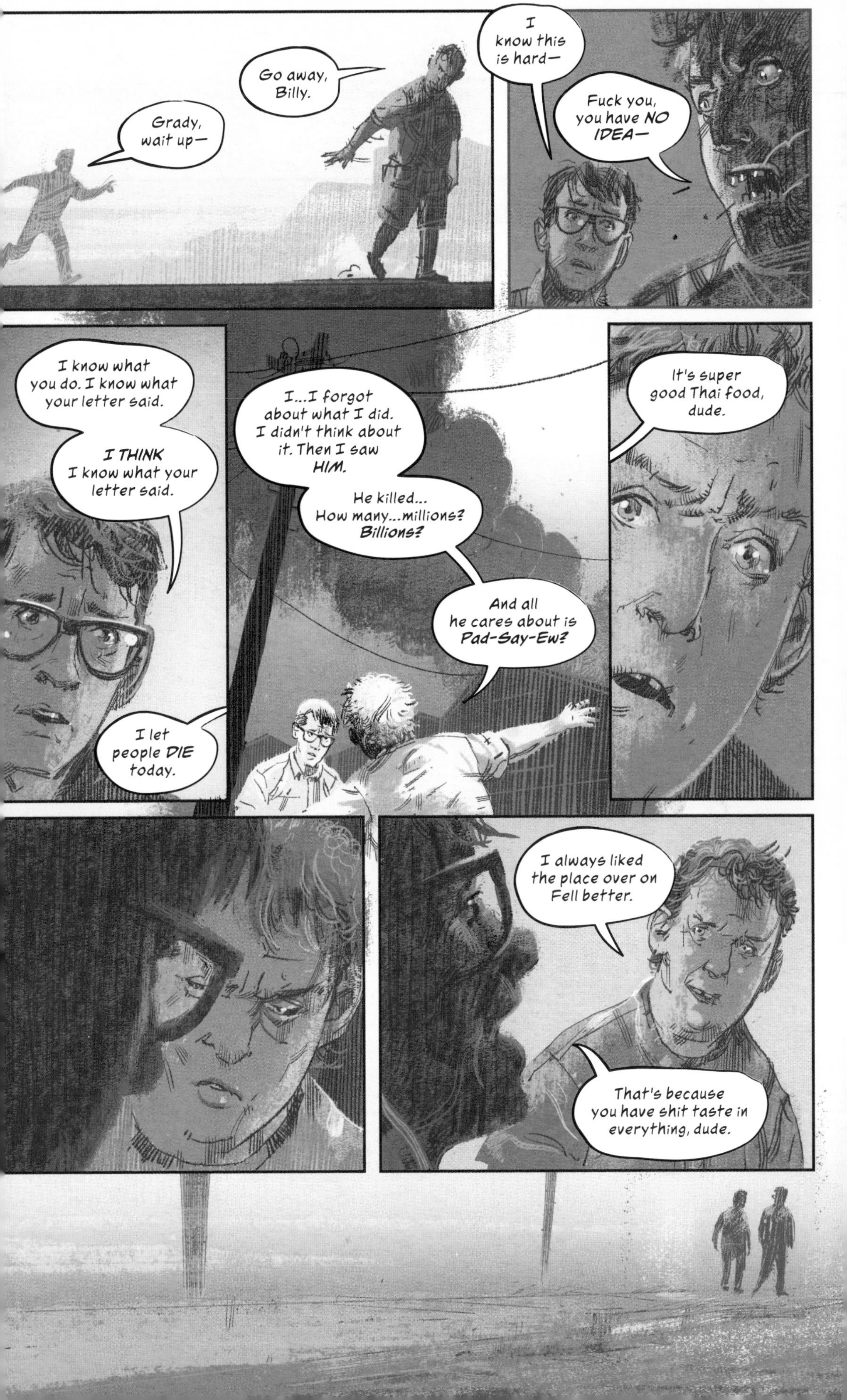
Grady, wait up—
Go away, Billy.
I know this is hard—
Fuck you, you have NO IDEA—
I know what you do. I know what your letter said.
I THINK I know what your letter said.
I let people DIE today.
I...I forgot about what I did. I didn't think about it. Then I saw HIM.
He killed... How many...millions? Billions?
And all he cares about is Pad-Say-Ew?
It's super good Thai food, dude.
I always liked the place over on Fell better.
That's because you have shit taste in everything, dude.

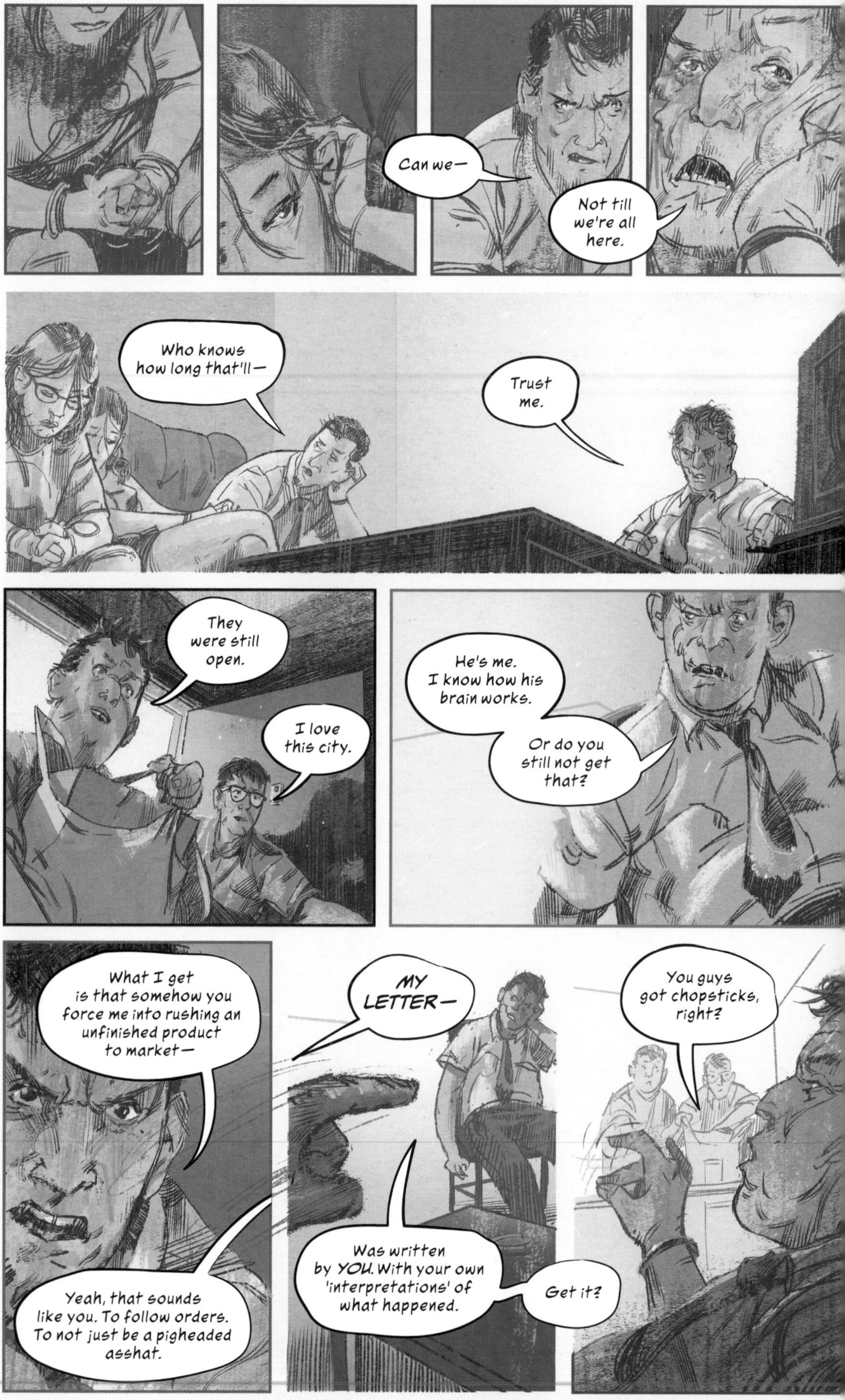

Can we—
Not till we're all here.
Who knows how long that'll—
Trust me.
They were still open.
I love this city.
He's me. I know how his brain works.
Or do you still not get that?
What I get is that somehow you force me into rushing an unfinished product to market—
Yeah, that sounds like you. To follow orders. To not just be a pigheaded asshat.
MY LETTER—
Was written by YOU. With your own 'interpretations' of what happened.
Get it?
You guys got chopsticks, right?

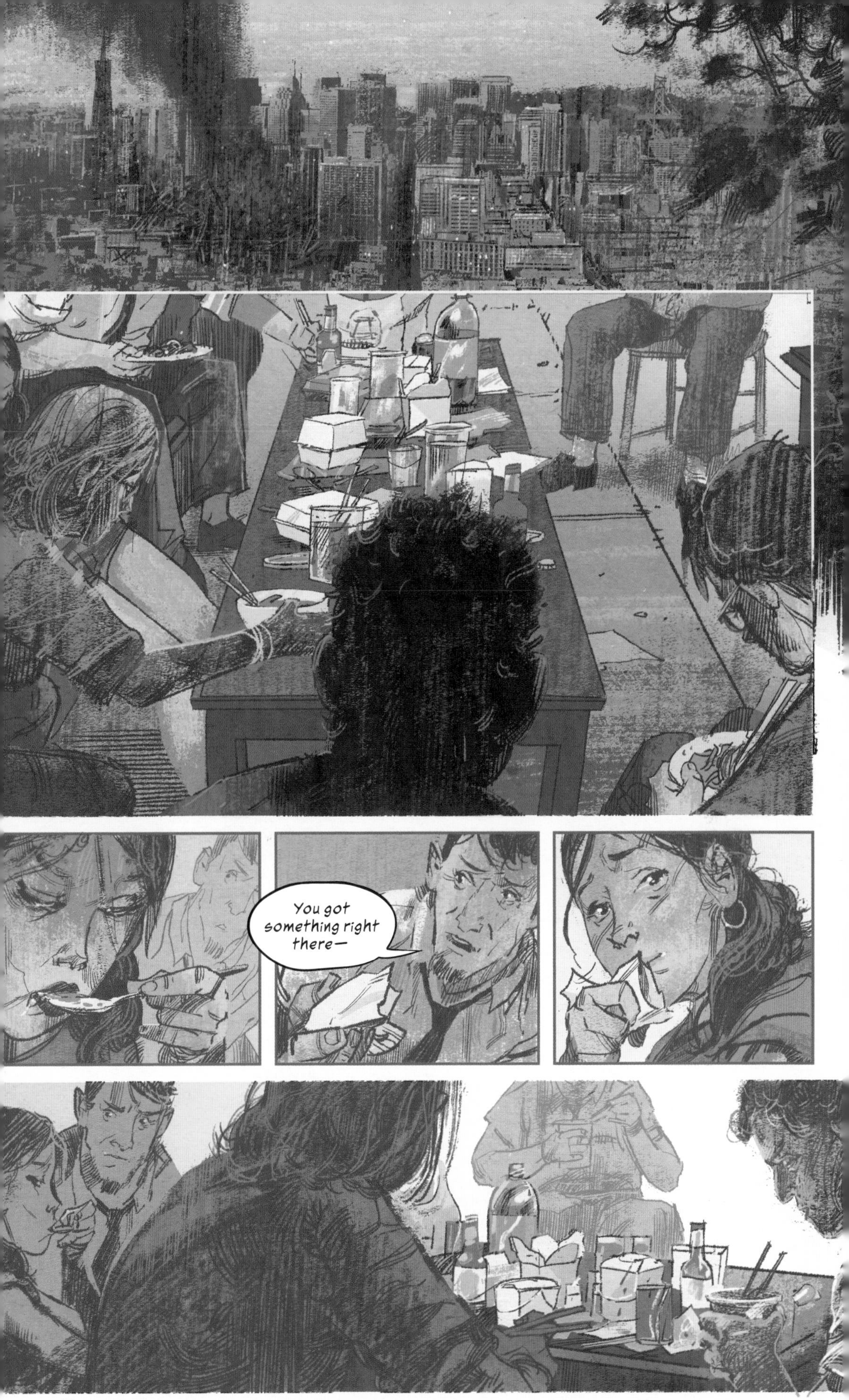
You got something right there—

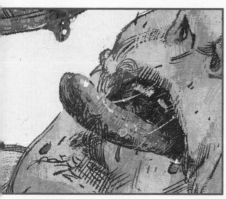

Oh God...

Alright.
Let's do this.

The planet has finite resources. We're overpopulated, and, we're on a collision course.

Now, without Daniel fucking up and killing everybody—

Dude, I told you—

Fine. Whatever. Without me forcing Daniel to fuck up and kill everybody, the species has, like, a couple hundred years to either move on or wipe out.

I don't need to tell you we won't be moving out anytime soon.

We should probably work on that, too—

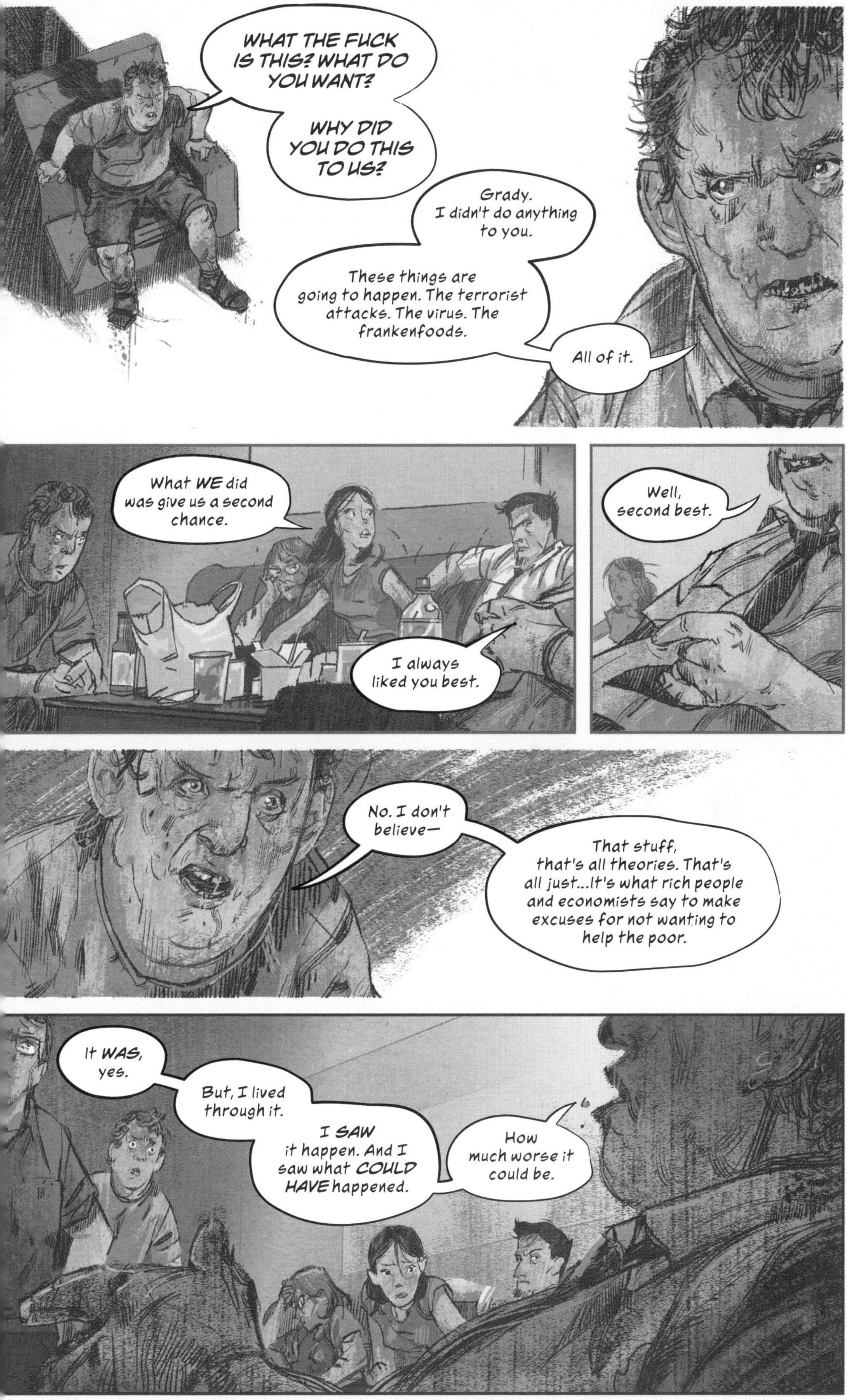
WHAT THE FUCK IS THIS? WHAT DO YOU WANT?
WHY DID YOU DO THIS TO US?
Grady. I didn't do anything to you.
These things are going to happen. The terrorist attacks. The virus. The frankenfoods.
All of it.
What WE did was give us a second chance.
I always liked you best.
Well, second best.
No. I don't believe—
That stuff, that's all theories. That's all just...It's what rich people and economists say to make excuses for not wanting to help the poor.
It WAS, yes.
But, I lived through it.
I SAW it happen. And I saw what COULD HAVE happened.
How much worse it could be.

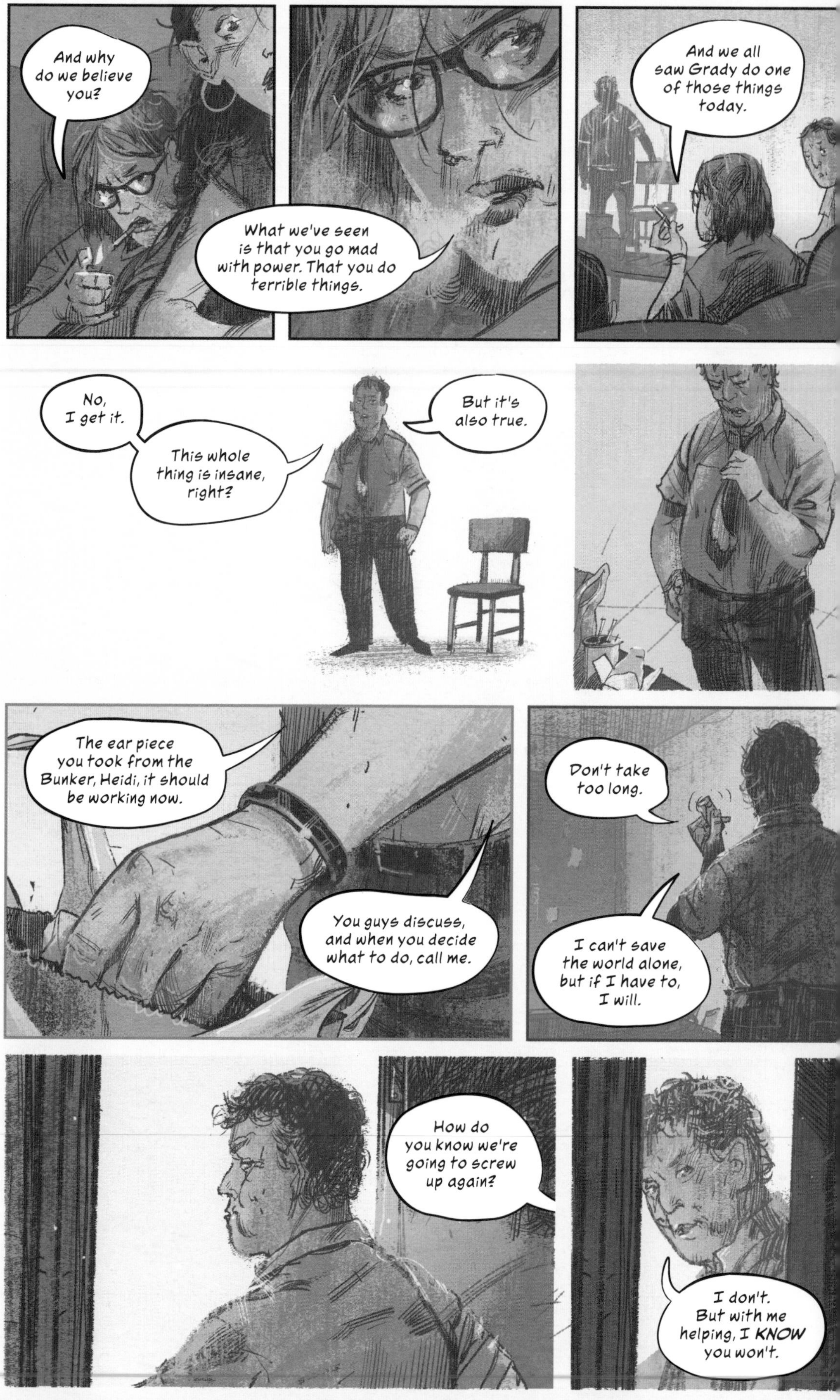
And why do we believe you?
What we've seen is that you go mad with power. That you do terrible things.
And we all saw Grady do one of those things today.
No, I get it.
This whole thing is insane, right?
But it's also true.
The ear piece you took from the Bunker, Heidi, it should be working now.
You guys discuss, and when you decide what to do, call me.
Don't take too long.
I can't save the world alone, but if I have to, I will.
How do you know we're going to screw up again?
I don't. But with me helping, I **KNOW** you won't.

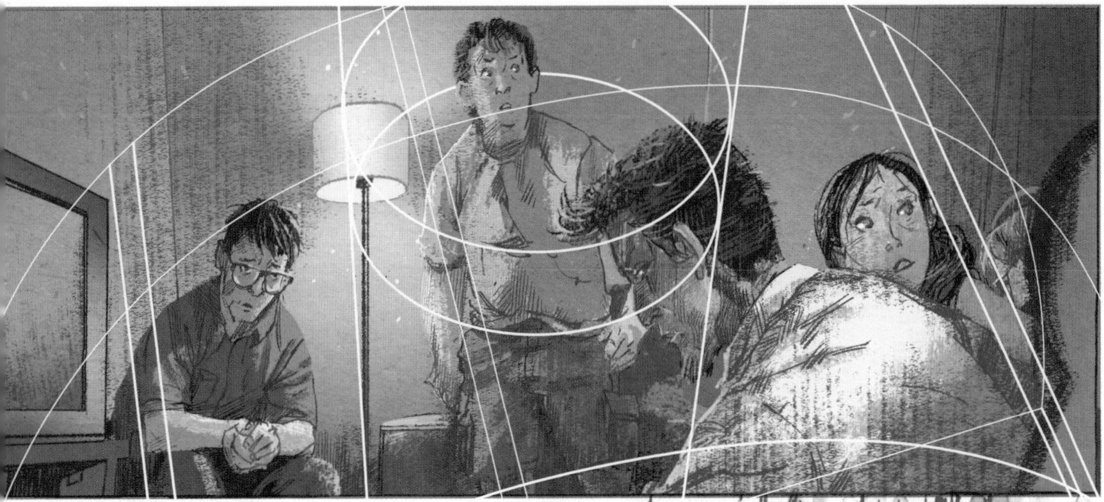

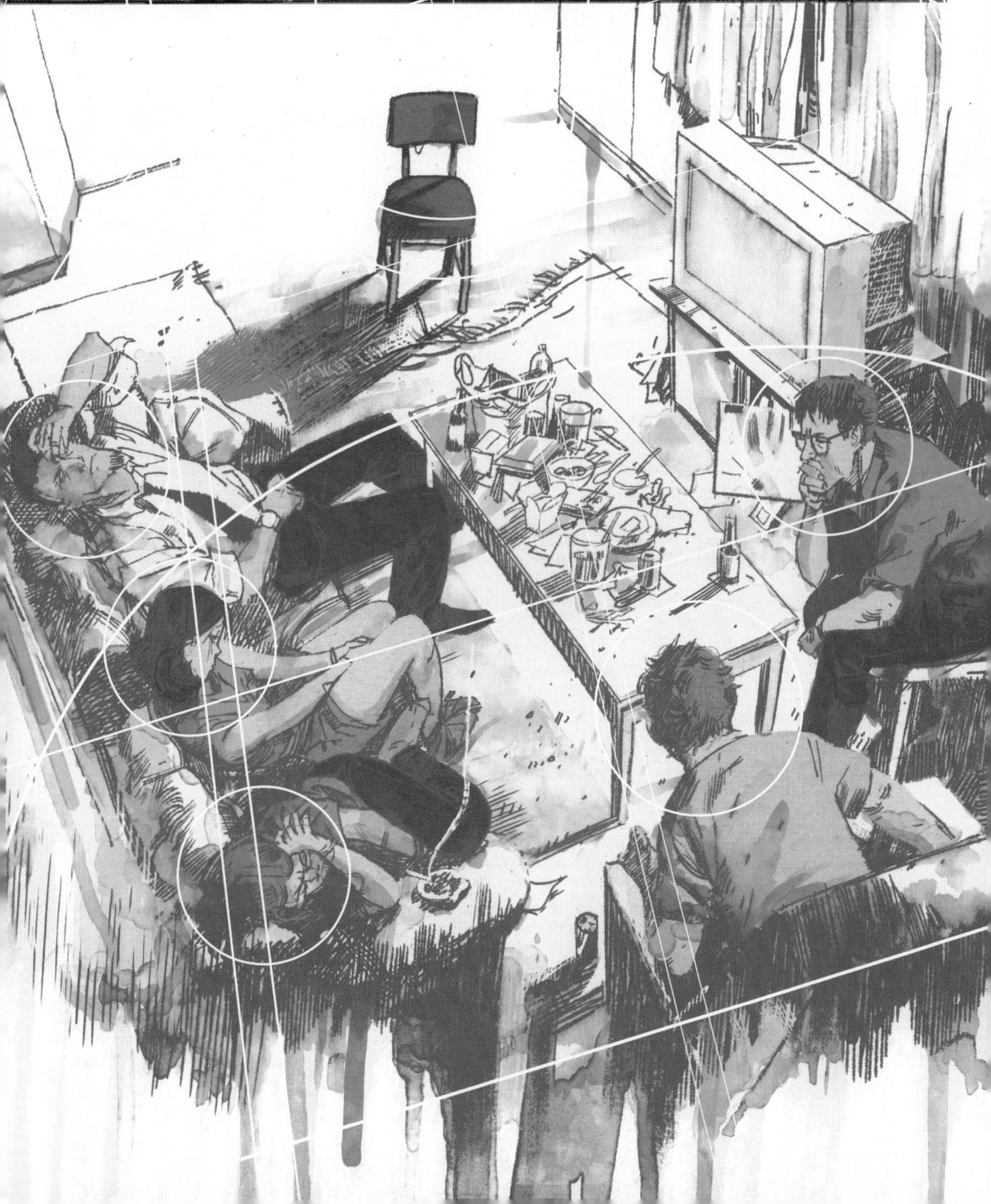

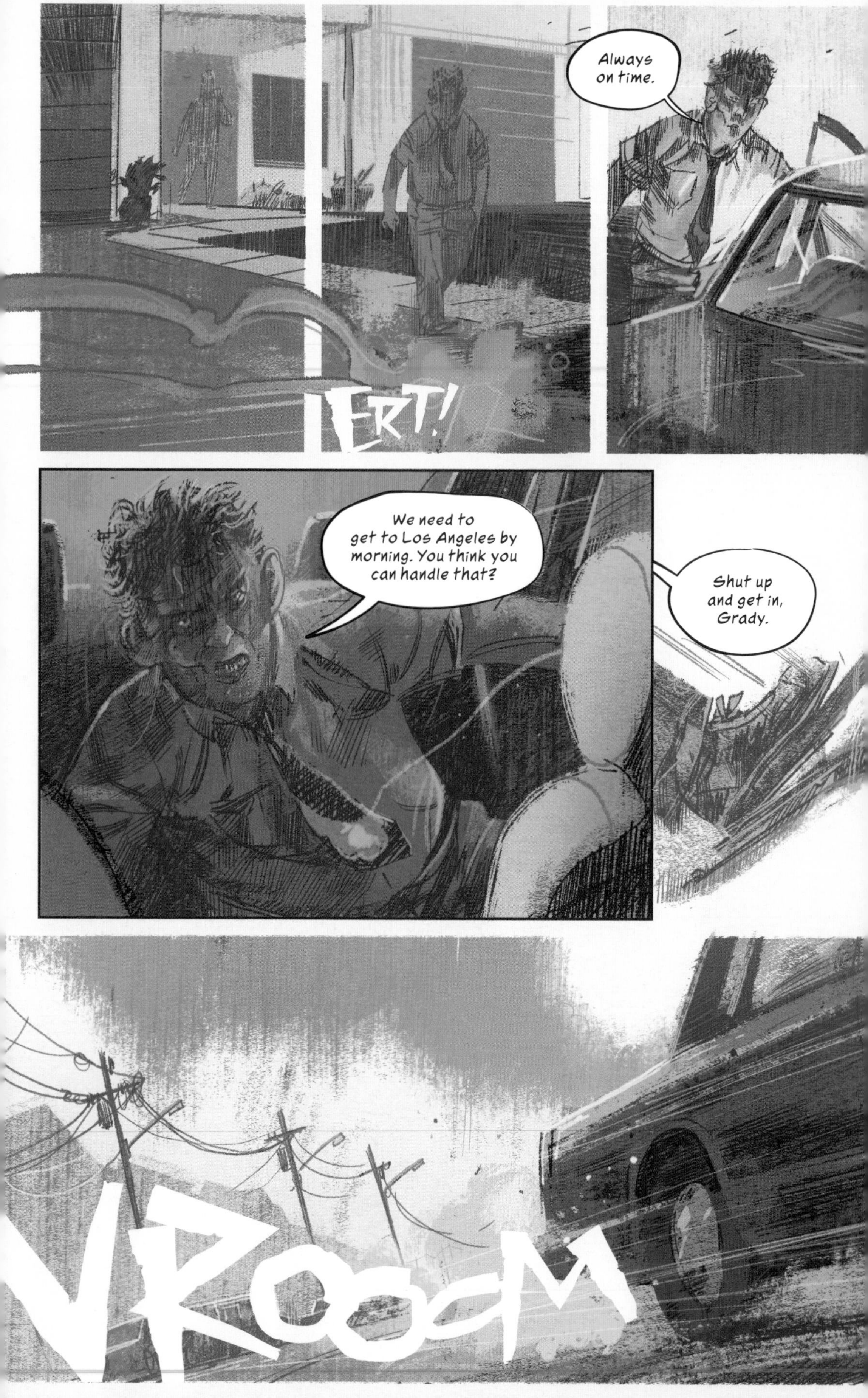
ERT!
Always on time.
We need to get to Los Angeles by morning. You think you can handle that?
Shut up and get in, Grady.
VROOOM

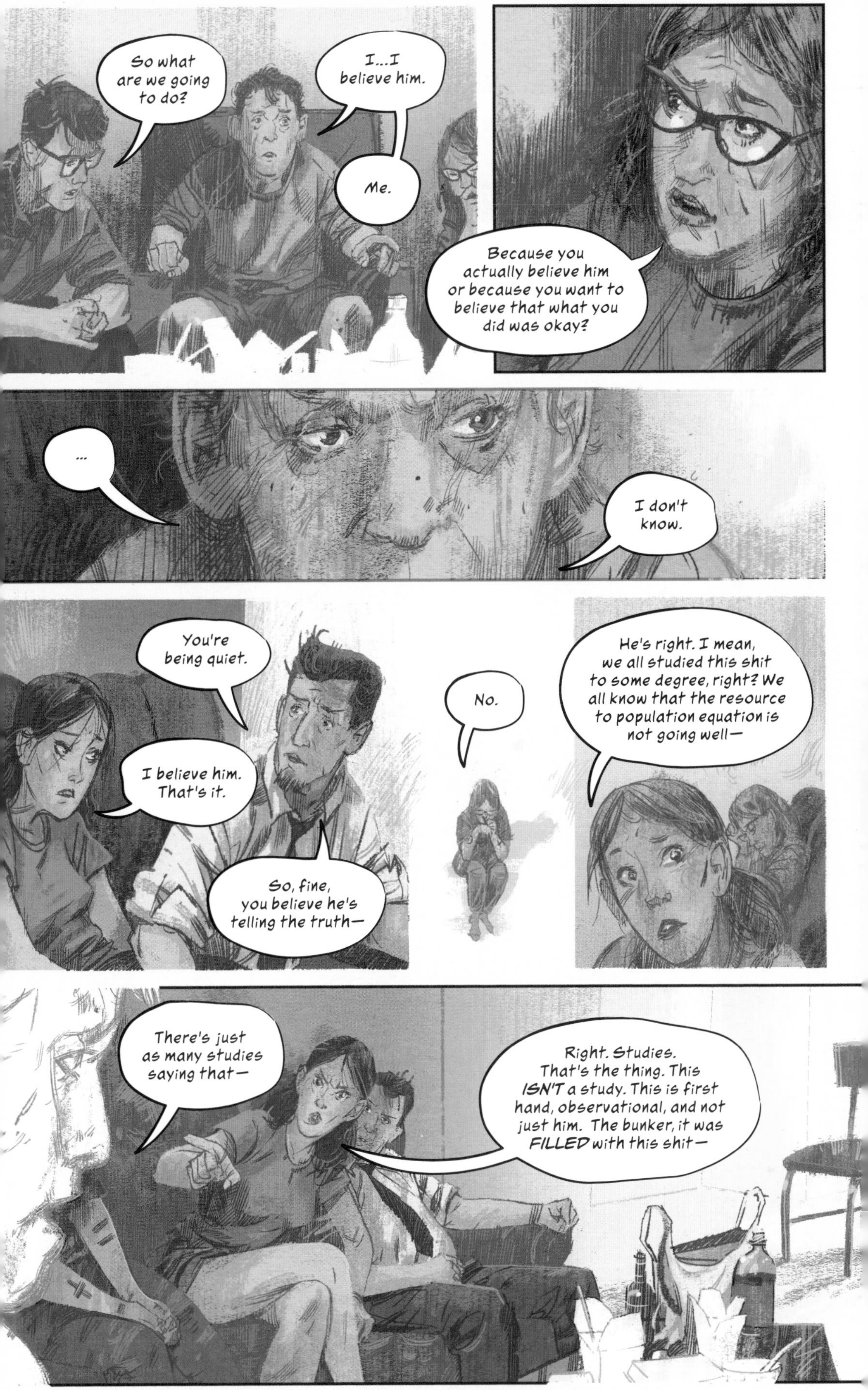
So what are we going to do?
I...I believe him.
Me.
Because you actually believe him or because you want to believe that what you did was okay?
...
I don't know.
You're being quiet.
I believe him. That's it.
So, fine, you believe he's telling the truth—
No.
He's right. I mean, we all studied this shit to some degree, right? We all know that the resource to population equation is not going well—
There's just as many studies saying that—
Right. Studies. That's the thing. This ISN'T a study. This is first hand, observational, and not just him. The bunker, it was FILLED with this shit—

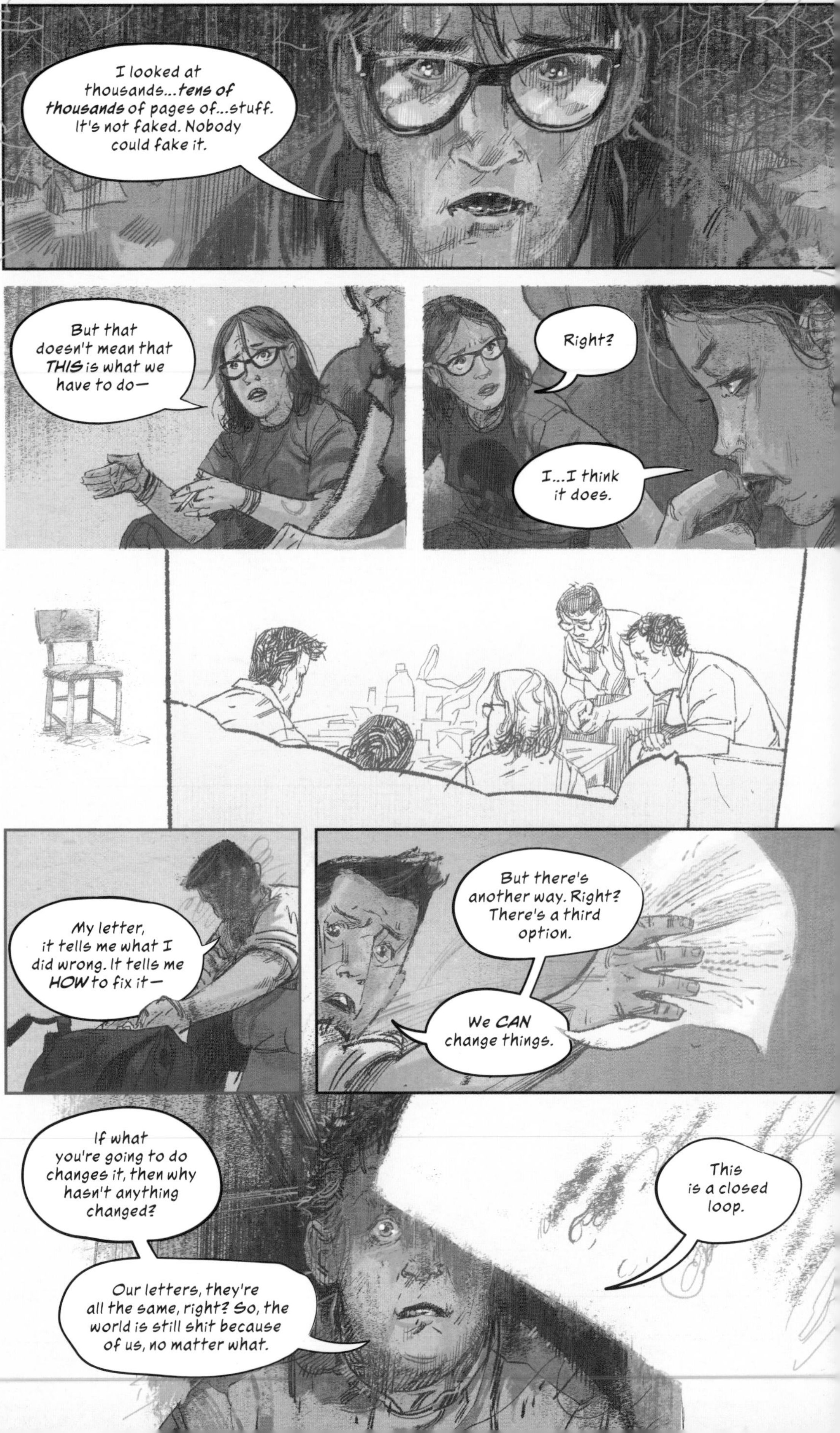
I looked at thousands...tens of thousands of pages of...stuff. It's not faked. Nobody could fake it.
But that doesn't mean that THIS is what we have to do—
Right?
I...I think it does.
My letter, it tells me what I did wrong. It tells me HOW to fix it—
But there's another way. Right? There's a third option.
We CAN change things.
If what you're going to do changes it, then why hasn't anything changed?
Our letters, they're all the same, right? So, the world is still shit because of us, no matter what.
This is a closed loop.

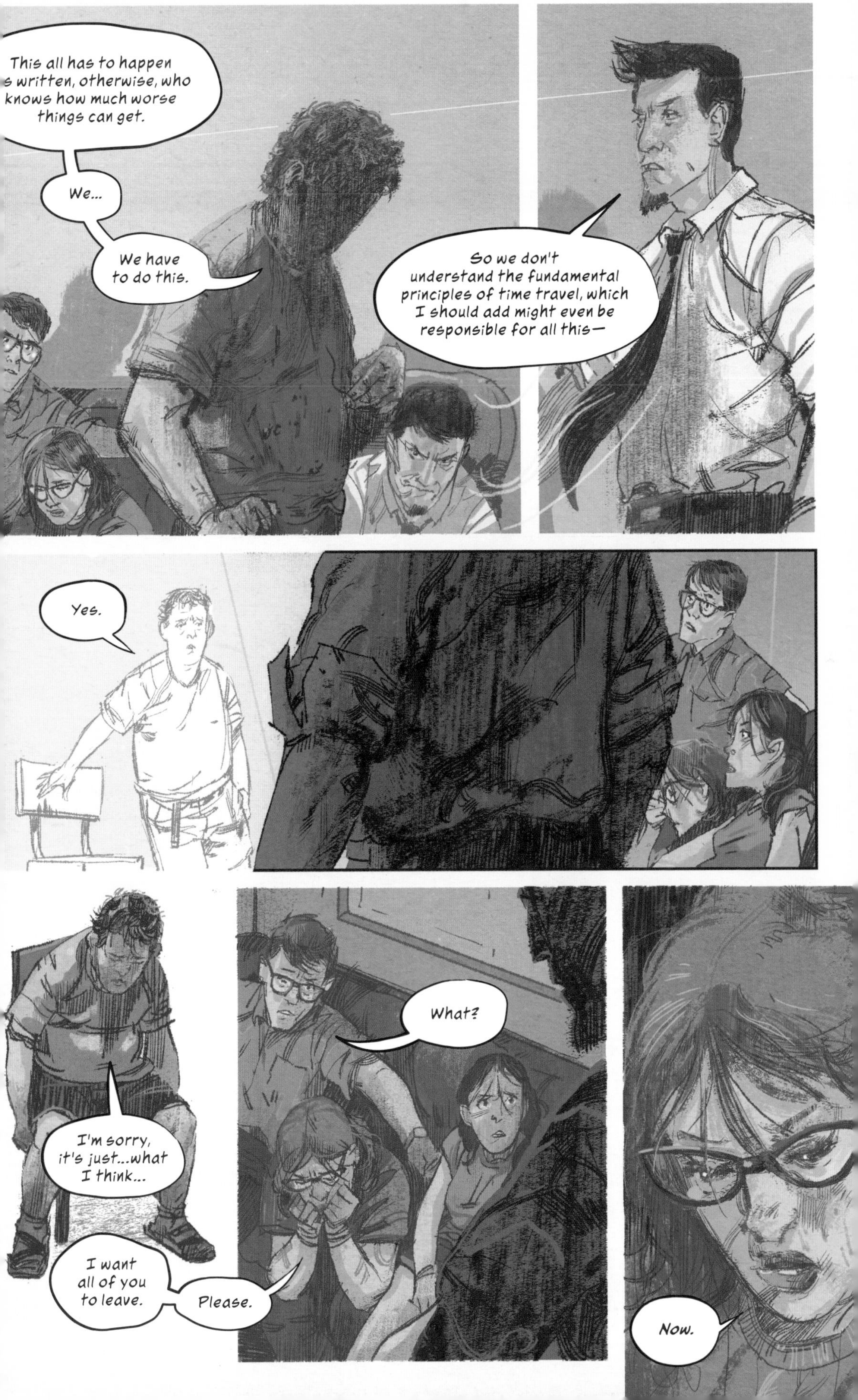
This all has to happen
s written, otherwise, who knows how much worse things can get.
We...
We have to do this.
So we don't understand the fundamental principles of time travel, which I should add might even be responsible for all this—
Yes.
I'm sorry, it's just...what I think...
I want all of you to leave.
Please.
What?
Now.

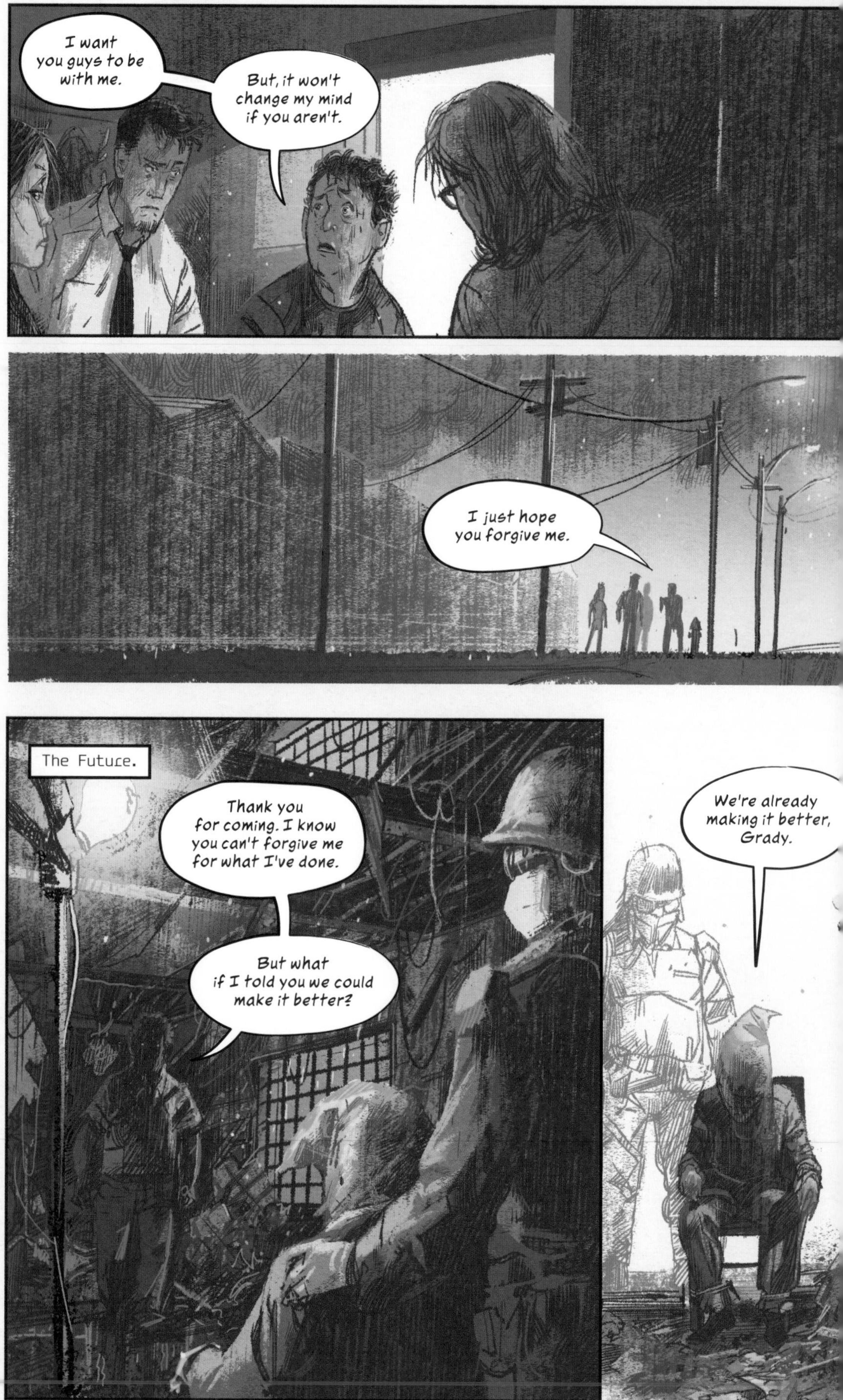
I want you guys to be with me.
But, it won't change my mind if you aren't.
I just hope you forgive me.
The Future.
Thank you for coming. I know you can't forgive me for what I've done.
But what if I told you we could make it better?
We're already making it better, Grady.

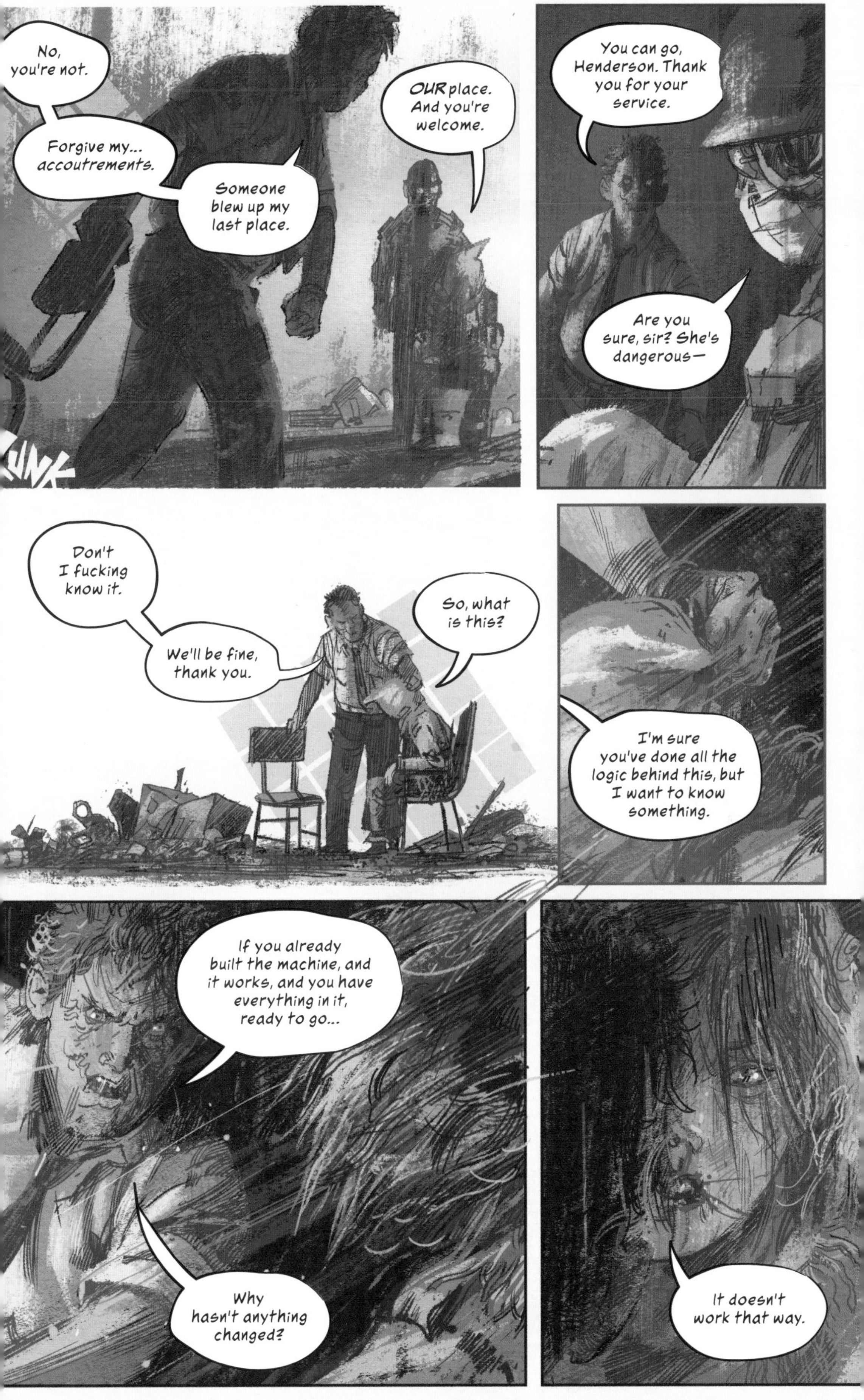

No, you're not.
Forgive my... accoutrements.
Someone blew up my last place.
OUR place. And you're welcome.
UNK
You can go, Henderson. Thank you for your service.
Are you sure, sir? She's dangerous—
Don't I fucking know it.
We'll be fine, thank you.
So, what is this?
I'm sure you've done all the logic behind this, but I want to know something.
If you already built the machine, and it works, and you have everything in it, ready to go...
Why hasn't anything changed?
It doesn't work that way.

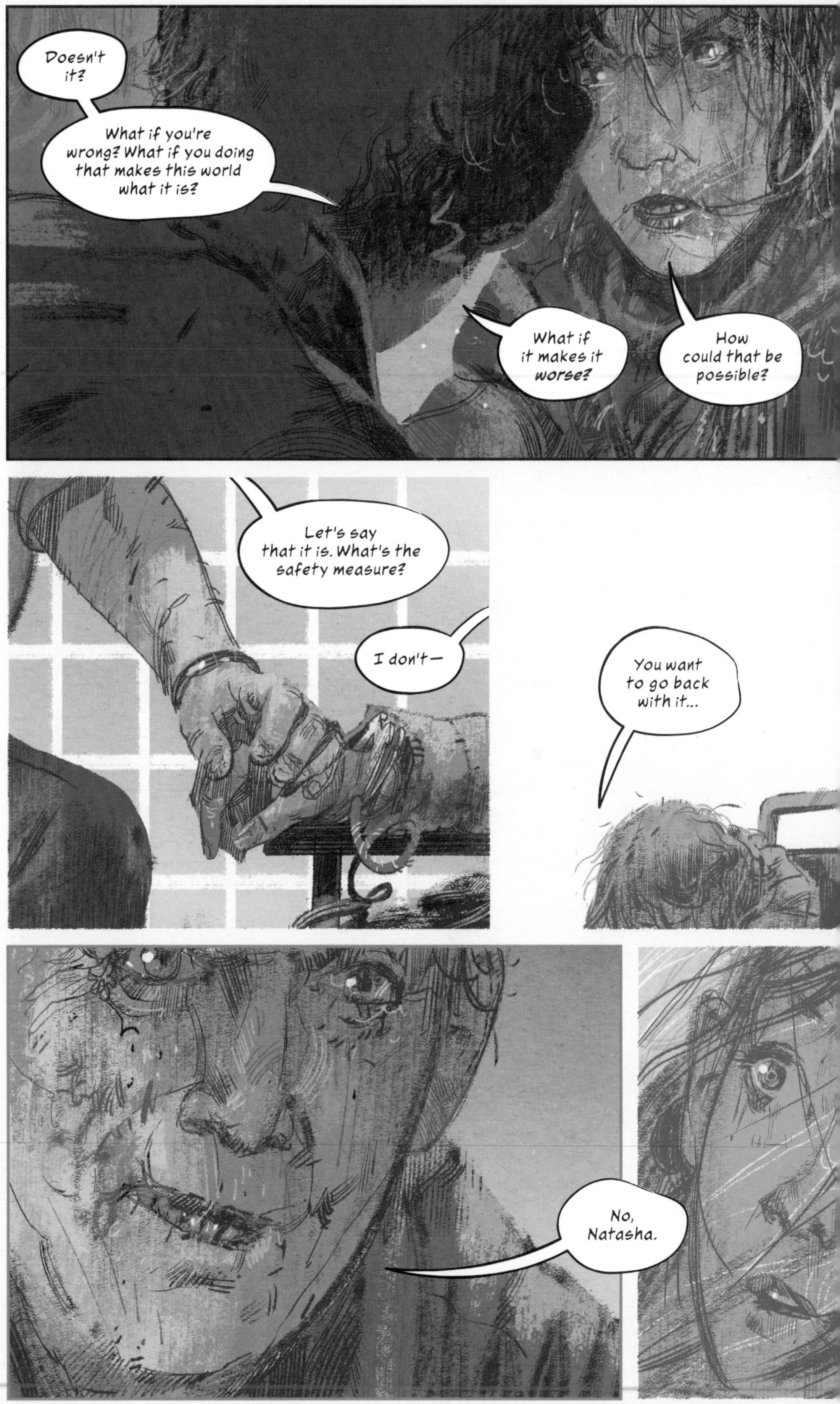
Doesn't it?
What if you're wrong? What if you doing that makes this world what it is?
What if it makes it *worse?*
How could that be possible?
Let's say that it is. What's the safety measure?
I don't—
You want to go back with it...
No, Natasha.

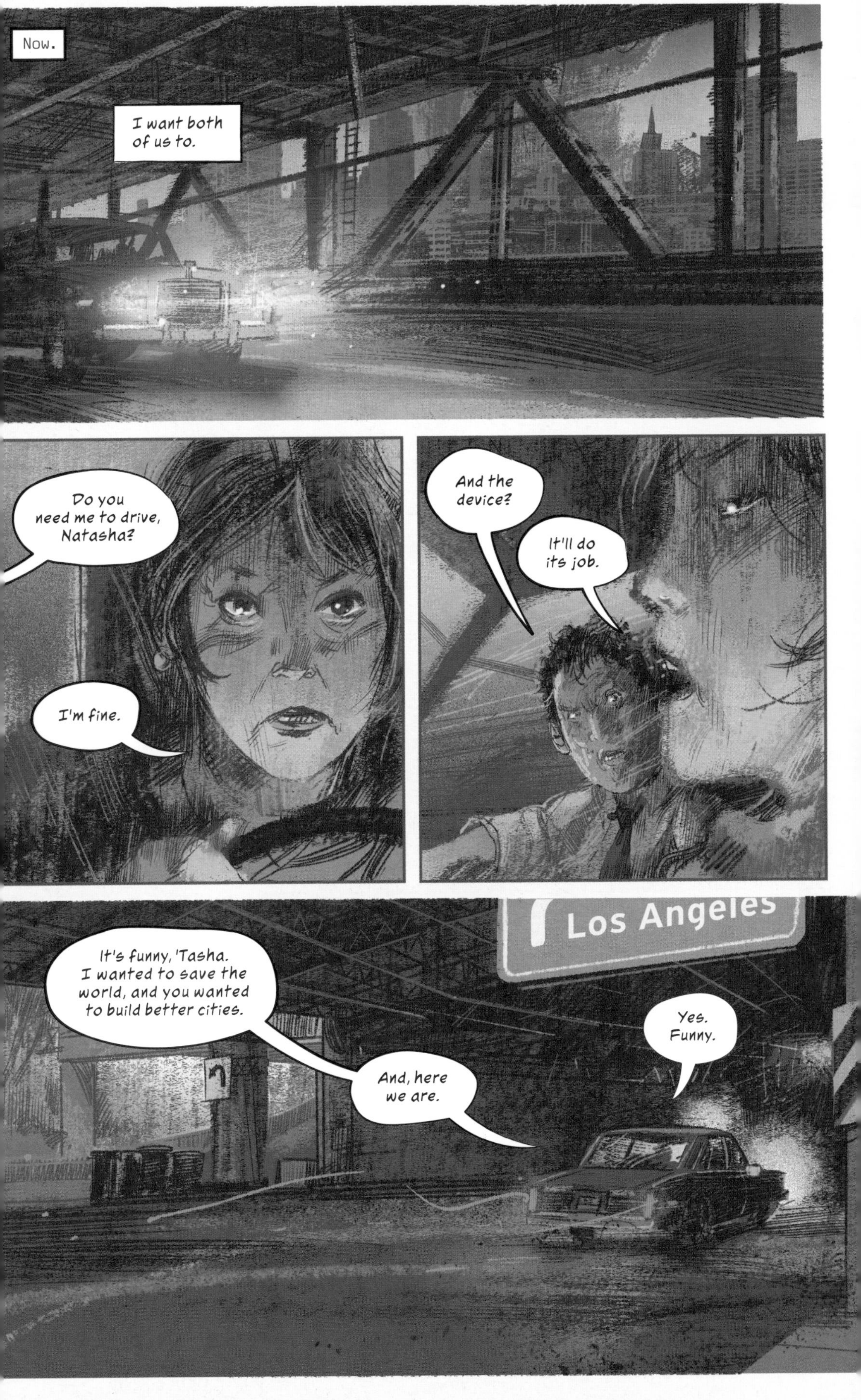

Now.
I want both of us to.
Do you need me to drive, Natasha?
I'm fine.
And the device?
It'll do its job.
Los Angeles
It's funny, 'Tasha. I wanted to save the world, and you wanted to build better cities.
And, here we are.
Yes. Funny.

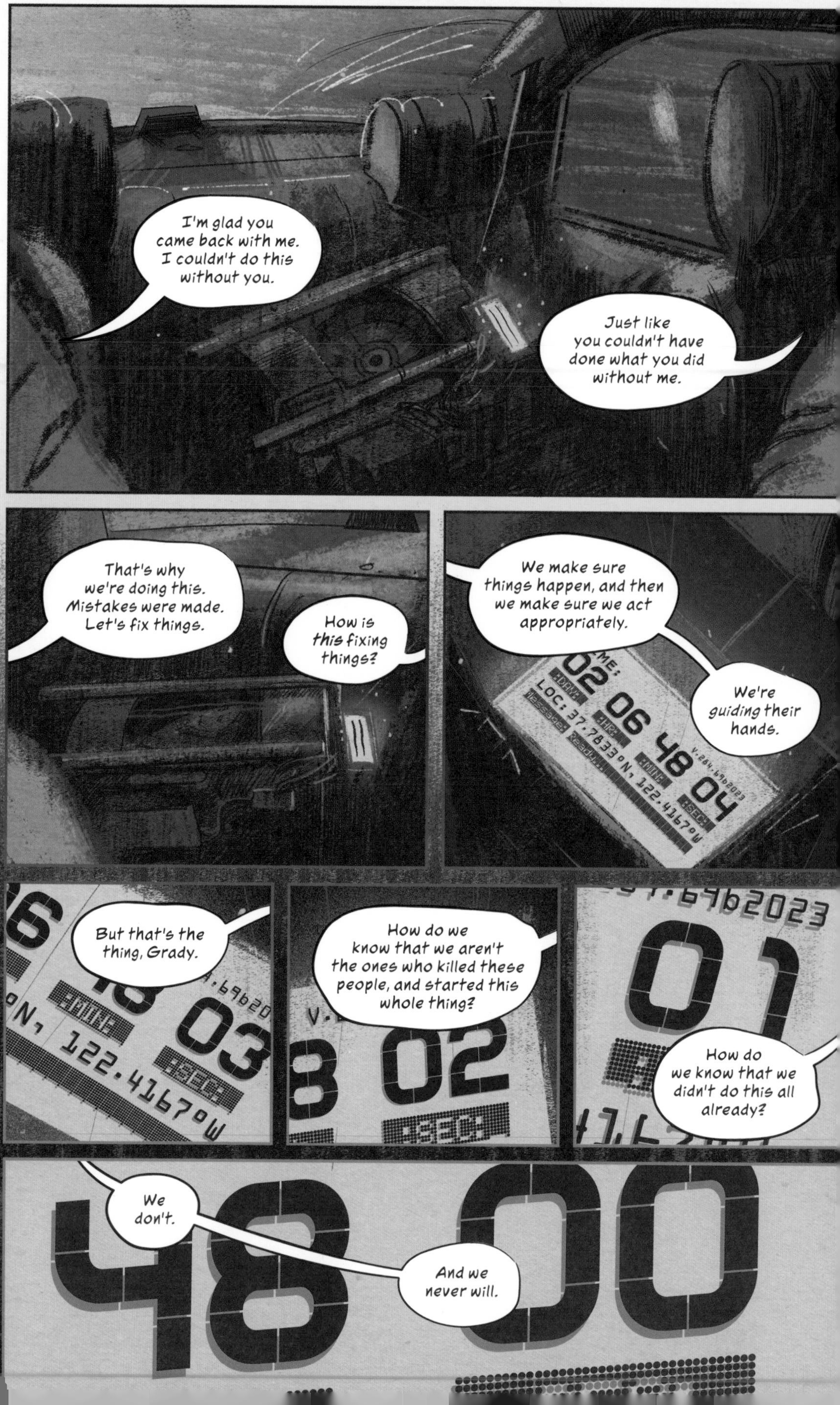
I'm glad you came back with me. I couldn't do this without you.
Just like you couldn't have done what you did without me.
That's why we're doing this. Mistakes were made. Let's fix things.
How is this fixing things?
We make sure things happen, and then we make sure we act appropriately.
We're guiding their hands.
But that's the thing, Grady.
How do we know that we aren't the ones who killed these people, and started this whole thing?
How do we know that we didn't do this all already?
We don't.
And we never will.

CHAPTER
06

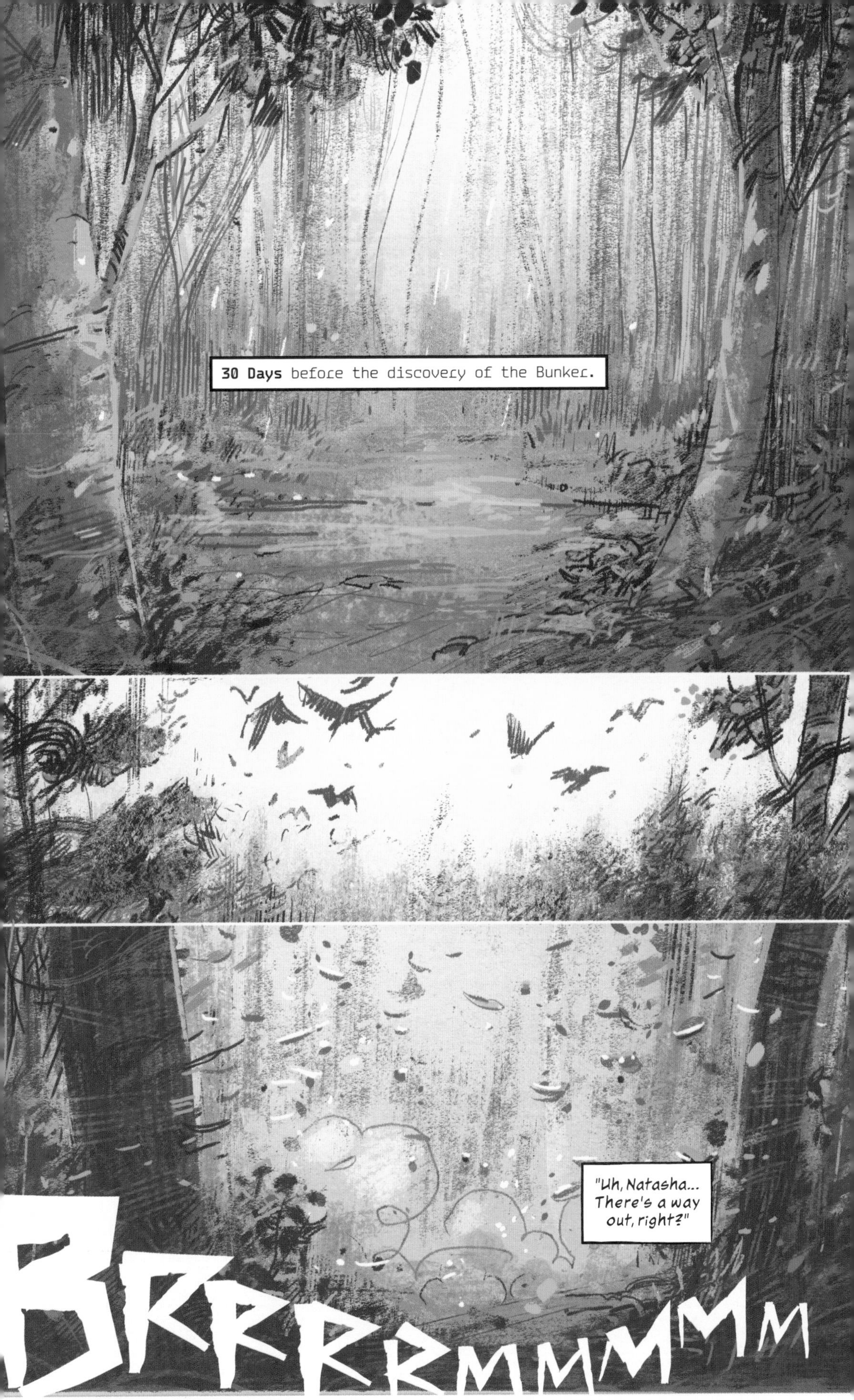
30 Days before the discovery of the Bunker.
"Uh, Natasha... There's a way out, right?"
BRRRRMMMMM

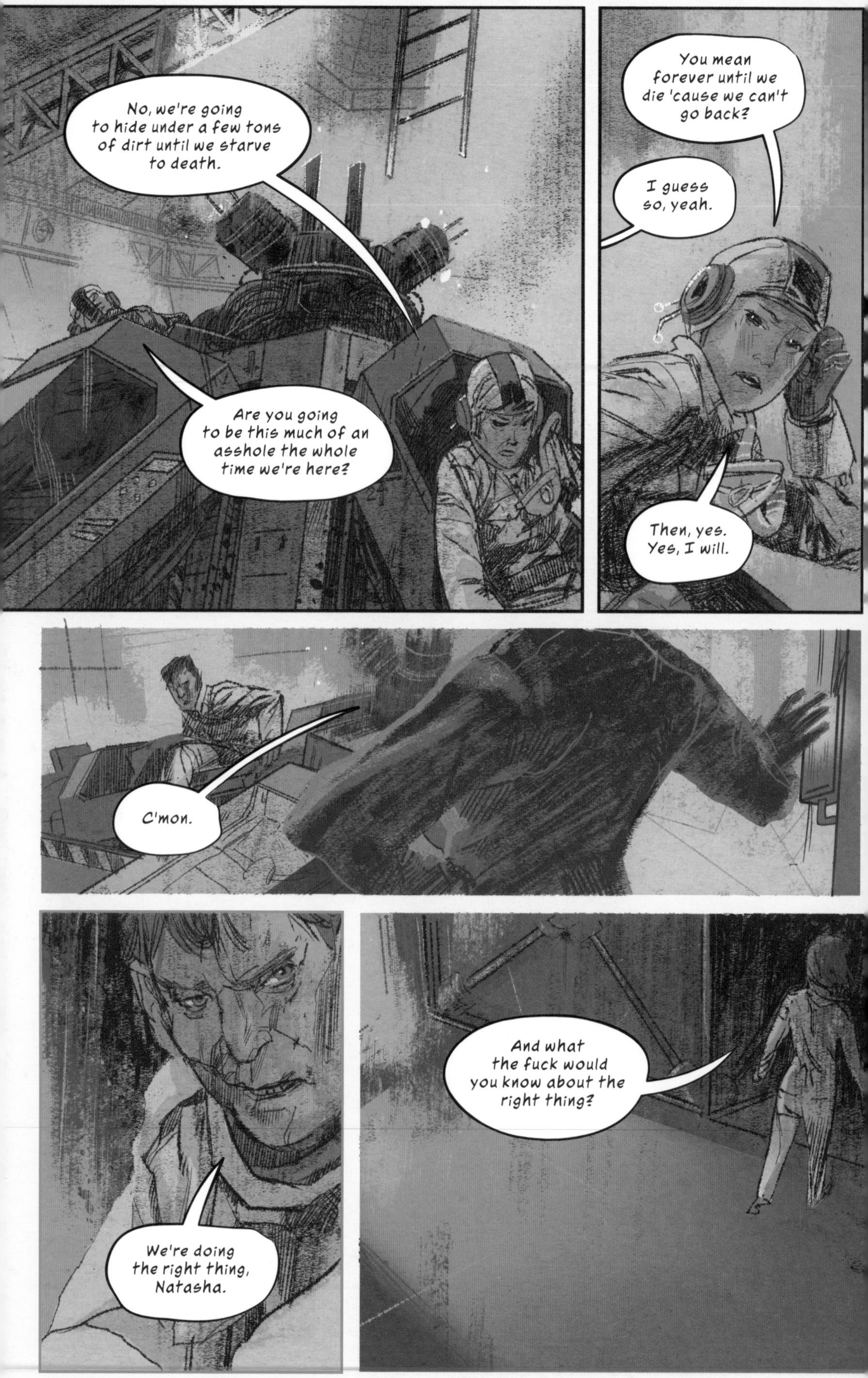
No, we're going to hide under a few tons of dirt until we starve to death.
Are you going to be this much of an asshole the whole time we're here?
You mean forever until we die 'cause we can't go back?
I guess so, yeah.
Then, yes. Yes, I will.
C'mon.
We're doing the right thing, Natasha.
And what the fuck would you know about the right thing?

You have no idea.

No? NO?

I approved Daniel's work. I vouched for it. I pushed it through.

I put you in office.

And I played house with you when I couldn't be more fucking disgusted by you.

You think YOU'RE the one who did all of this? You think YOU are going to save the world?

Fuck.

You.

This was me.

One hundred percent me.

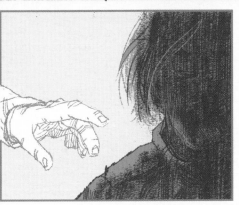

Don't touch me. Ever again.

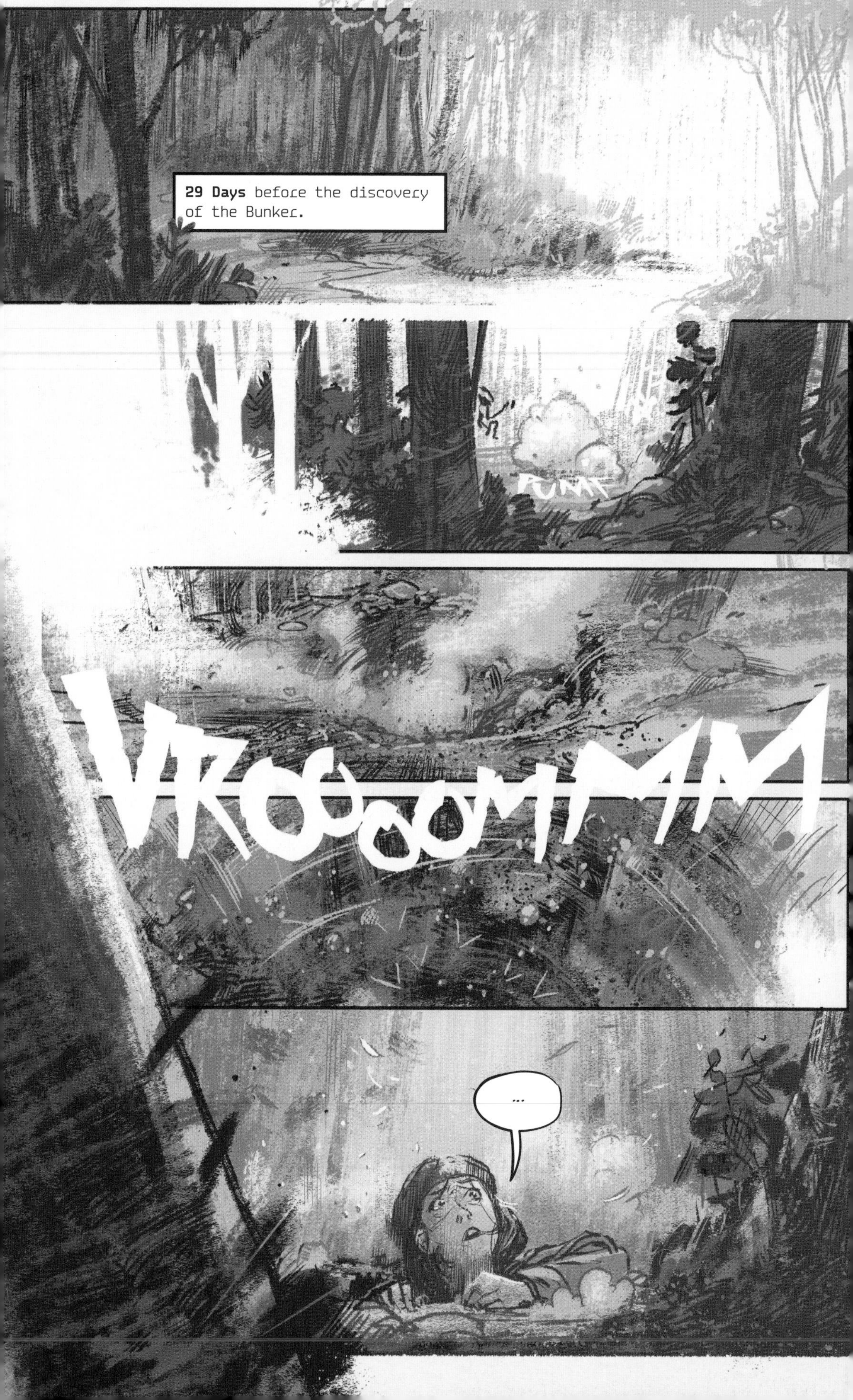
29 Days before the discovery of the Bunker.
PUMF
VROOOOOMMM
...

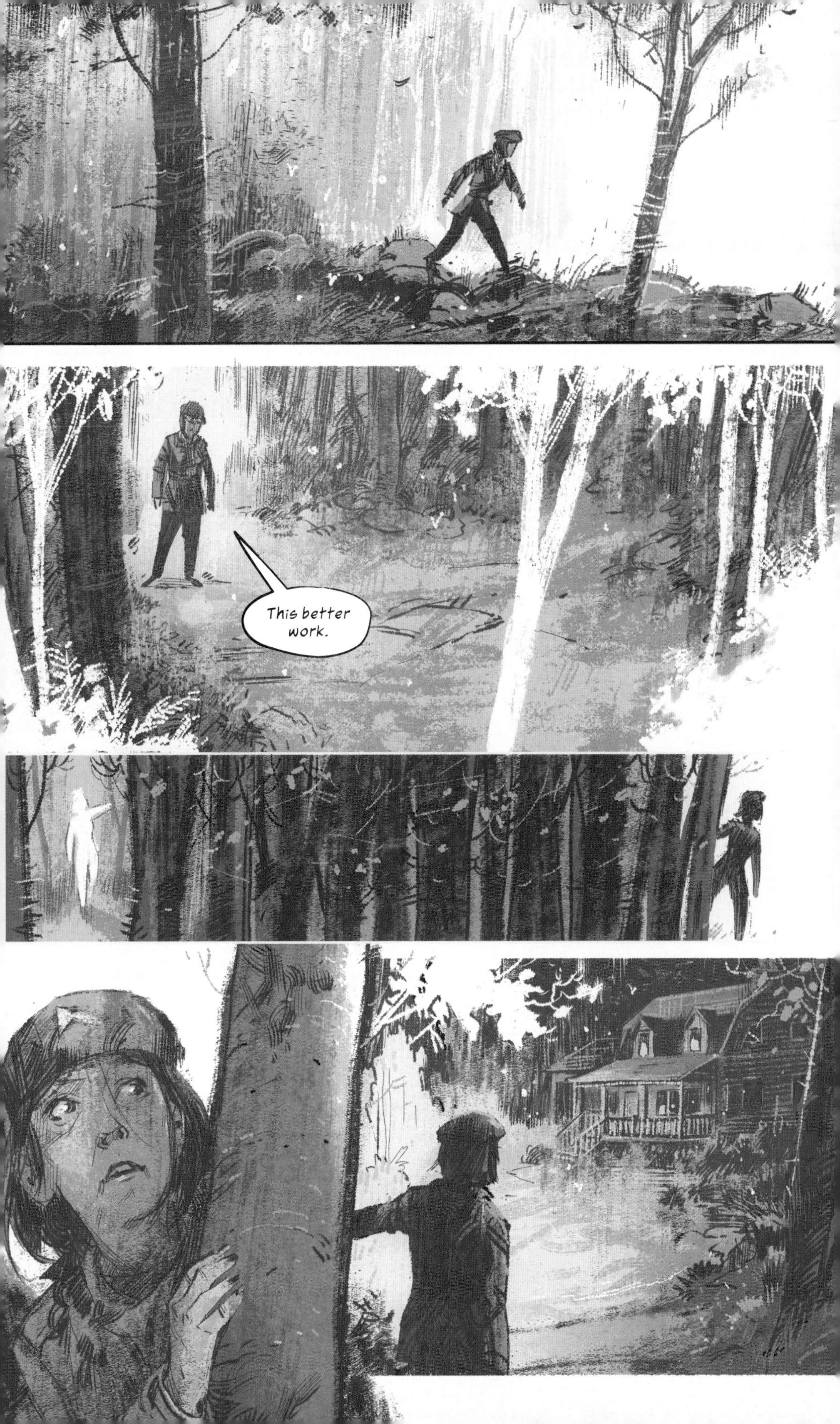
This better work.

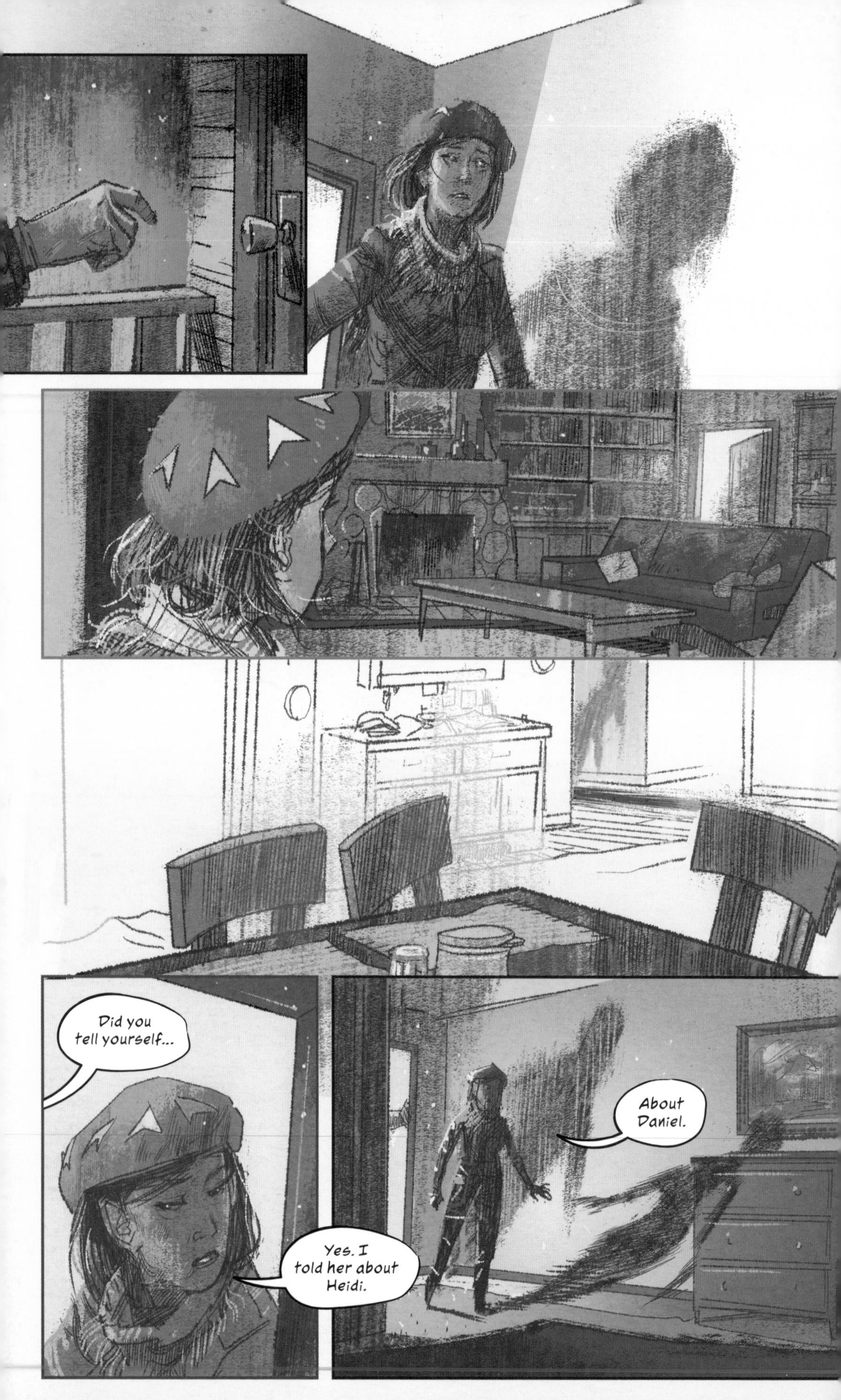
Did you tell yourself...
Yes. I told her about Heidi.
About Daniel.

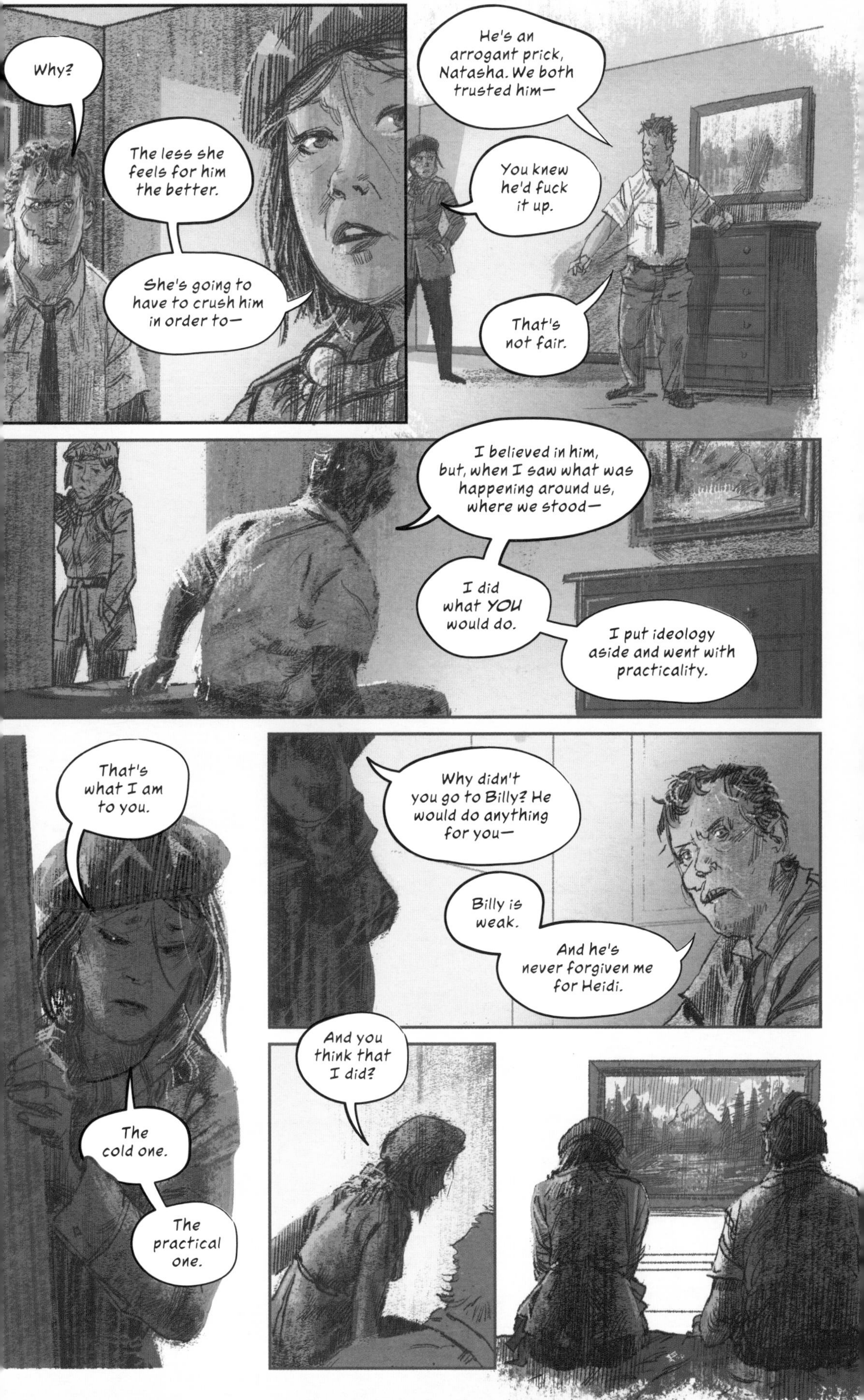
Why?
The less she feels for him the better.
She's going to have to crush him in order to—
He's an arrogant prick, Natasha. We both trusted him—
You knew he'd fuck it up.
That's not fair.
I believed in him, but, when I saw what was happening around us, where we stood—
I did what YOU would do.
I put ideology aside and went with practicality.
That's what I am to you.
The cold one.
The practical one.
Why didn't you go to Billy? He would do anything for you—
Billy is weak.
And he's never forgiven me for Heidi.
And you think that I did?

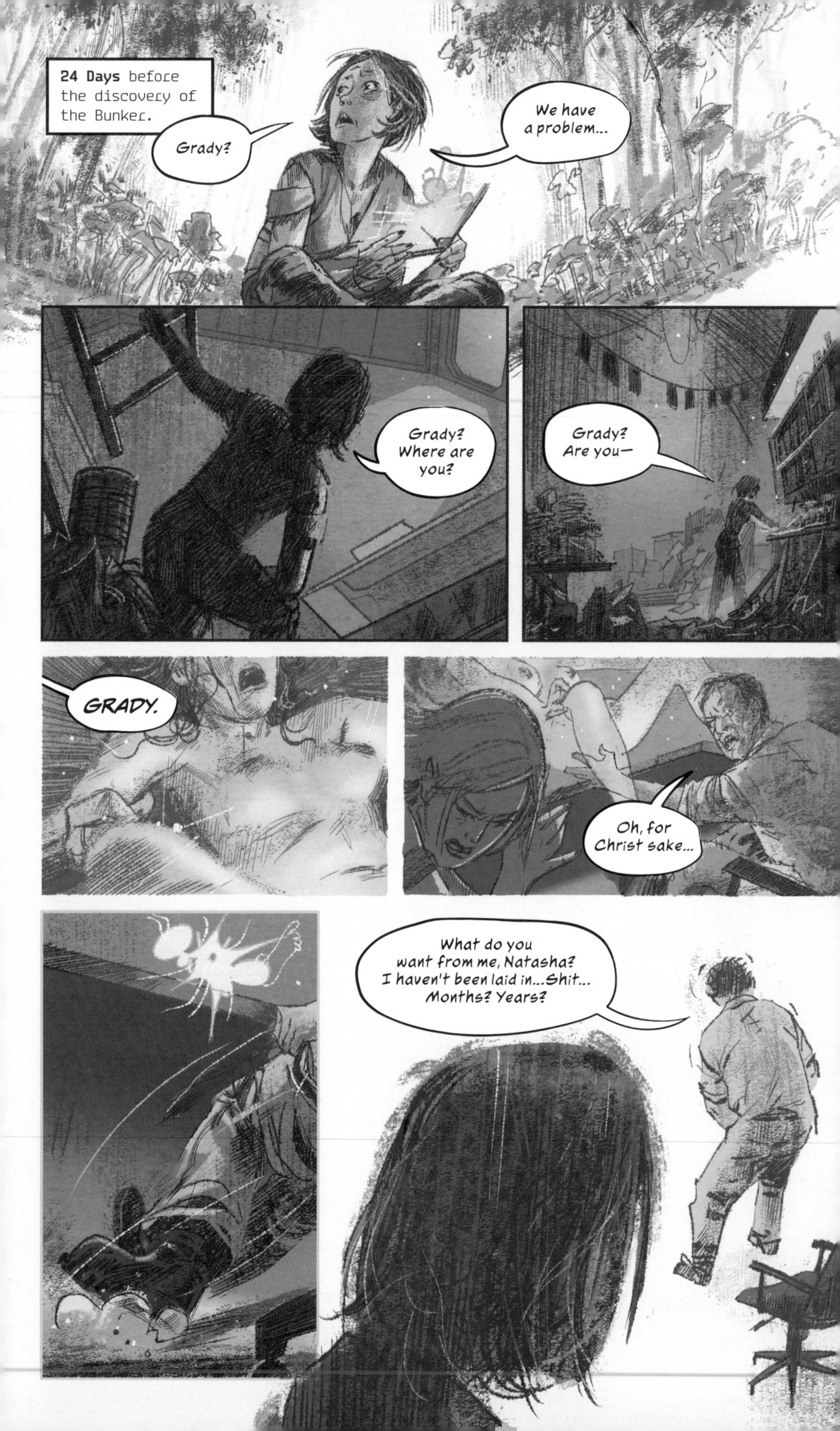

24 Days before the discovery of the Bunker.
Grady?
We have a problem...
Grady? Where are you?
Grady? Are you—
GRADY.
Oh, for Christ sake...
What do you want from me, Natasha? I haven't been laid in...Shit... Months? Years?

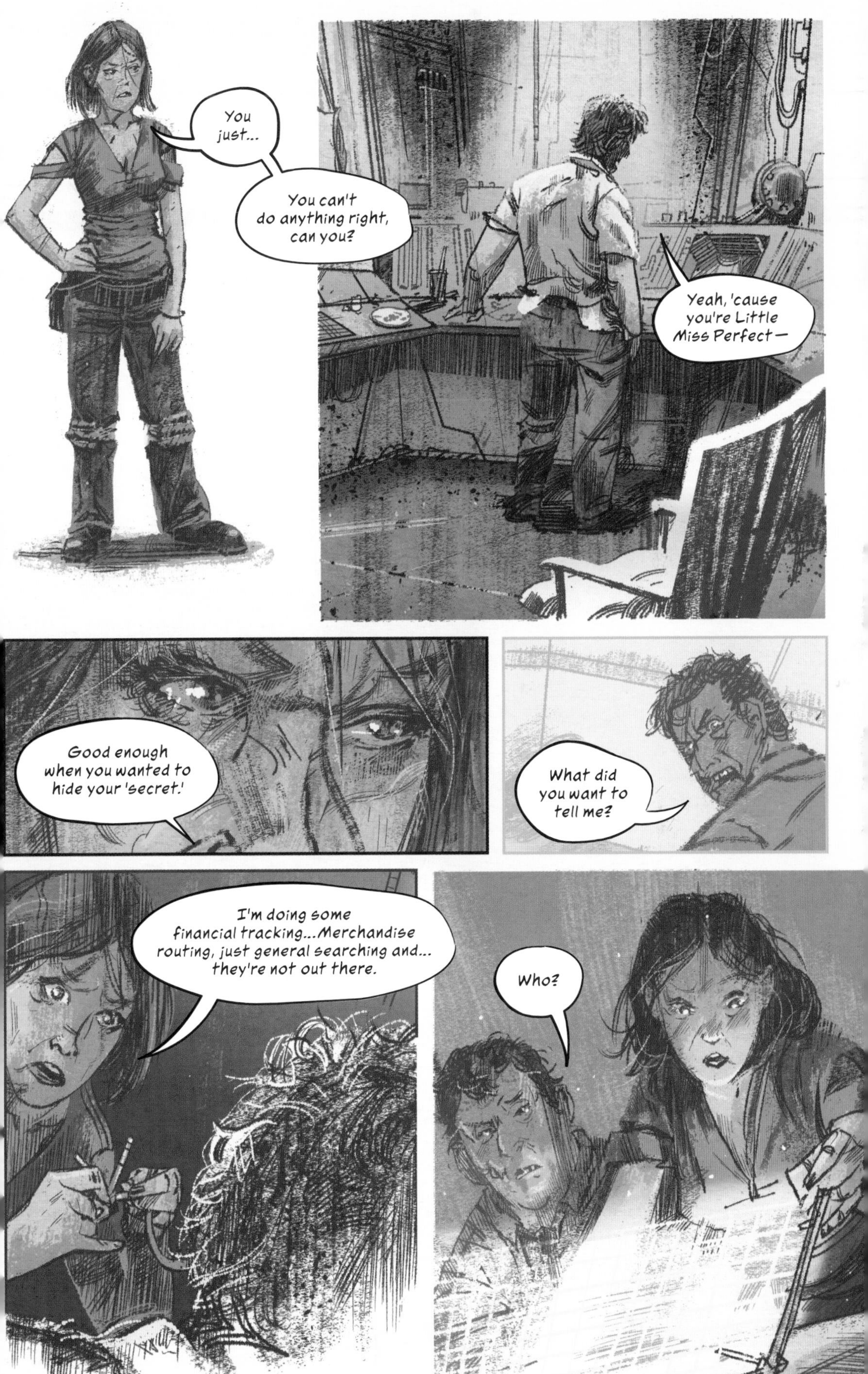
You just...
You can't do anything right, can you?
Yeah, 'cause you're Little Miss Perfect—
Good enough when you wanted to hide your 'secret.'
What did you want to tell me?
I'm doing some financial tracking... Merchandise routing, just general searching and... they're not out there.
Who?

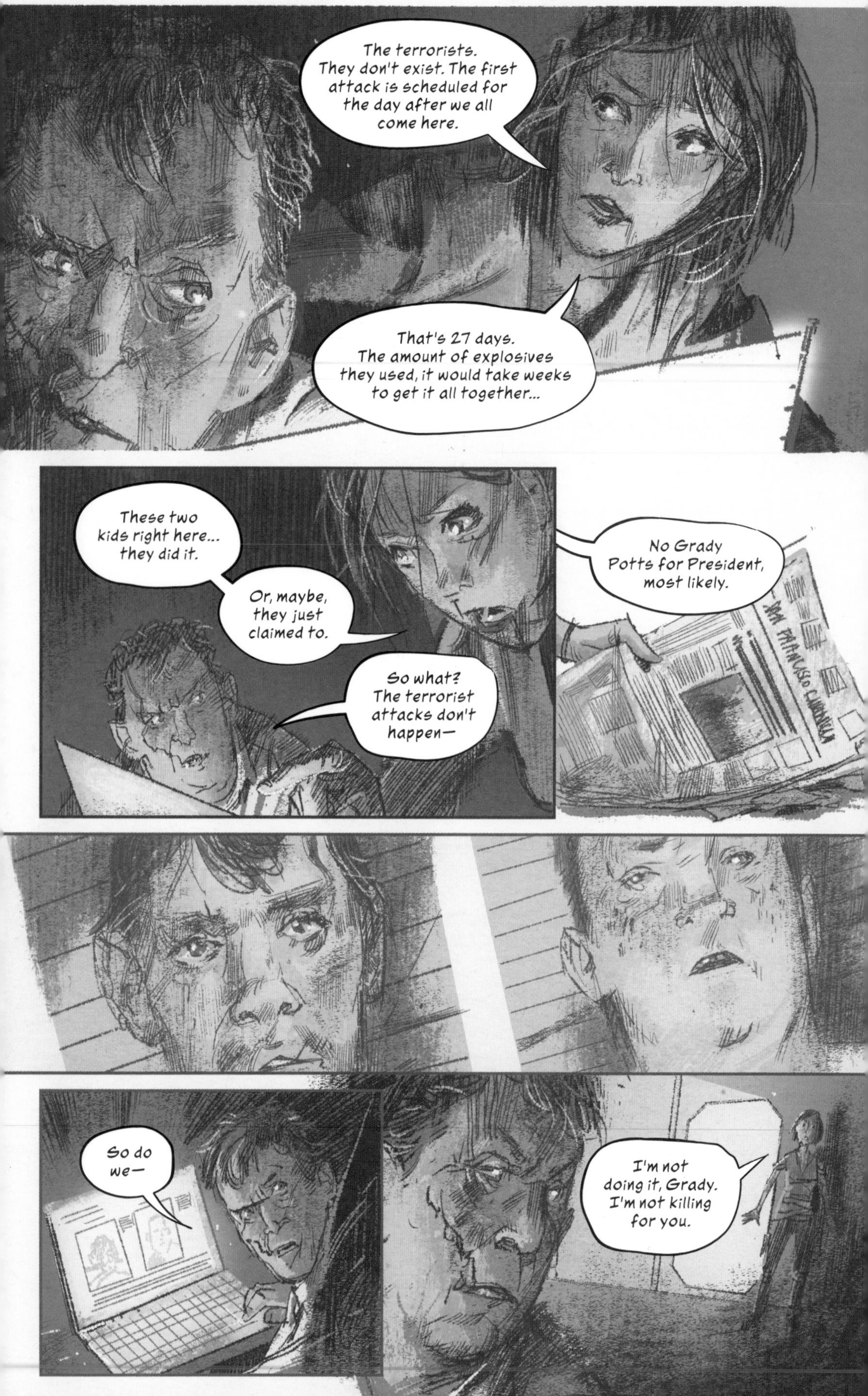
The terrorists. They don't exist. The first attack is scheduled for the day after we all come here.
That's 27 days. The amount of explosives they used, it would take weeks to get it all together...
These two kids right here... they did it.
Or, maybe, they just claimed to.
No Grady Potts for President, most likely.
So what? The terrorist attacks don't happen—
So do we—
I'm not doing it, Grady. I'm not killing for you.

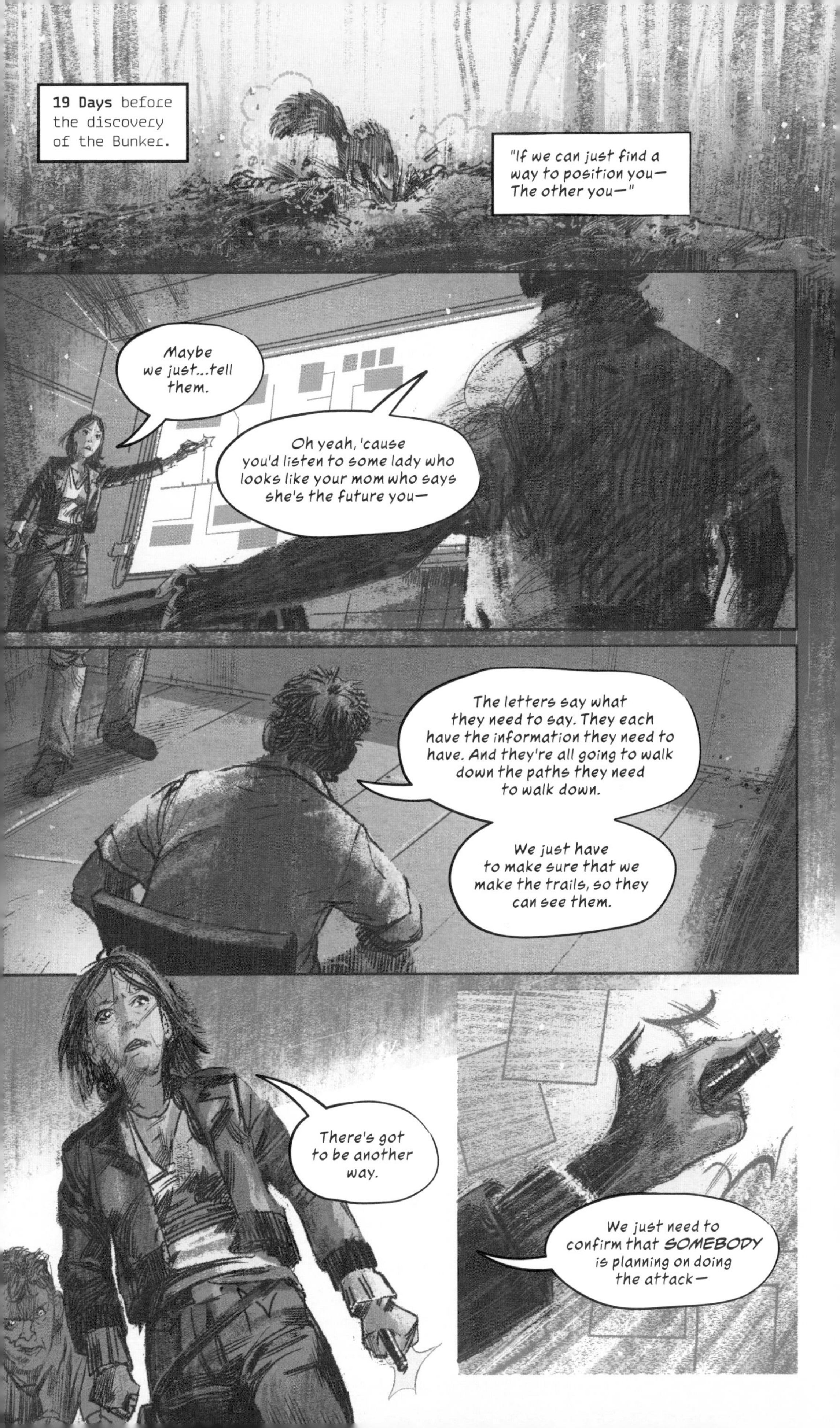
19 Days before the discovery of the Bunker.
"If we can just find a way to position you— The other you—"
Maybe we just...tell them.
Oh yeah, 'cause you'd listen to some lady who looks like your mom who says she's the future you—
The letters say what they need to say. They each have the information they need to have. And they're all going to walk down the paths they need to walk down.
We just have to make sure that we make the trails, so they can see them.
There's got to be another way.
We just need to confirm that *SOMEBODY* is planning on doing the attack—

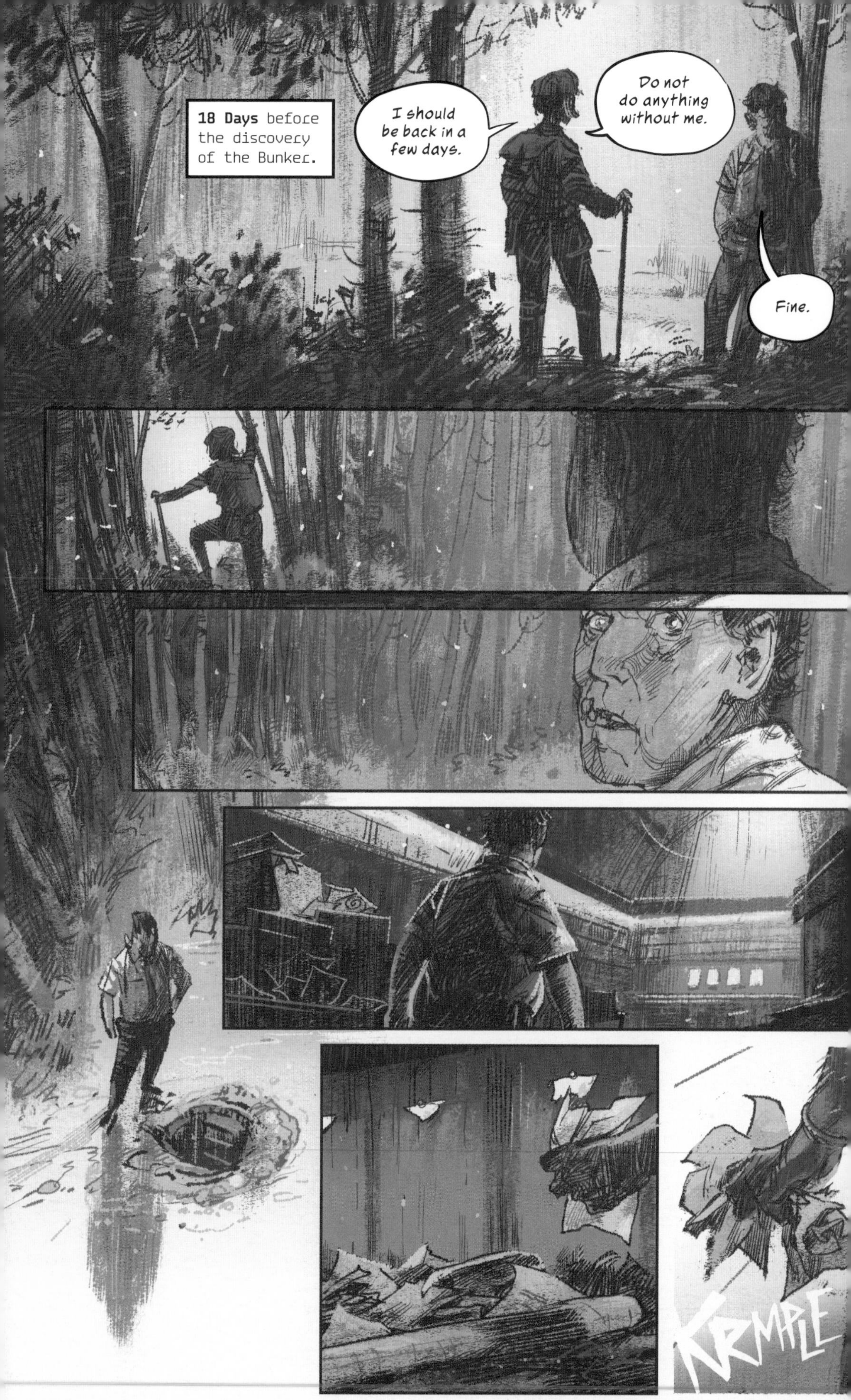
18 Days before the discovery of the Bunker.
I should be back in a few days.
Do not do anything without me.
Fine.
KRMPLE

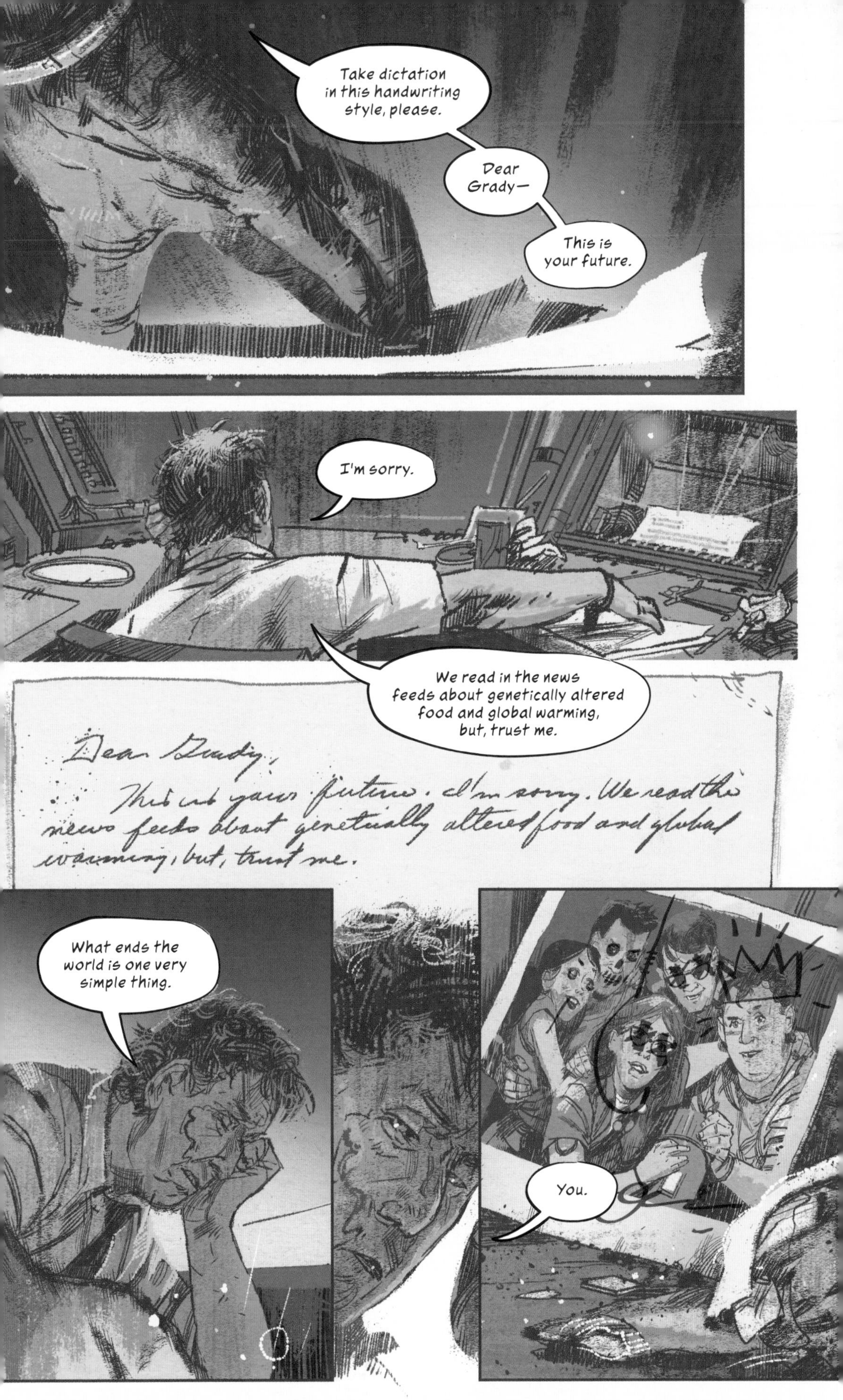
Take dictation in this handwriting style, please.
Dear Grady—
This is your future.
I'm sorry.
We read in the news feeds about genetically altered food and global warming, but, trust me.
Dear Grady:
This is your future. I'm sorry. We read the news feeds about genetically altered food and global warming, but, trust me.
What ends the world is one very simple thing.
You.

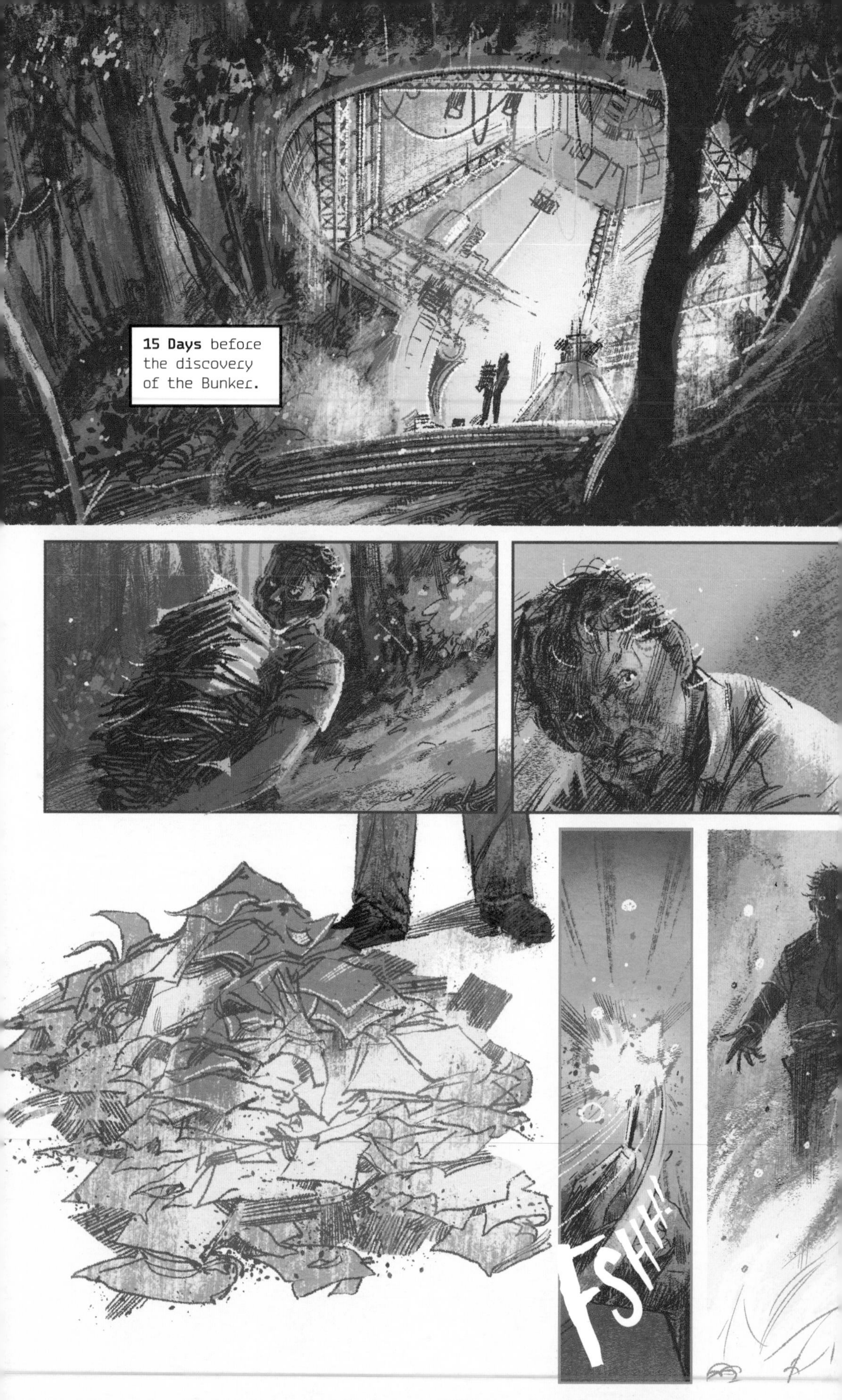
15 Days before the discovery of the Bunker.
FSHH!

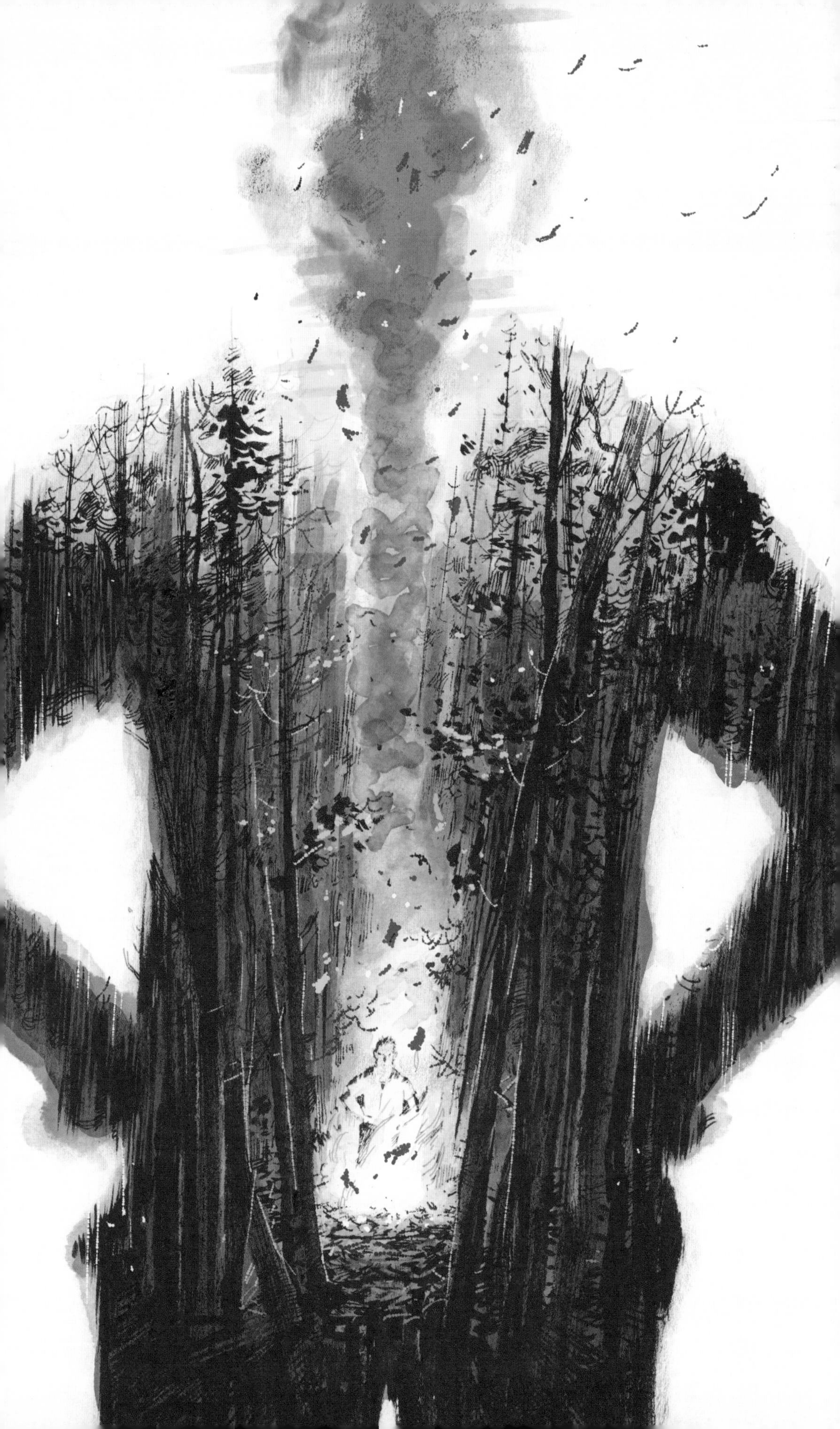

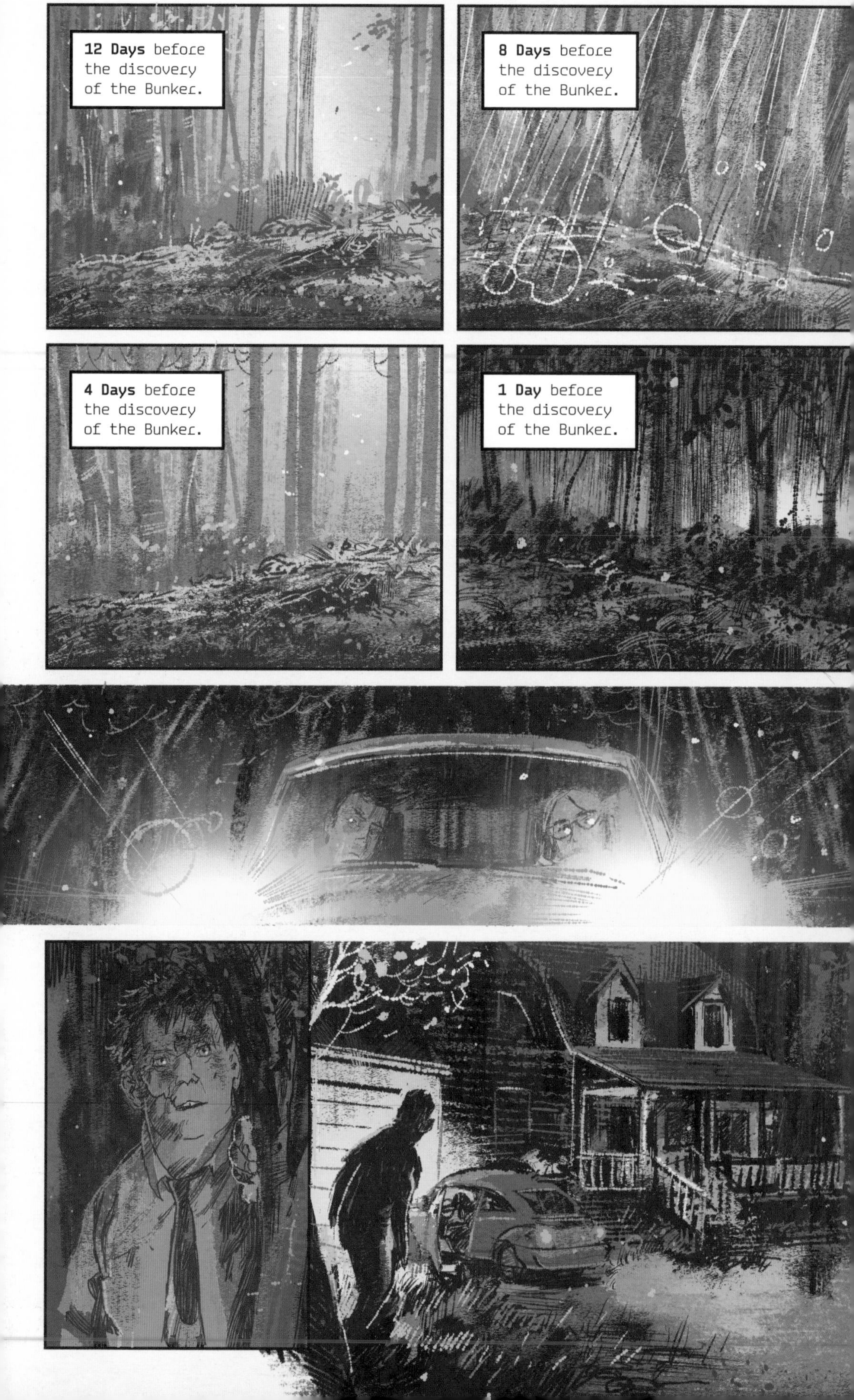
12 Days before the discovery of the Bunker.
8 Days before the discovery of the Bunker.
4 Days before the discovery of the Bunker.
1 Day before the discovery of the Bunker.

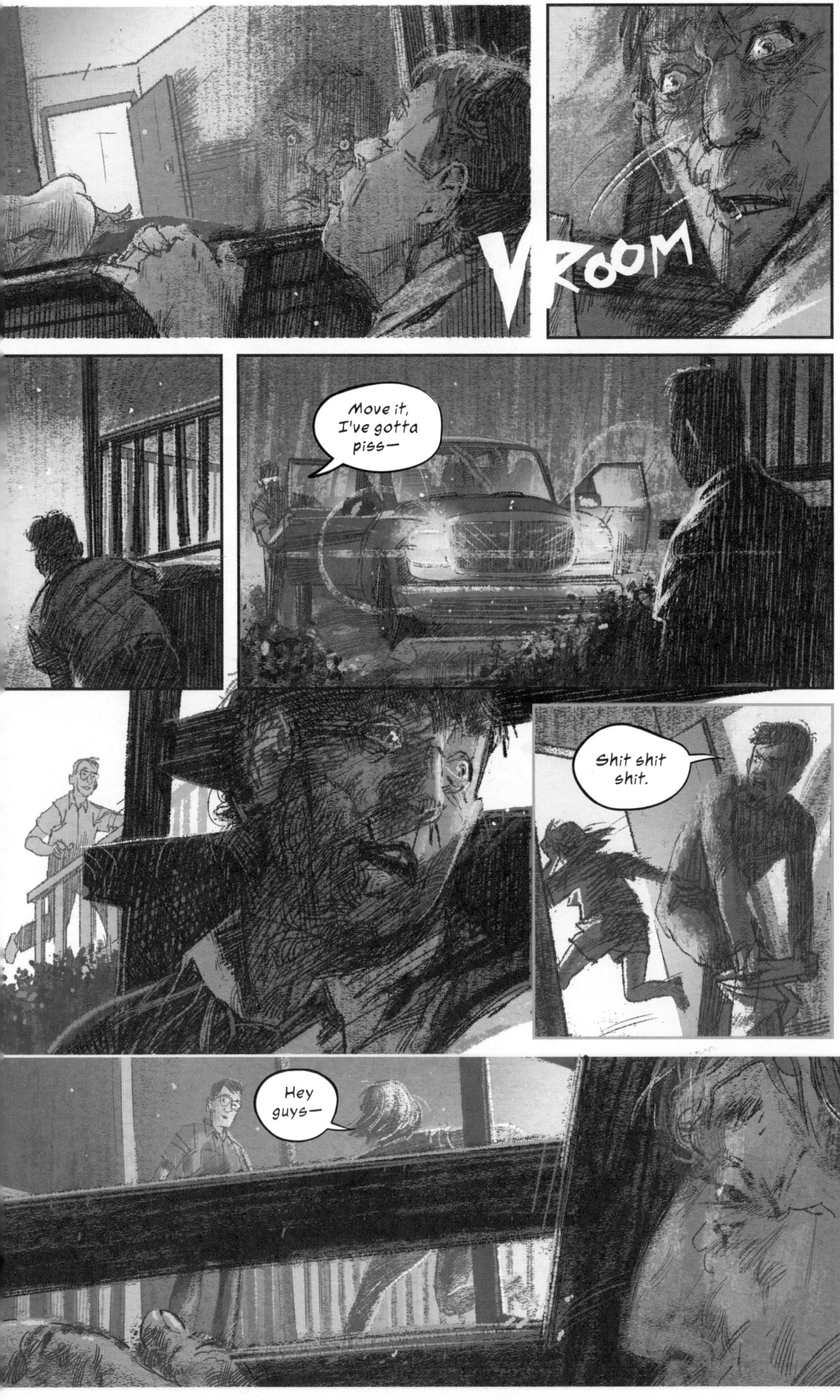
VROOM
Move it, I've gotta piss—
Shit shit shit.
Hey guys—

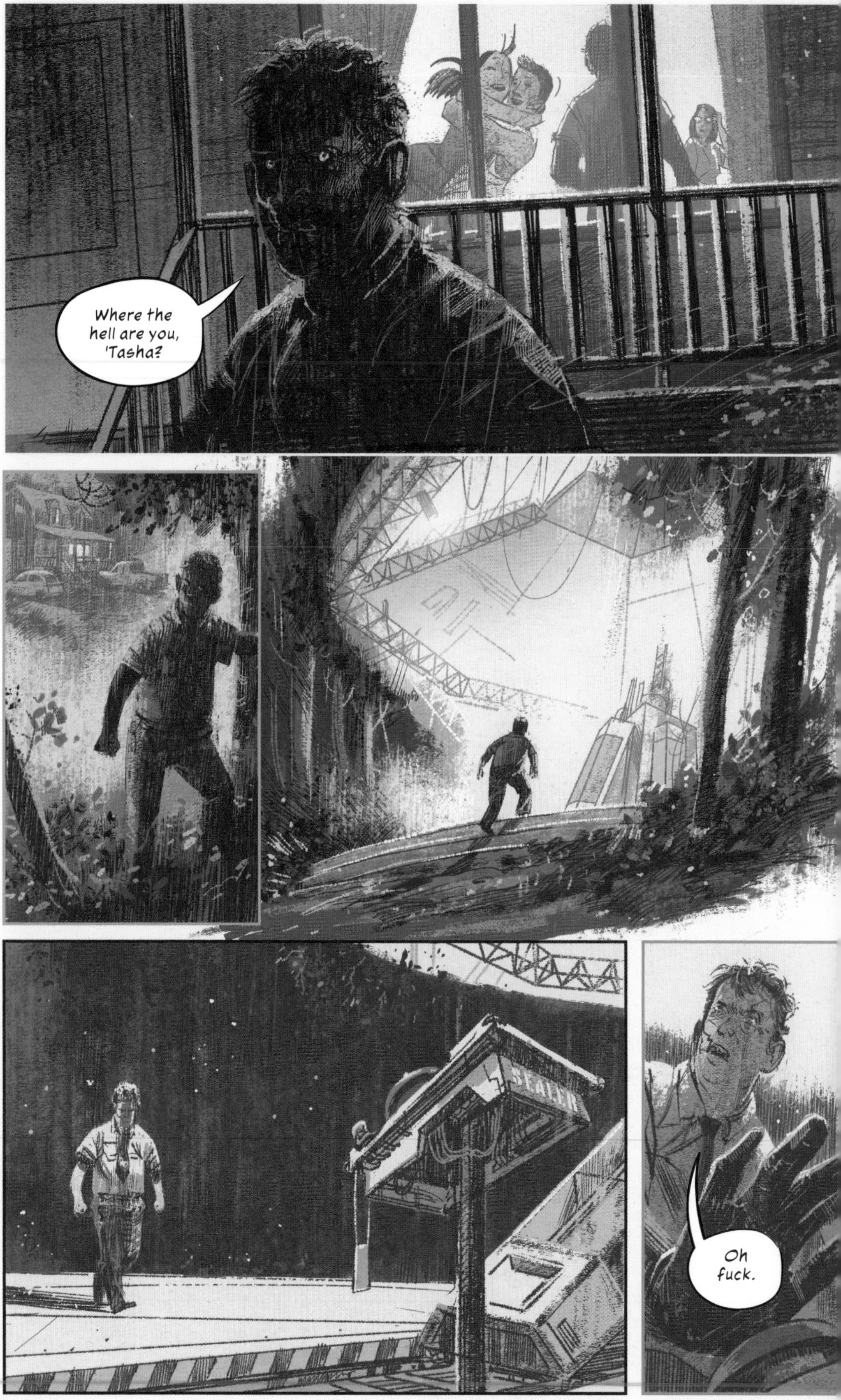
Where the hell are you, 'Tasha?
SEALER
Oh fuck.

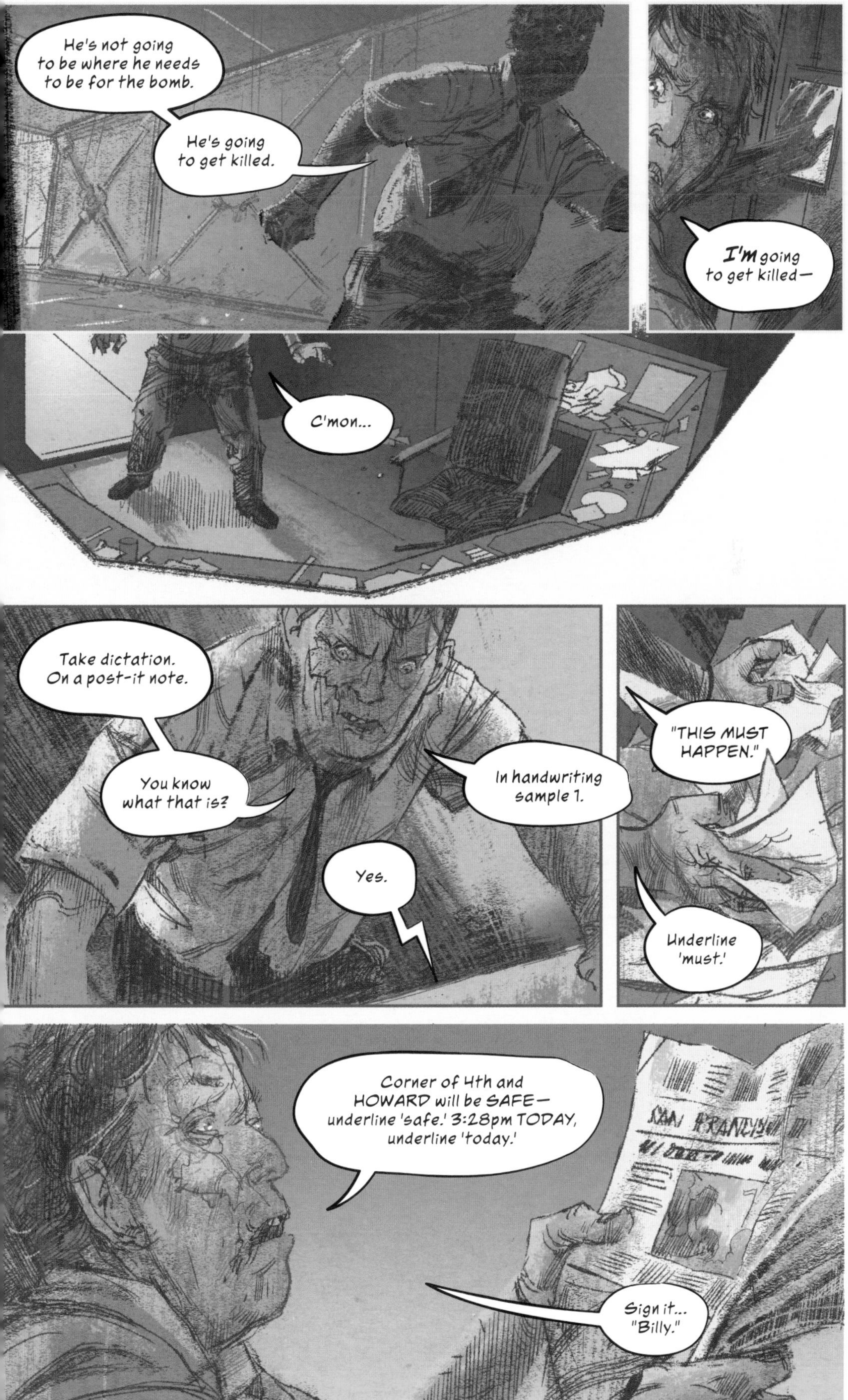
He's not going to be where he needs to be for the bomb.
He's going to get killed.
I'M going to get killed—
C'mon...
Take dictation. On a post-it note.
You know what that is?
In handwriting sample 1.
Yes.
"THIS MUST HAPPEN."
Underline 'must.'
Corner of 4th and HOWARD will be SAFE— underline 'safe.' 3:28pm TODAY, underline 'today.'
Sign it... "Billy."

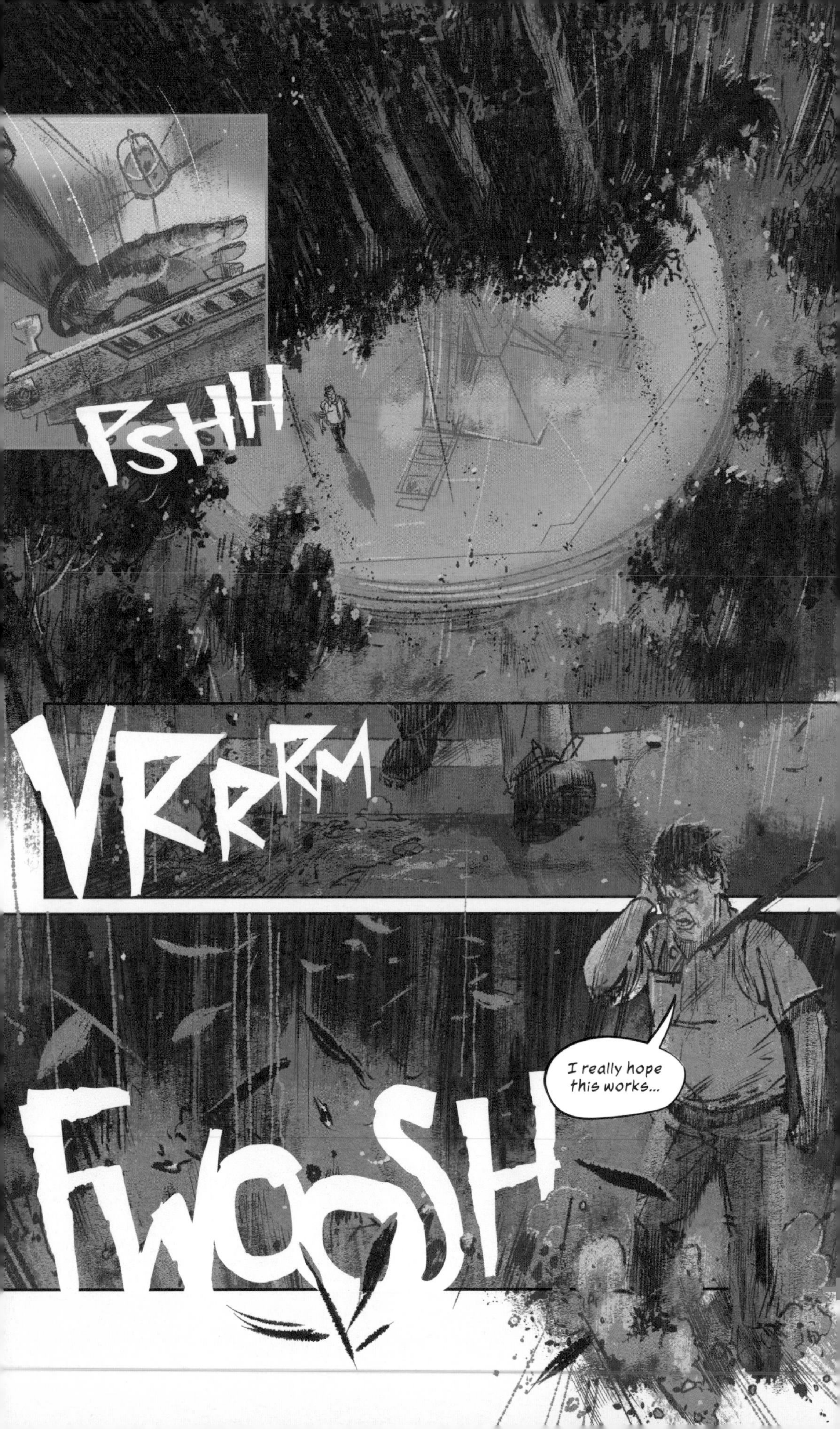
PSHH
VRRRM
I really hope this works...
FWOOSH

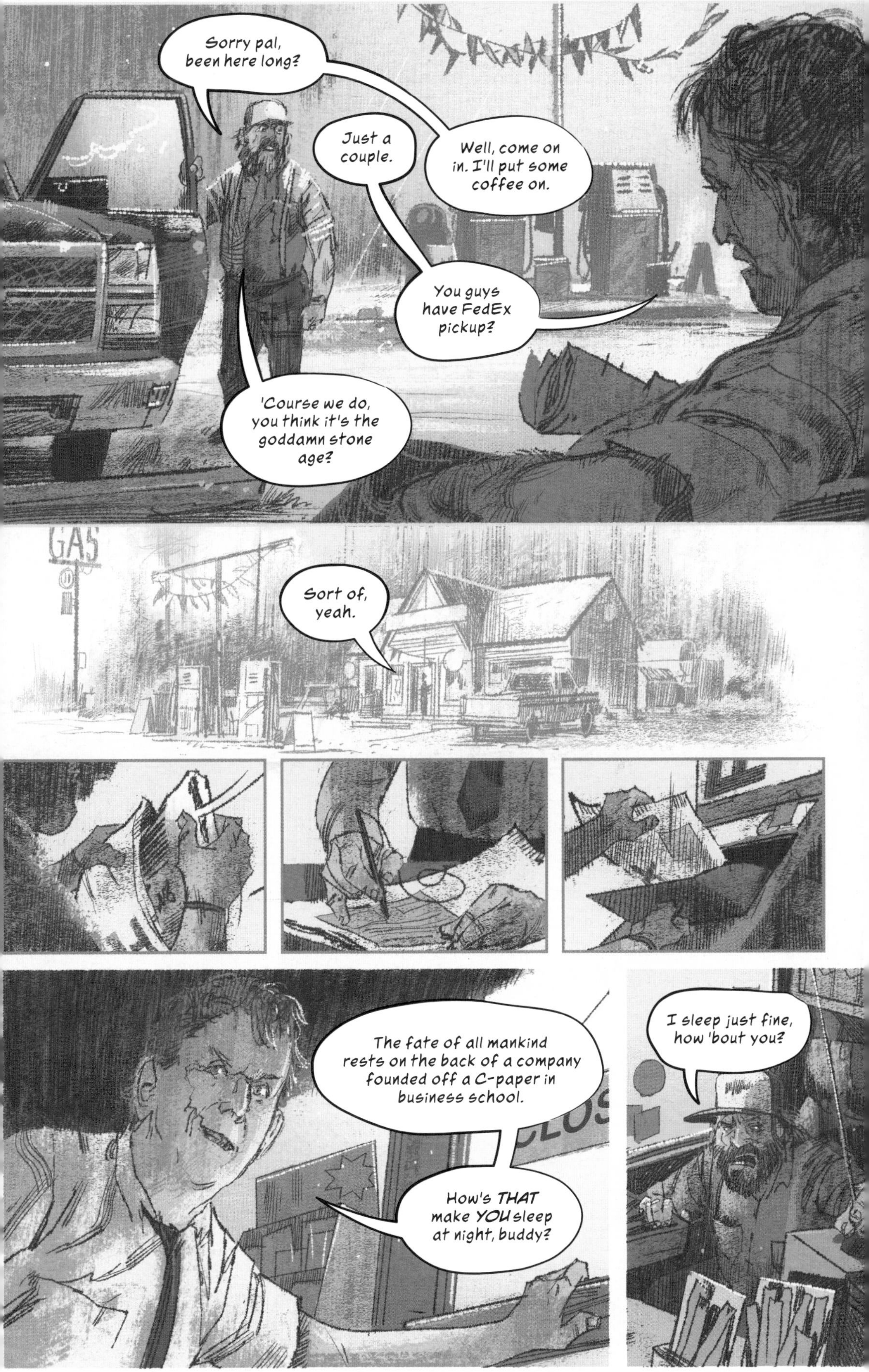
Sorry pal, been here long?
Just a couple.
Well, come on in. I'll put some coffee on.
You guys have FedEx pickup?
'Course we do, you think it's the goddamn stone age?
GAS
Sort of, yeah.
The fate of all mankind rests on the back of a company founded off a C-paper in business school.
How's *THAT* make *YOU* sleep at night, buddy?
I sleep just fine, how 'bout you?

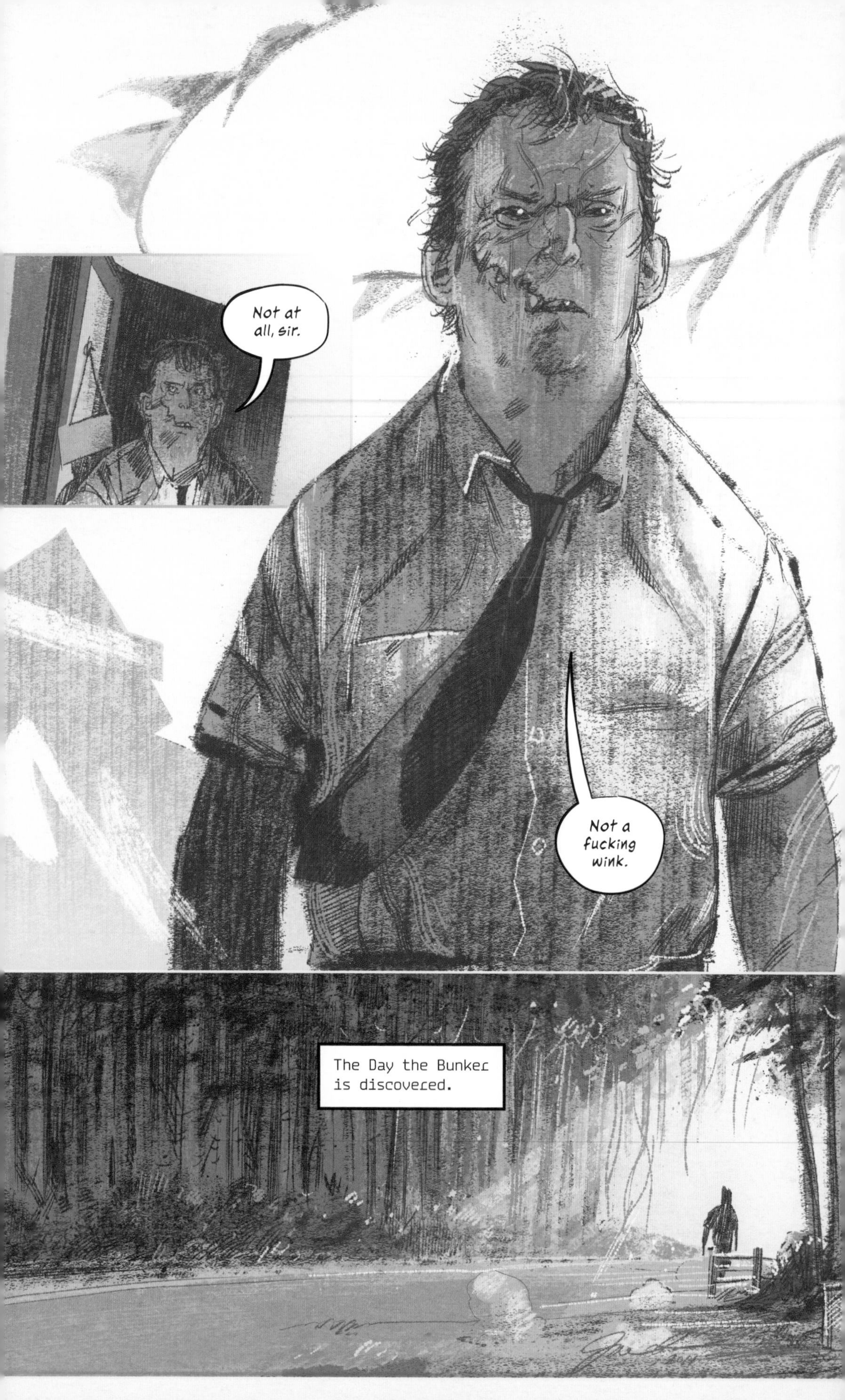

Not at all, sir.
Not a fucking wink.
The Day the Bunker is discovered.

CHAPTER
07

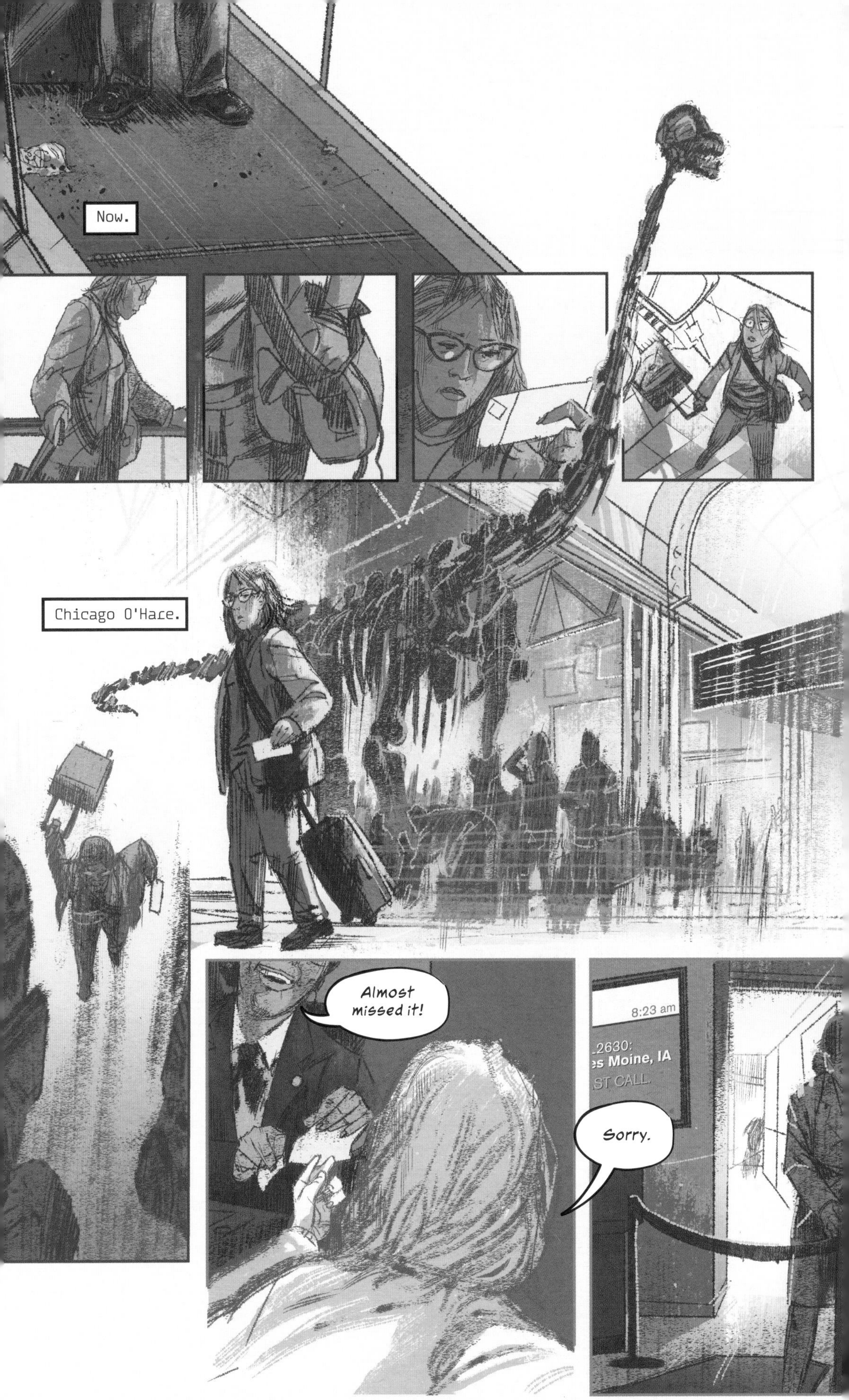
Now.
Chicago O'Hare.
Almost missed it!
8:23 am
2630:
es Moine, IA
ST CALL.
Sorry.

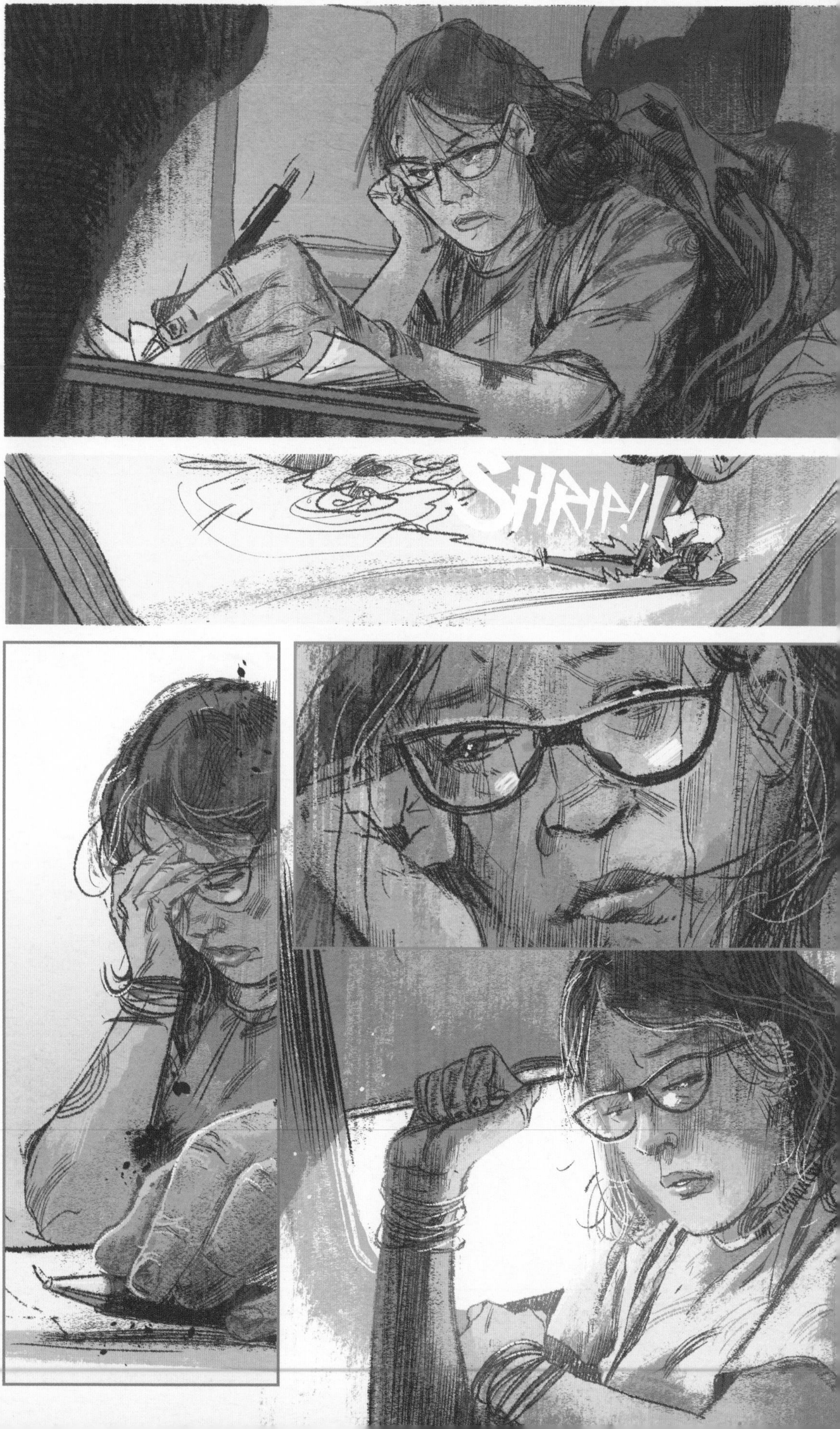
SHRIP!

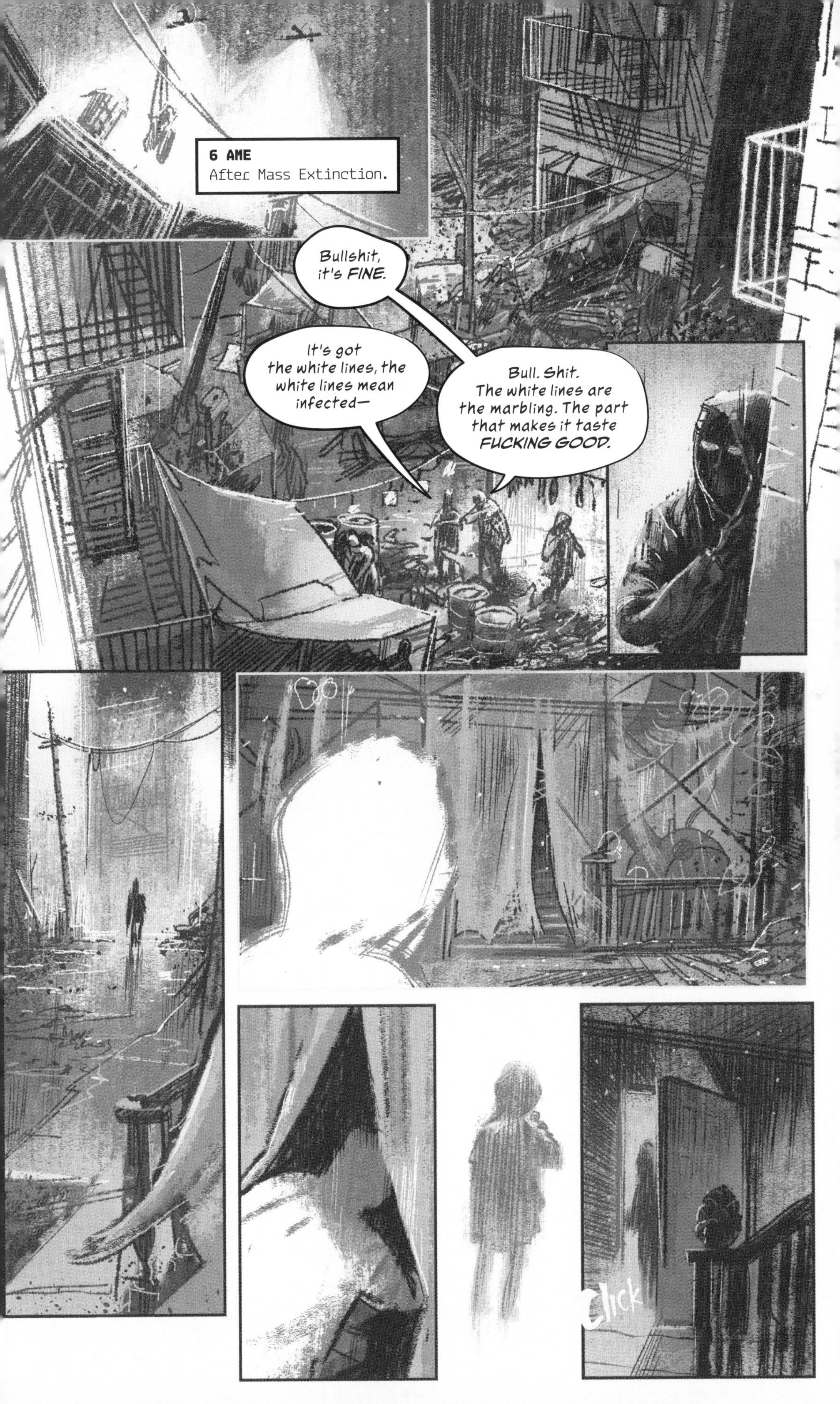
6 AME
After Mass Extinction.
Bullshit, it's FINE.
It's got the white lines, the white lines mean infected—
Bull. Shit. The white lines are the marbling. The part that makes it taste FUCKING GOOD.
CLICK

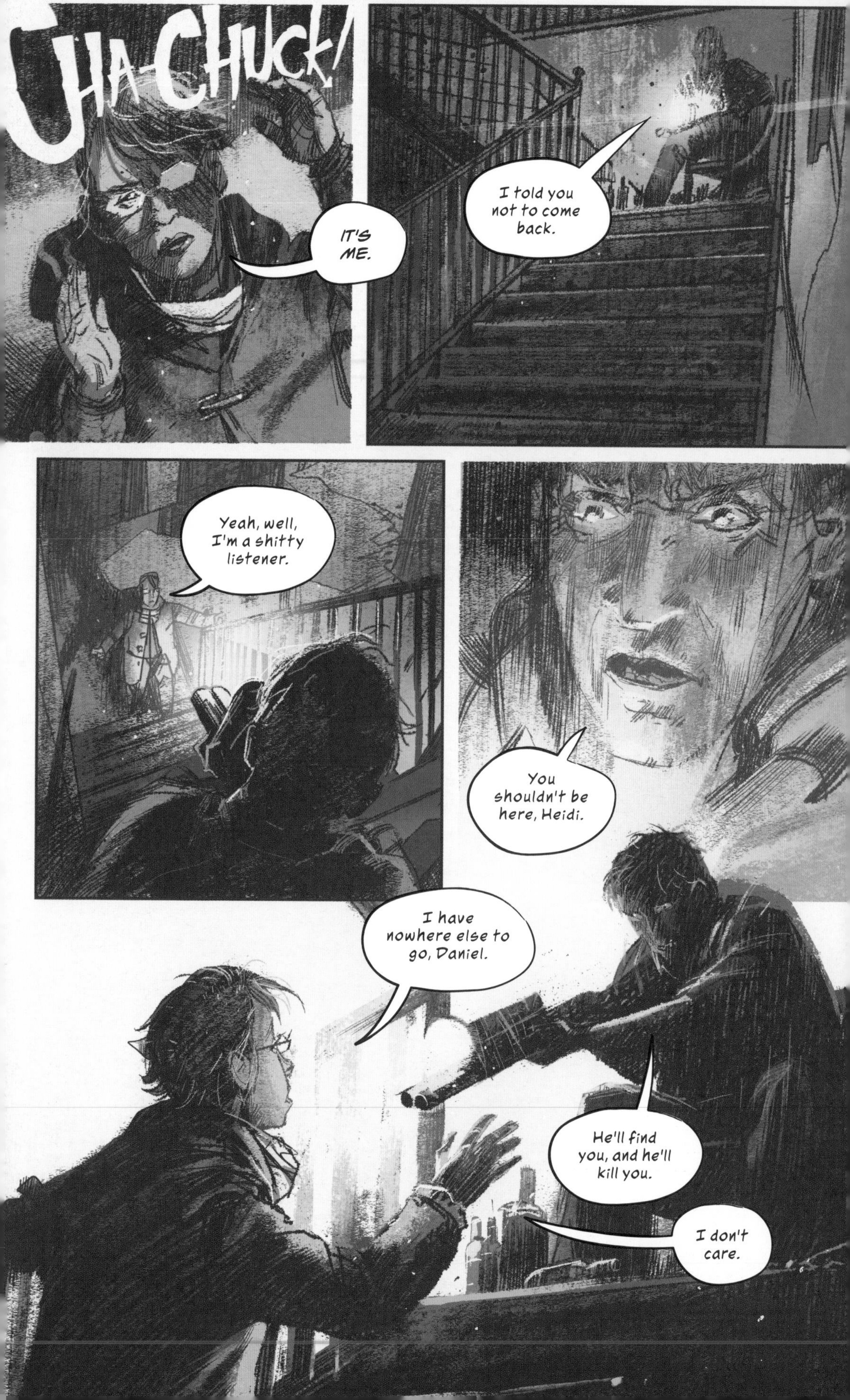
CHA-CHUCK!
IT'S ME.
I told you not to come back.
Yeah, well, I'm a shitty listener.
You shouldn't be here, Heidi.
I have nowhere else to go, Daniel.
He'll find you, and he'll kill you.
I don't care.

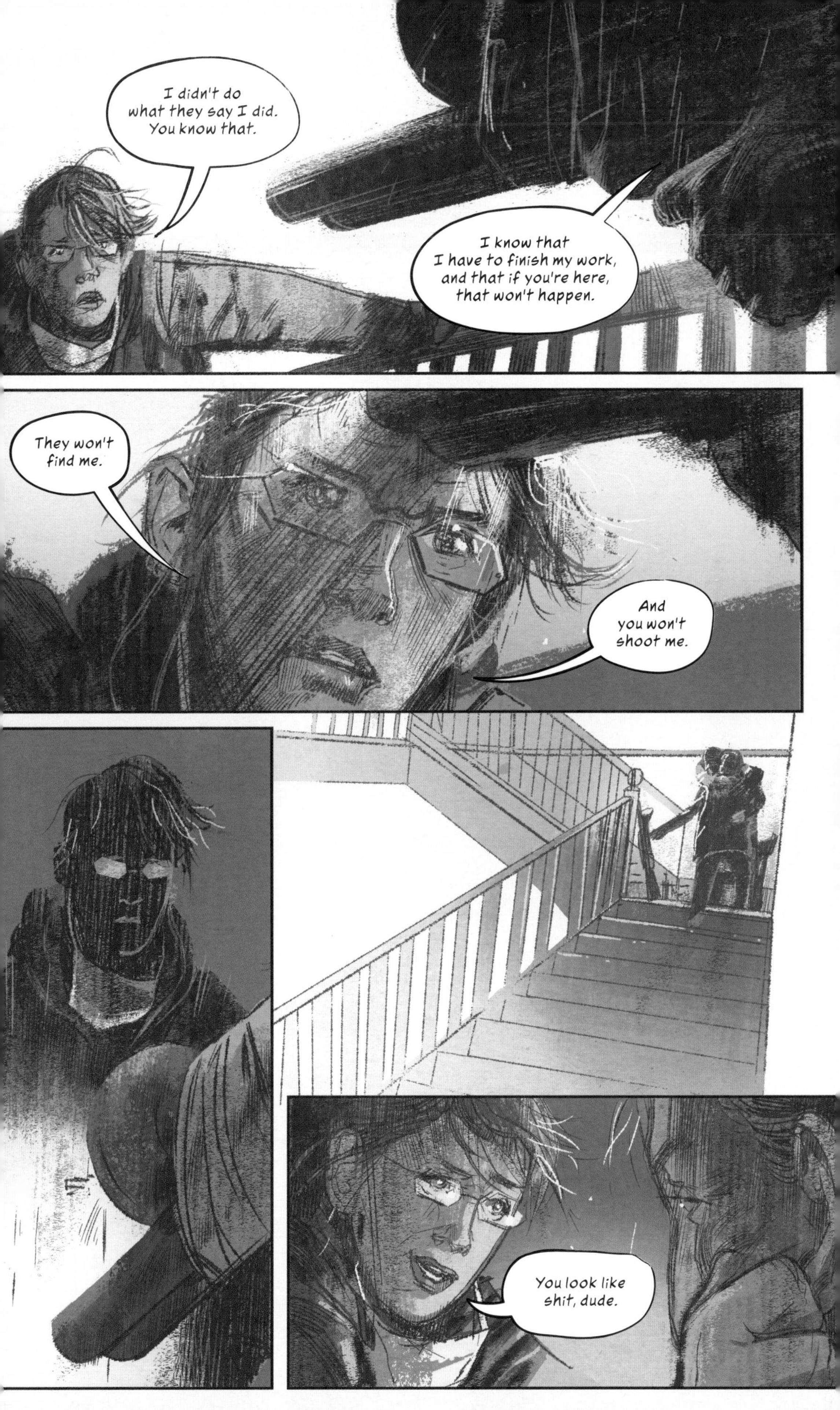
I didn't do what they say I did. You know that.
I know that I have to finish my work, and that if you're here, that won't happen.
They won't find me.
And you won't shoot me.
You look like shit, dude.

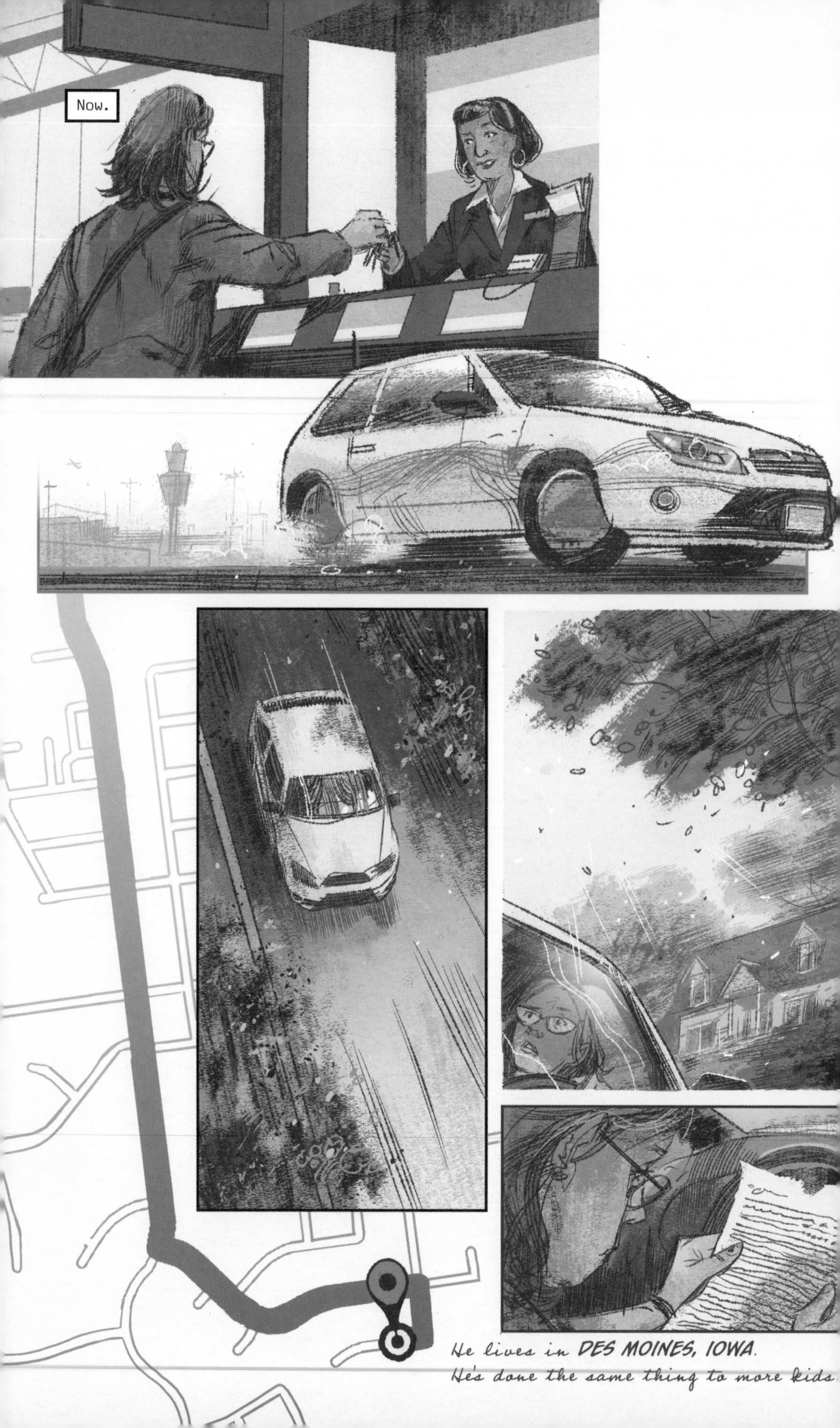
Now.
He lives in DES MOINES, IOWA.
He's done the same thing to more kids

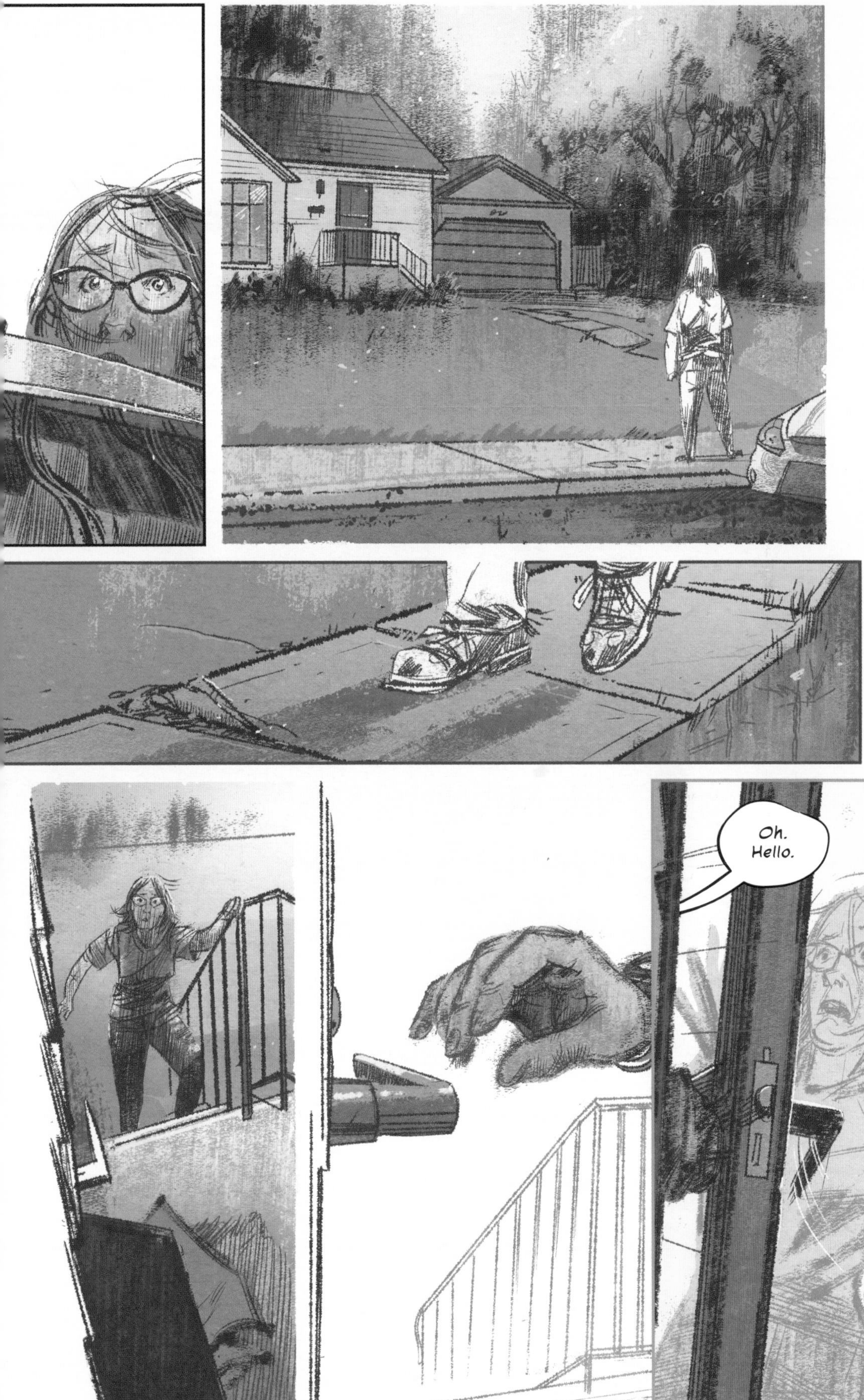
Oh. Hello.

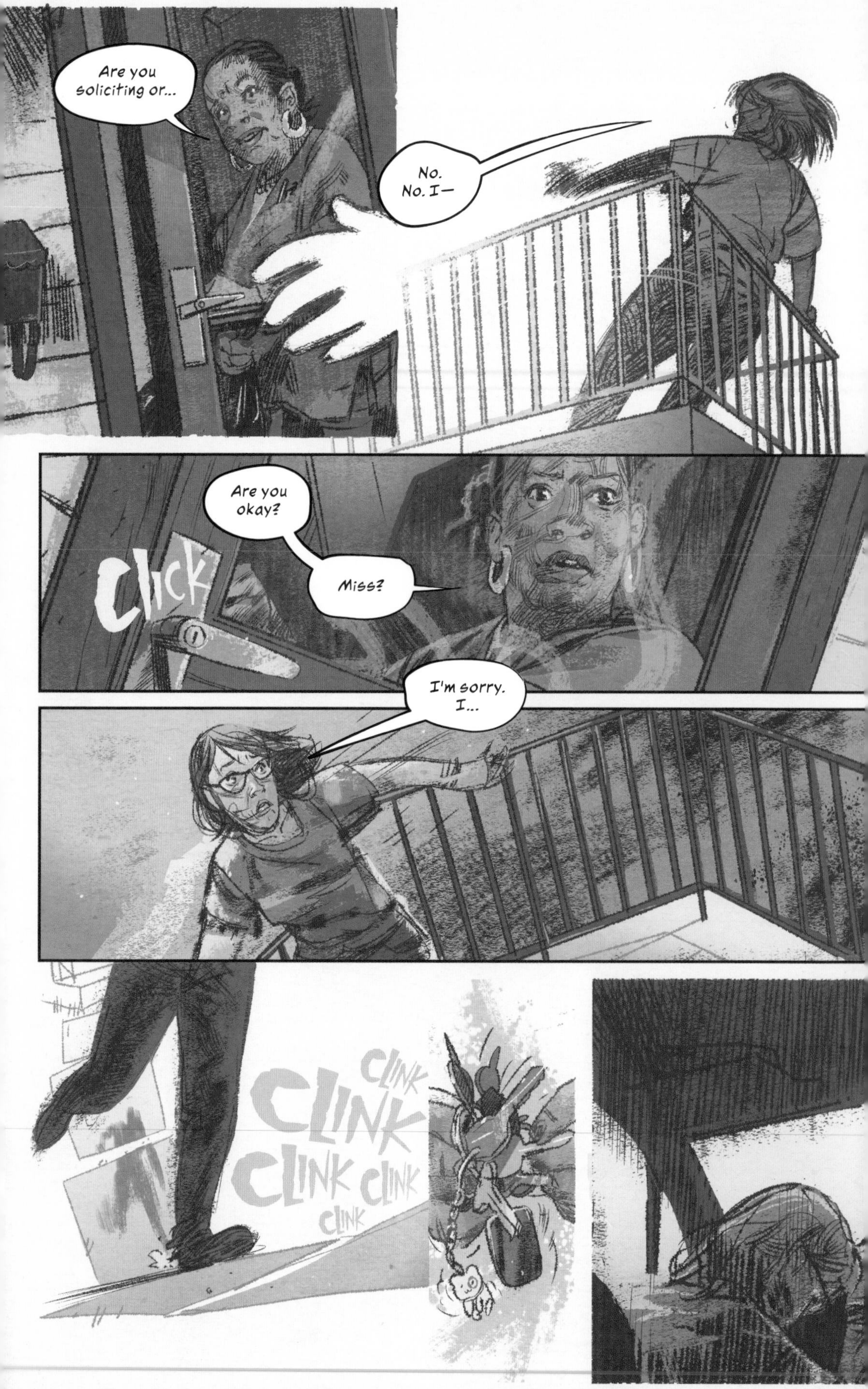
Are you soliciting or...
No. No. I—
Are you okay?
Miss?
CLICK
I'm sorry. I...
CLINK
CLINK
CLINK CLINK
CLINK

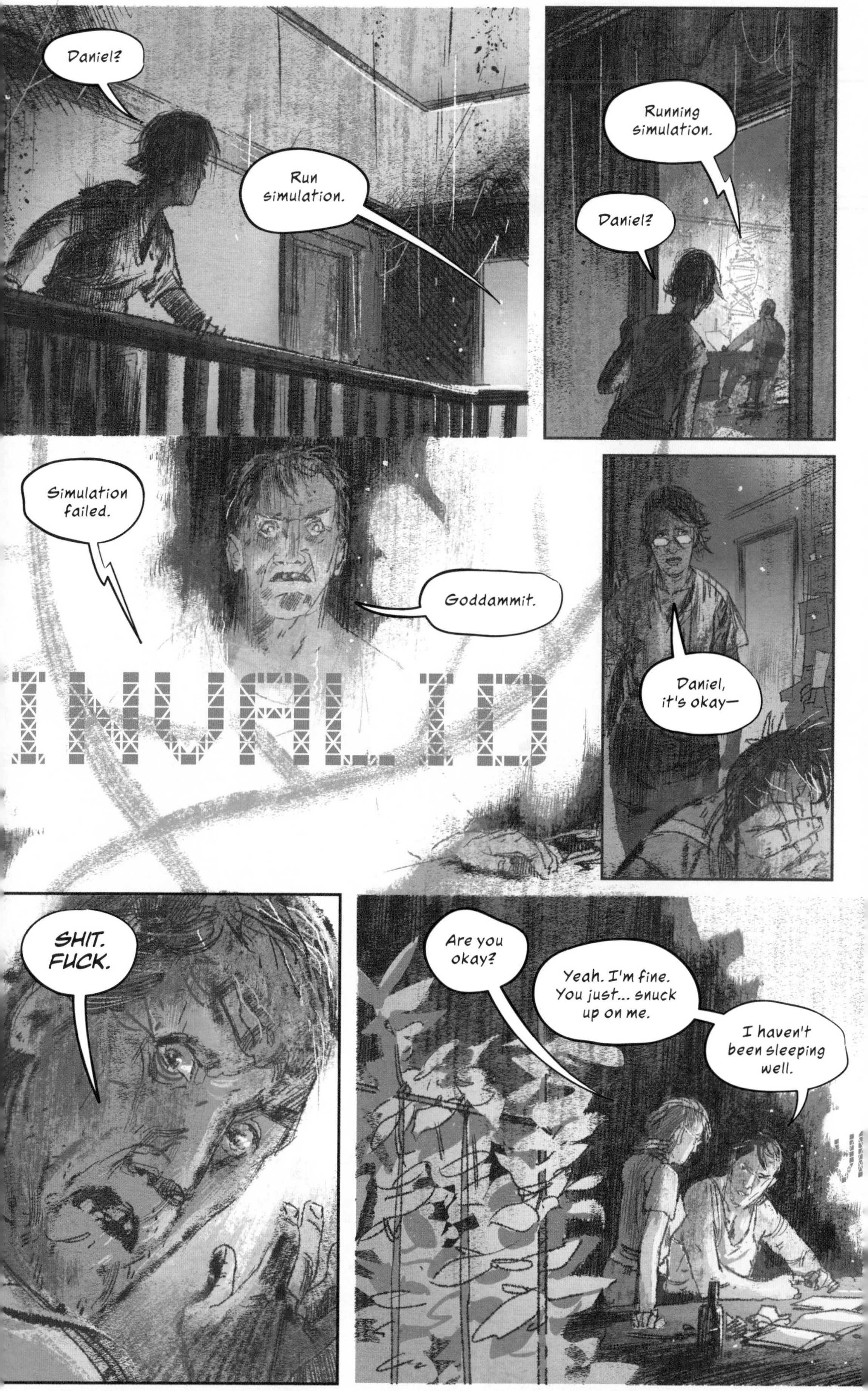
Daniel?
Run simulation.
Running simulation.
Daniel?
Simulation failed.
Goddammit.
INVALID
Daniel, it's okay—
SHIT. FUCK.
Are you okay?
Yeah. I'm fine. You just... snuck up on me.
I haven't been sleeping well.

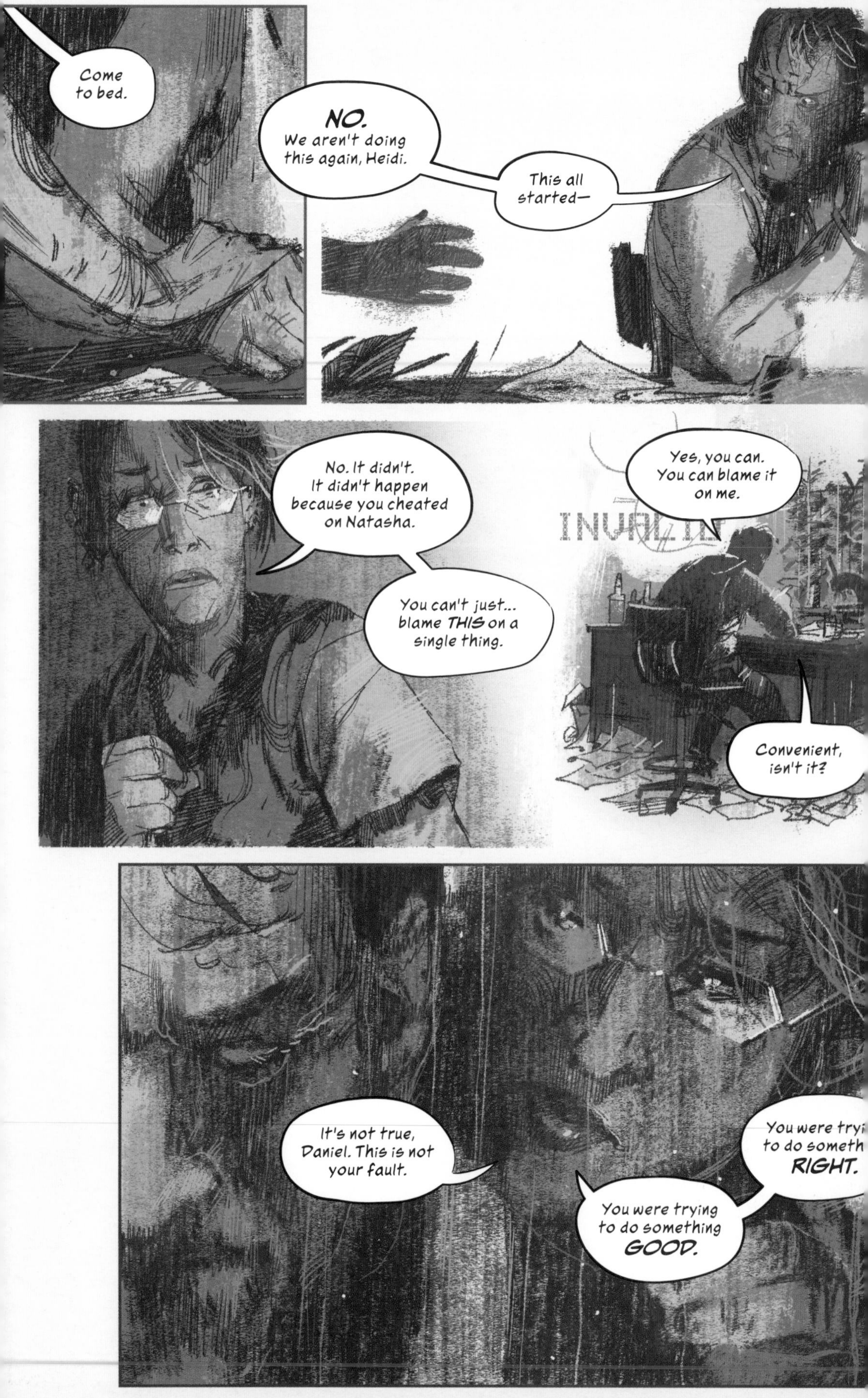
Come to bed.
NO. We aren't doing this again, Heidi.
This all started—
No. It didn't. It didn't happen because you cheated on Natasha.
You can't just... blame THIS on a single thing.
INVALID
Yes, you can. You can blame it on me.
Convenient, isn't it?
It's not true, Daniel. This is not your fault.
You were trying to do something GOOD.
You were tryi to do someth RIGHT.

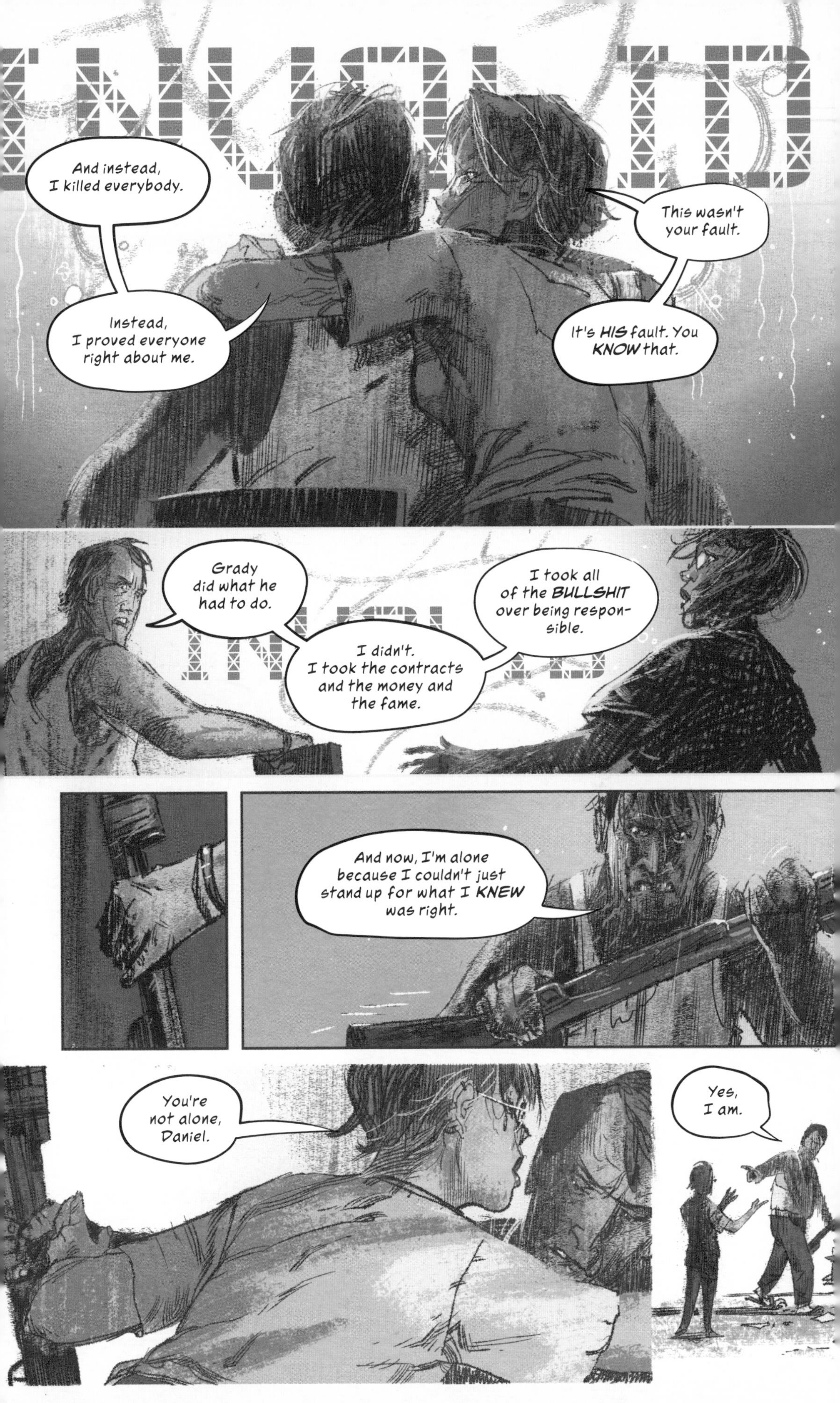
And instead, I killed everybody.
Instead, I proved everyone right about me.
This wasn't your fault.
It's HIS fault. You KNOW that.
Grady did what he had to do.
I didn't. I took the contracts and the money and the fame.
I took all of the BULLSHIT over being respon-sible.
And now, I'm alone because I couldn't just stand up for what I KNEW was right.
You're not alone, Daniel.
Yes, I am.

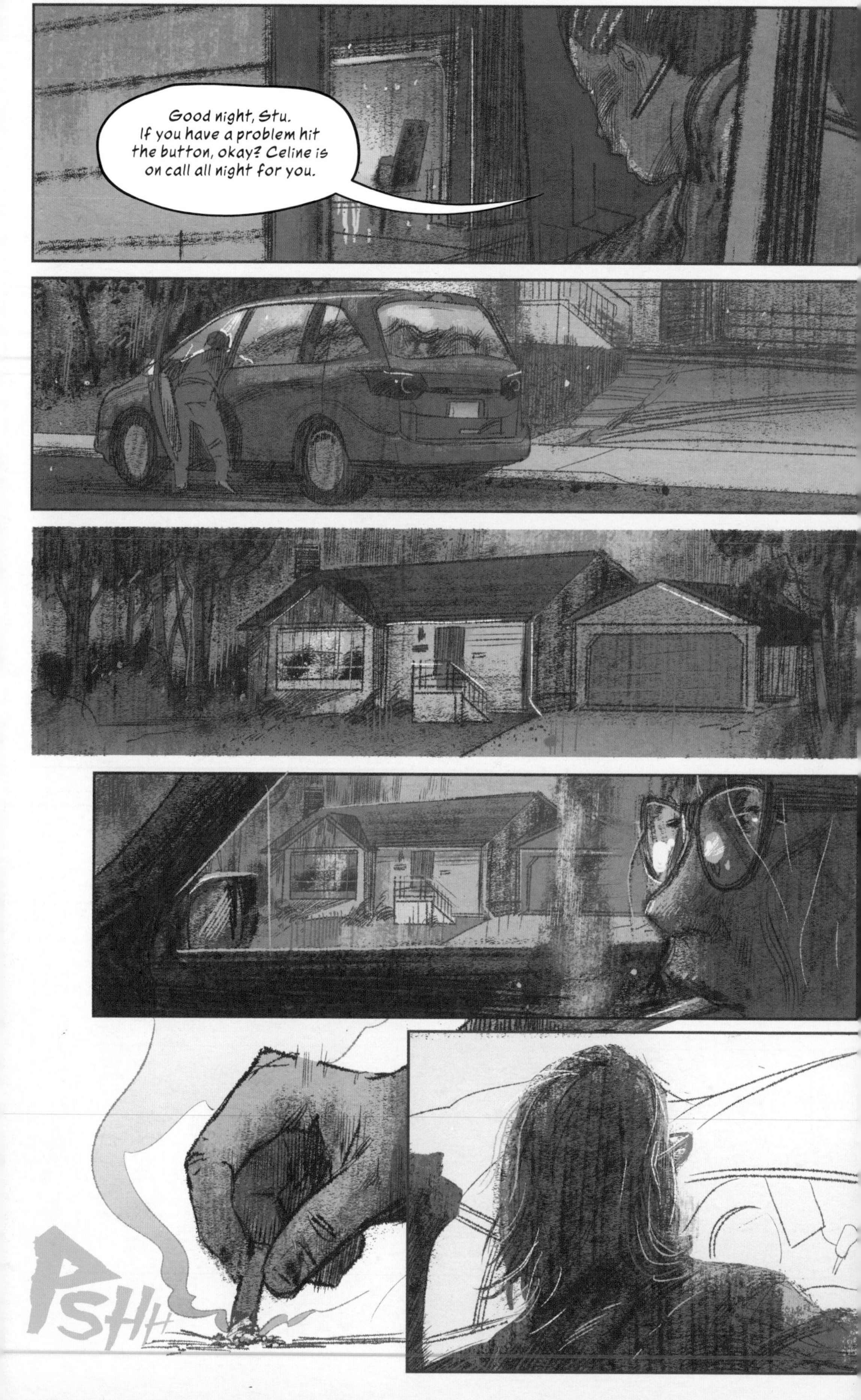
Good night, Stu. If you have a problem hit the button, okay? Celine is on call all night for you.
PSHH

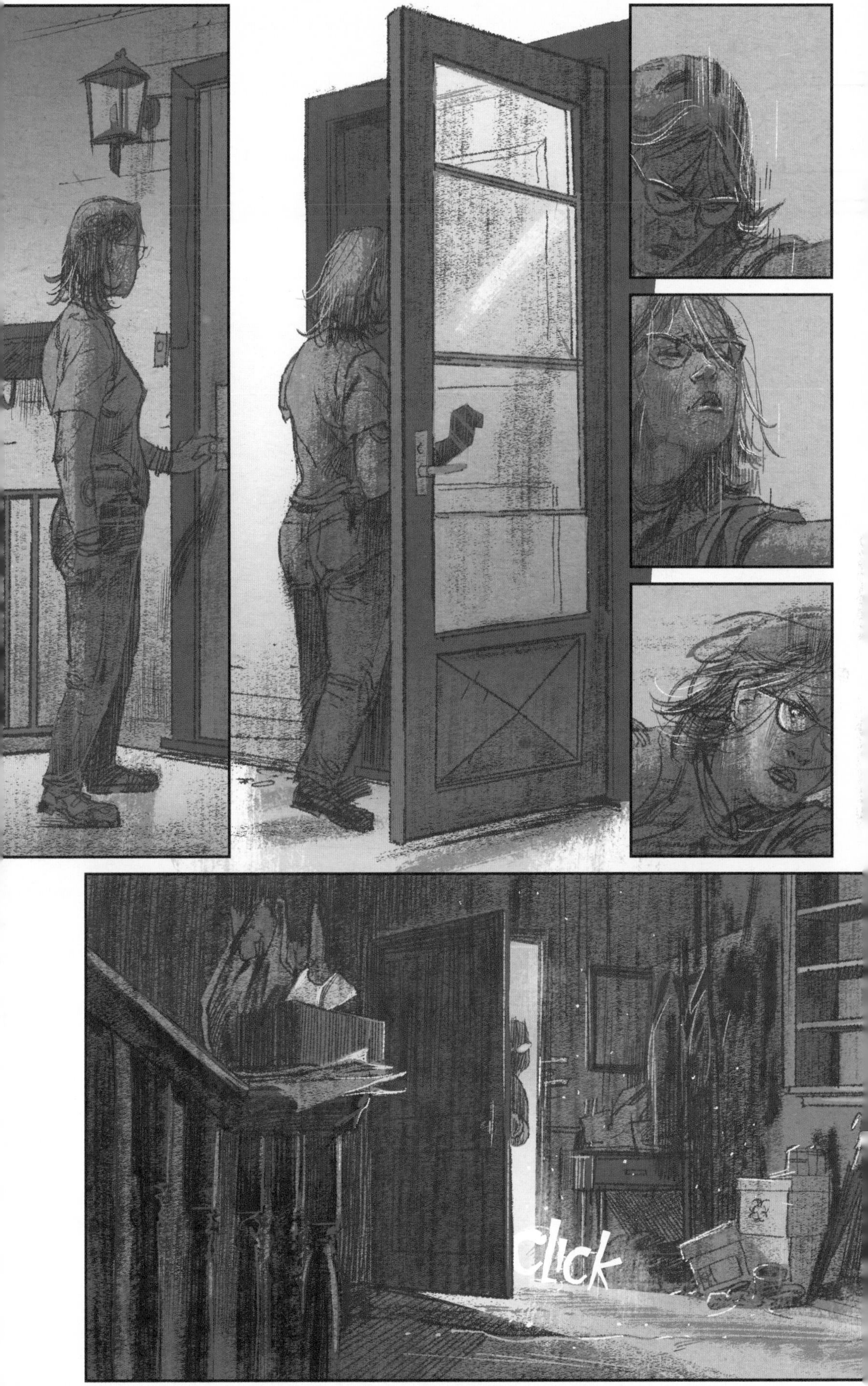
CLICK

SKRITCH SKRT

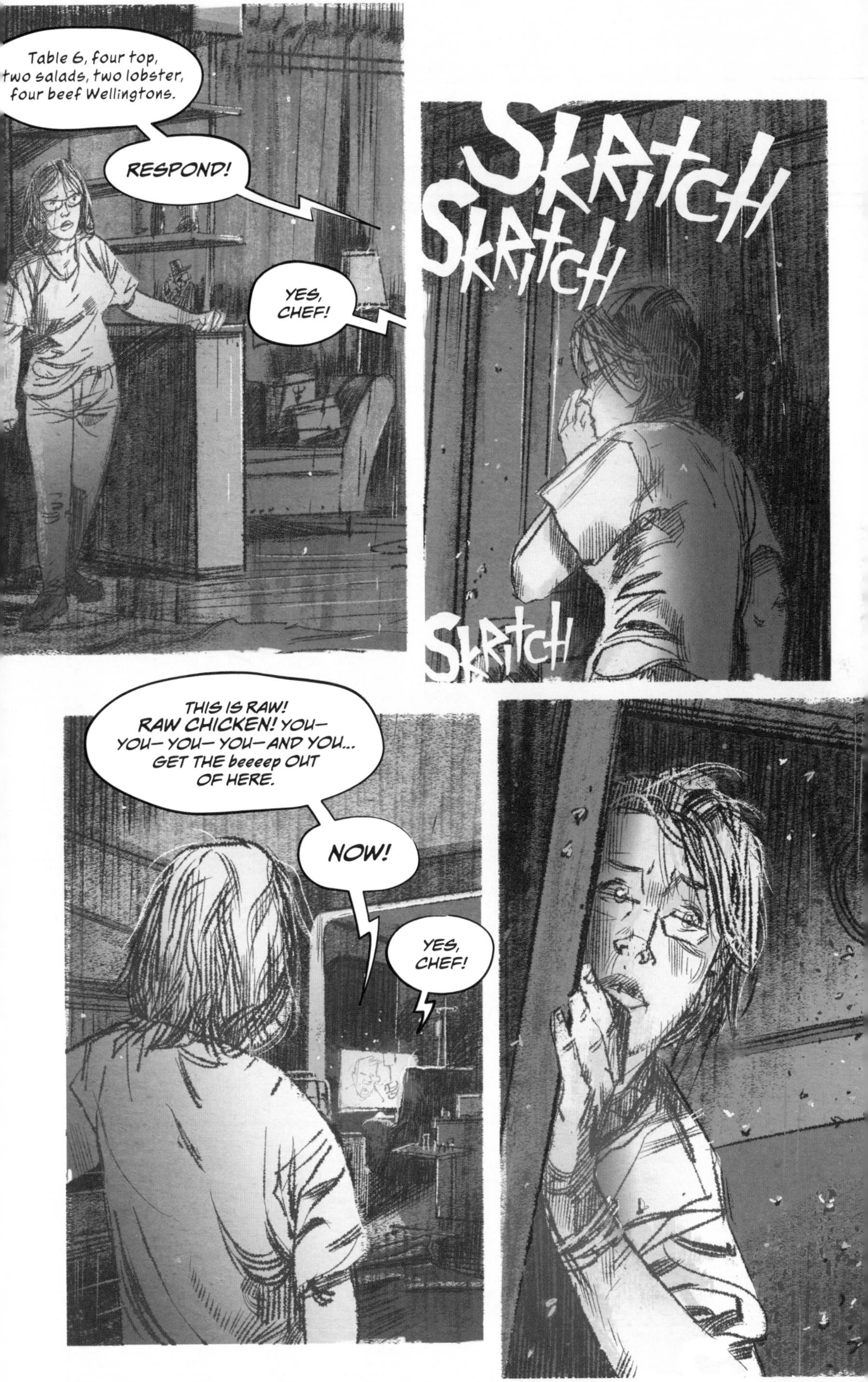

Table 6, four top, two salads, two lobster, four beef Wellingtons.
RESPOND!
YES, CHEF!
SKRITCH
SKRITCH
SKRITCH
THIS IS RAW! RAW CHICKEN! YOU— YOU— YOU— YOU— AND YOU... GET THE beeeep OUT OF HERE.
NOW!
YES, CHEF!

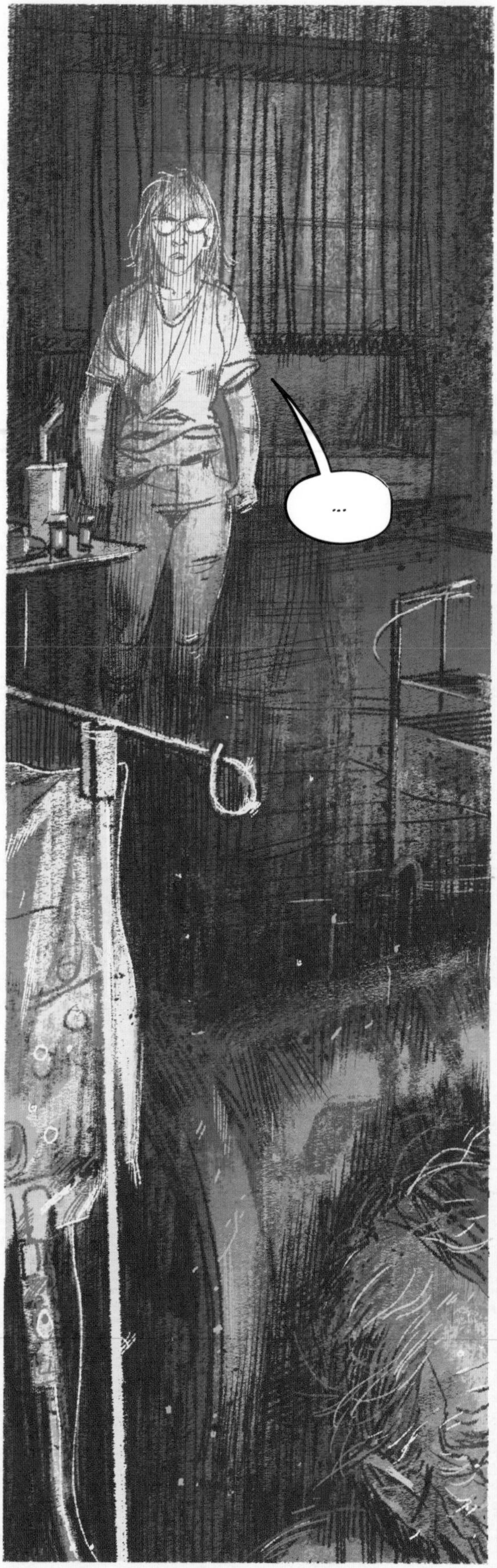
...

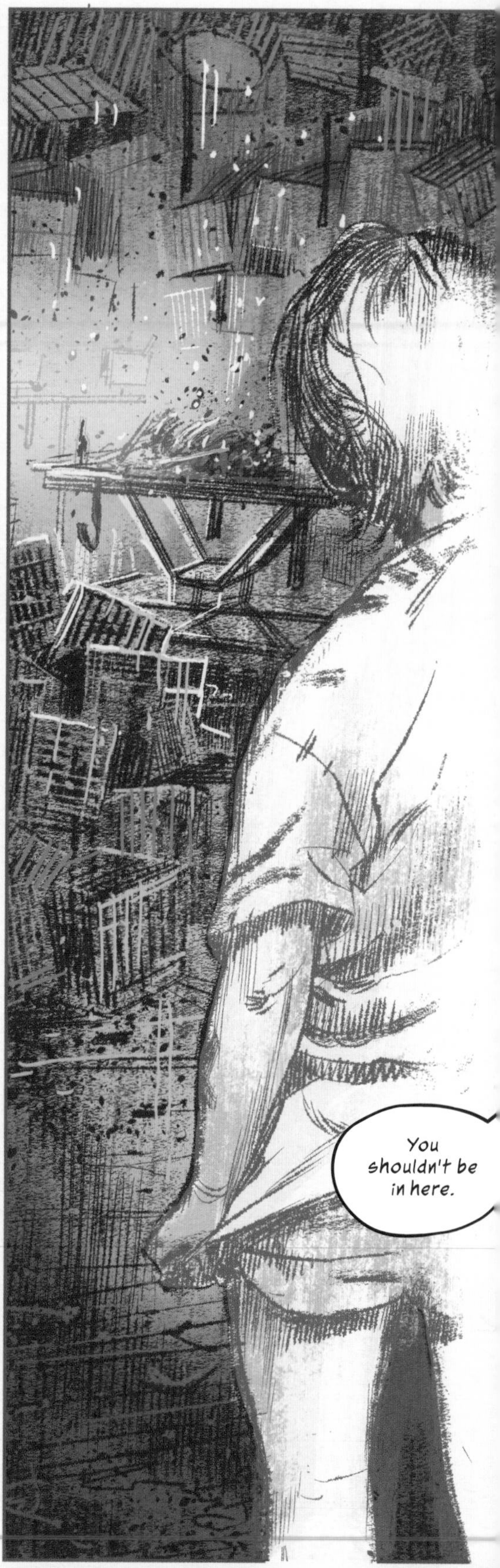
You shouldn't be in here.

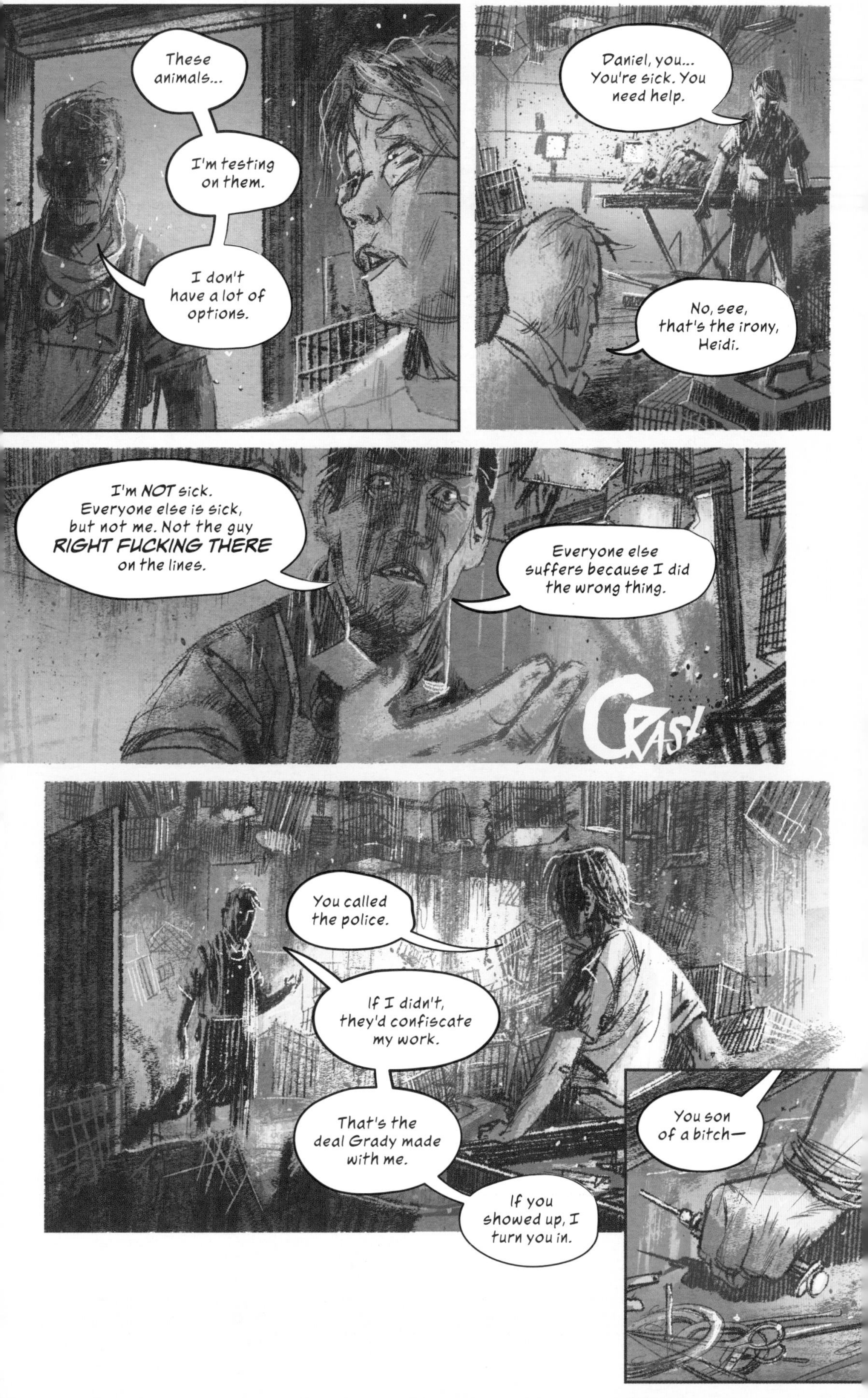
These animals...
I'm testing on them.
I don't have a lot of options.
Daniel, you... You're sick. You need help.
No, see, that's the irony, Heidi.
I'm NOT sick. Everyone else is sick, but not me. Not the guy RIGHT FUCKING THERE on the lines.
Everyone else suffers because I did the wrong thing.
CRASH
You called the police.
If I didn't, they'd confiscate my work.
That's the deal Grady made with me.
If you showed up, I turn you in.
You son of a bitch—

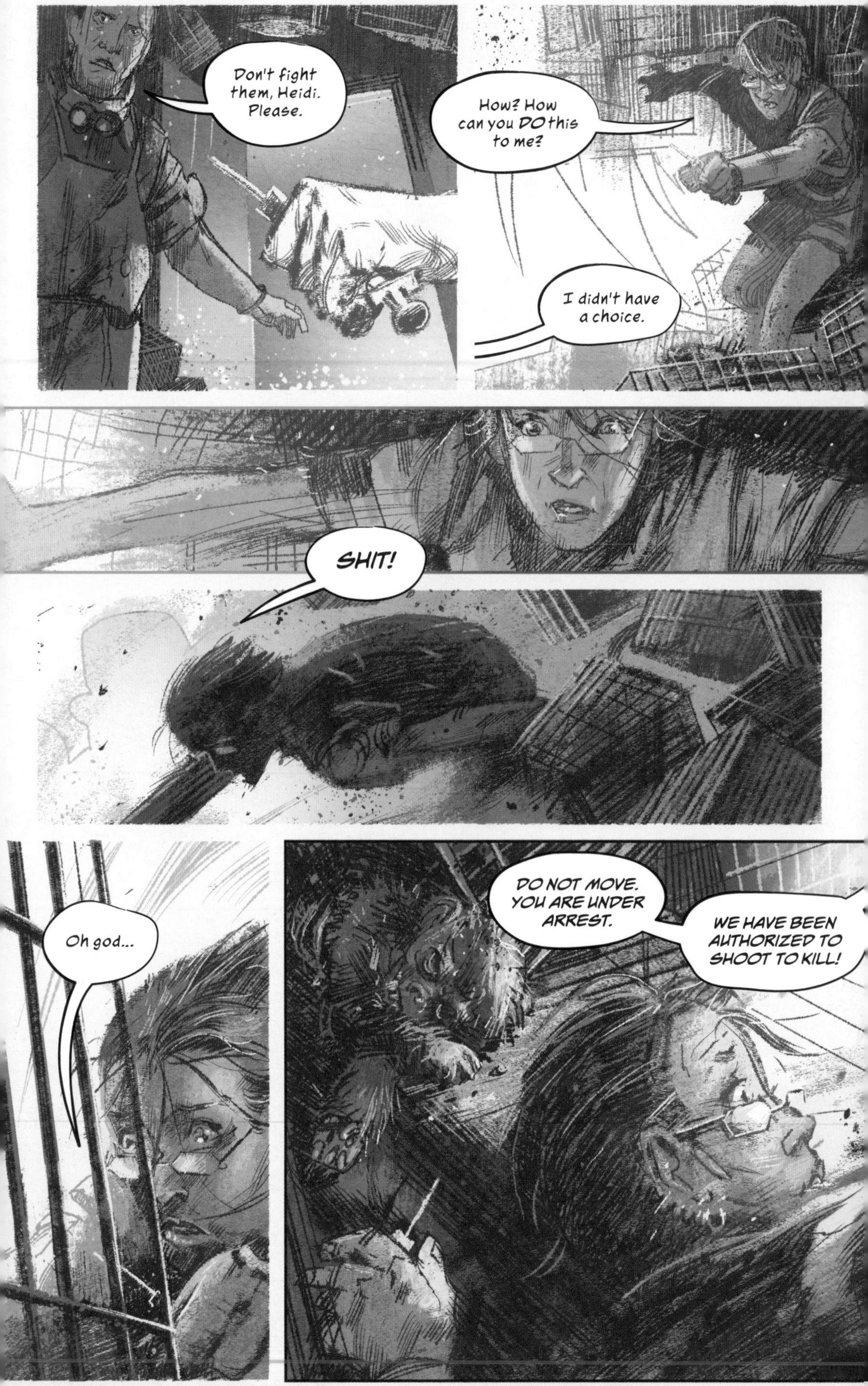
Don't fight them, Heidi. Please.
How? How can you DO this to me?
I didn't have a choice.
SHIT!
Oh god...
DO NOT MOVE. YOU ARE UNDER ARREST.
WE HAVE BEEN AUTHORIZED TO SHOOT TO KILL!

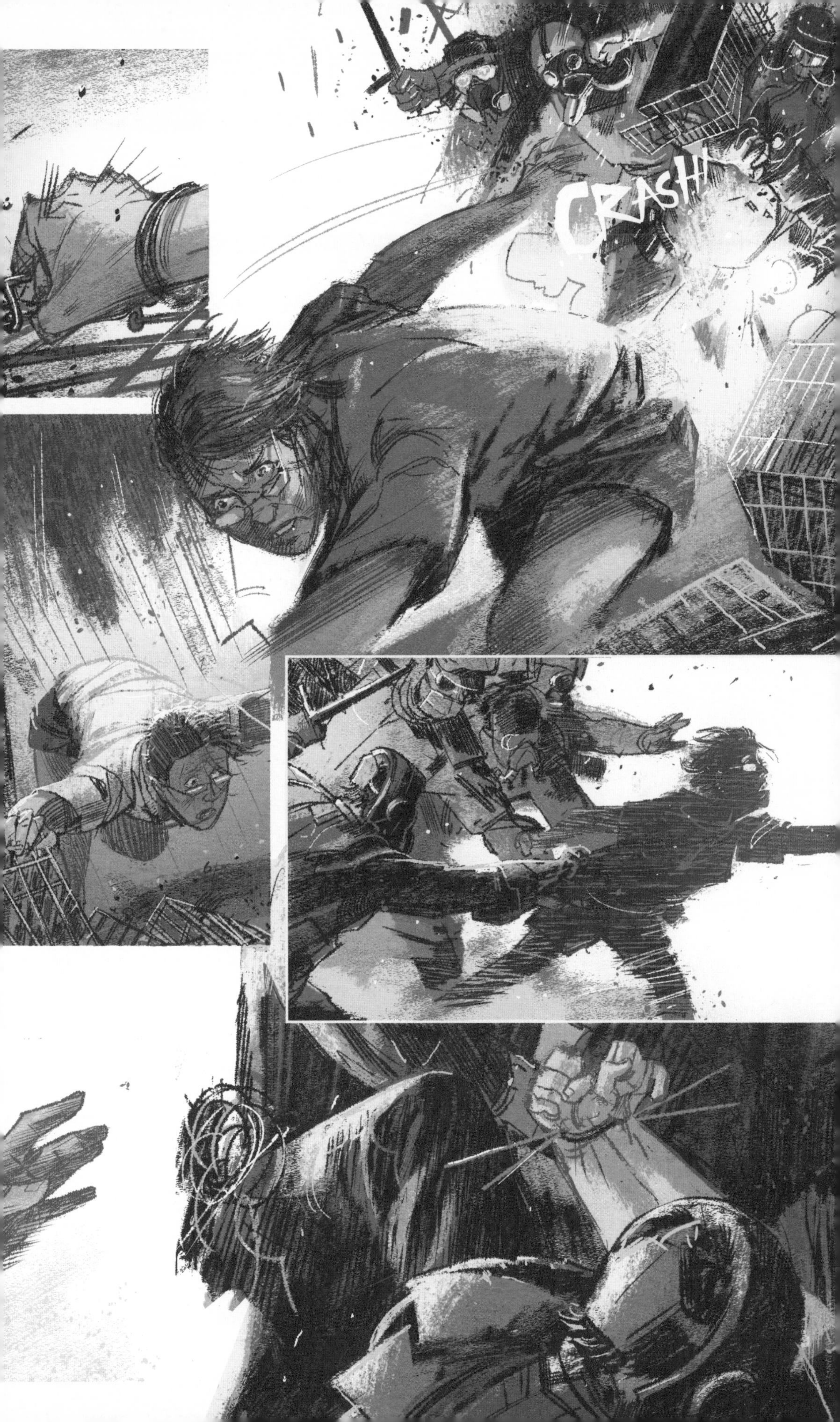
CRASH!

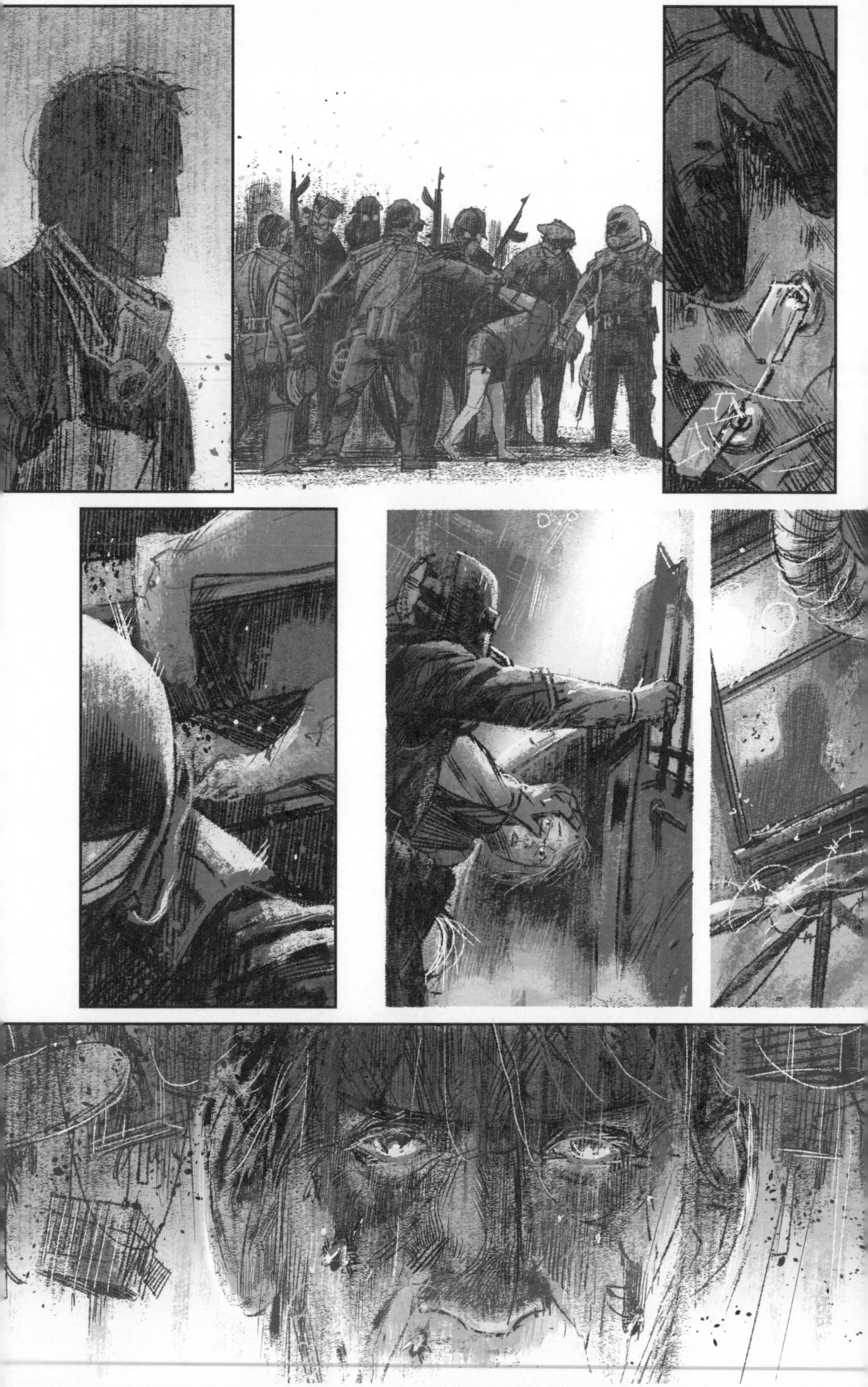

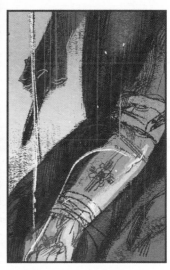

You motherfucker.

FUCK!

SHUT YOUR MOUTH.

Please...

If you ever lay a hand on another child ever again, I will come back and I will slash your throat.

Do you understand?

I... I haven't done that in years. I made a mistake. One time.

You. Ever. Do. It. Again. I. Will. Kill. You. Do. You. Under. Stand.

SFFT

ONE TIME—

Yes. Yes. God. Please.

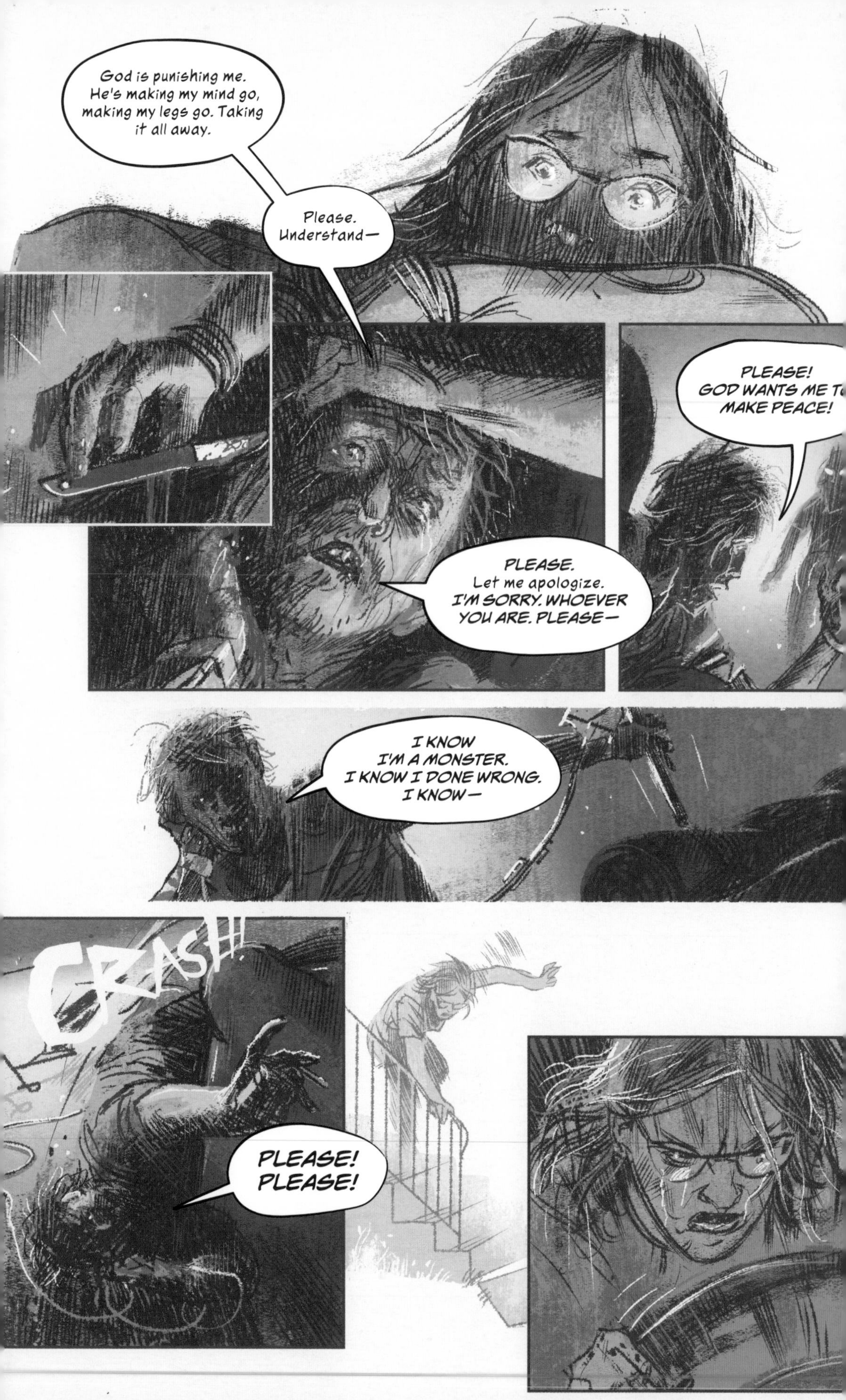
God is punishing me. He's making my mind go, making my legs go. Taking it all away.
Please. Understand—
PLEASE! GOD WANTS ME T
MAKE PEACE!
PLEASE. Let me apologize. I'M SORRY. WHOEVER YOU ARE. PLEASE—
I KNOW I'M A MONSTER. I KNOW I DONE WRONG. I KNOW—
CRASH!
PLEASE! PLEASE!

CHAPTER
08

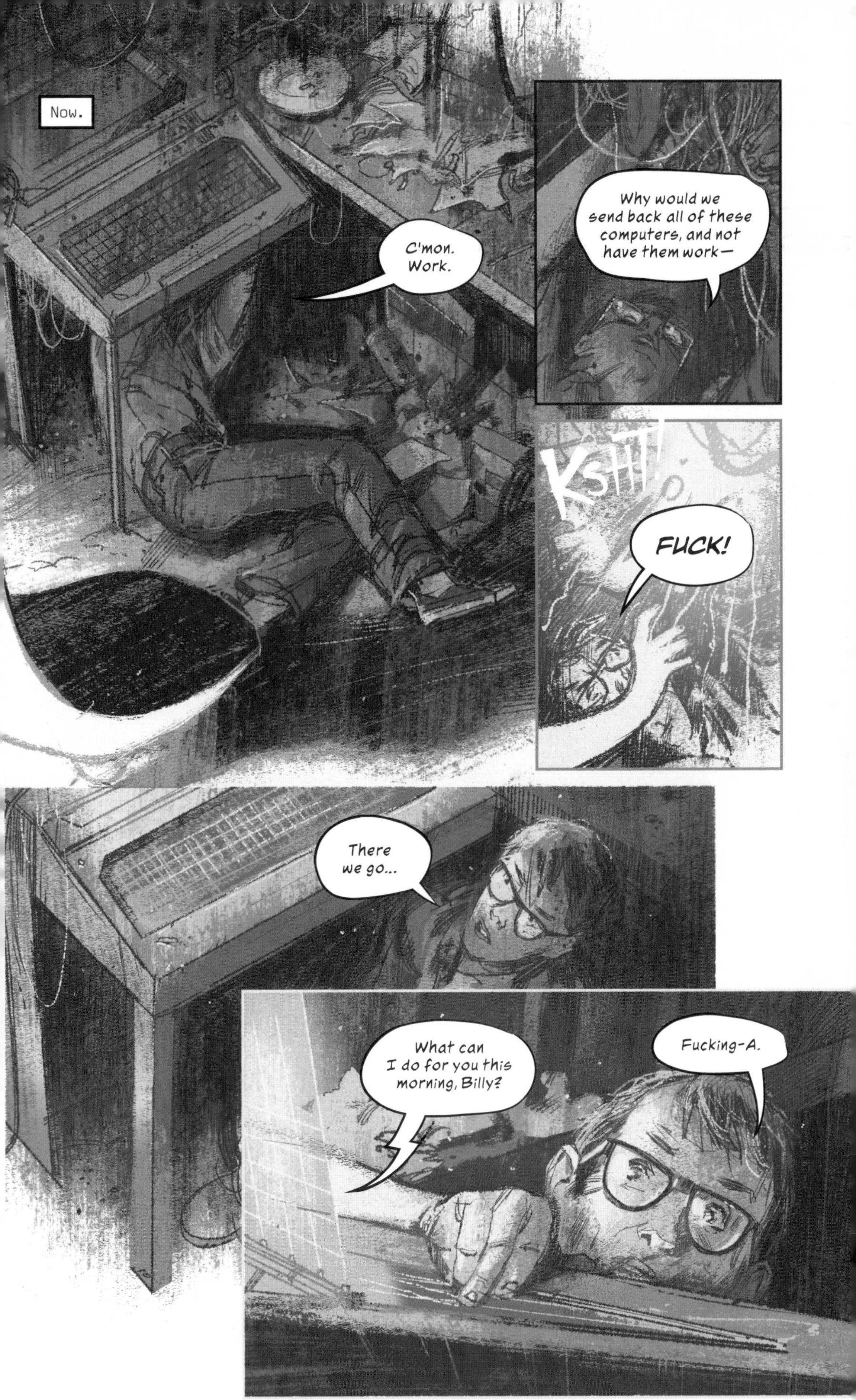
Now.
C'mon. Work.
Why would we send back all of these computers, and not have them work—
KSHT!
FUCK!
There we go...
What can I do for you this morning, Billy?
Fucking-A.

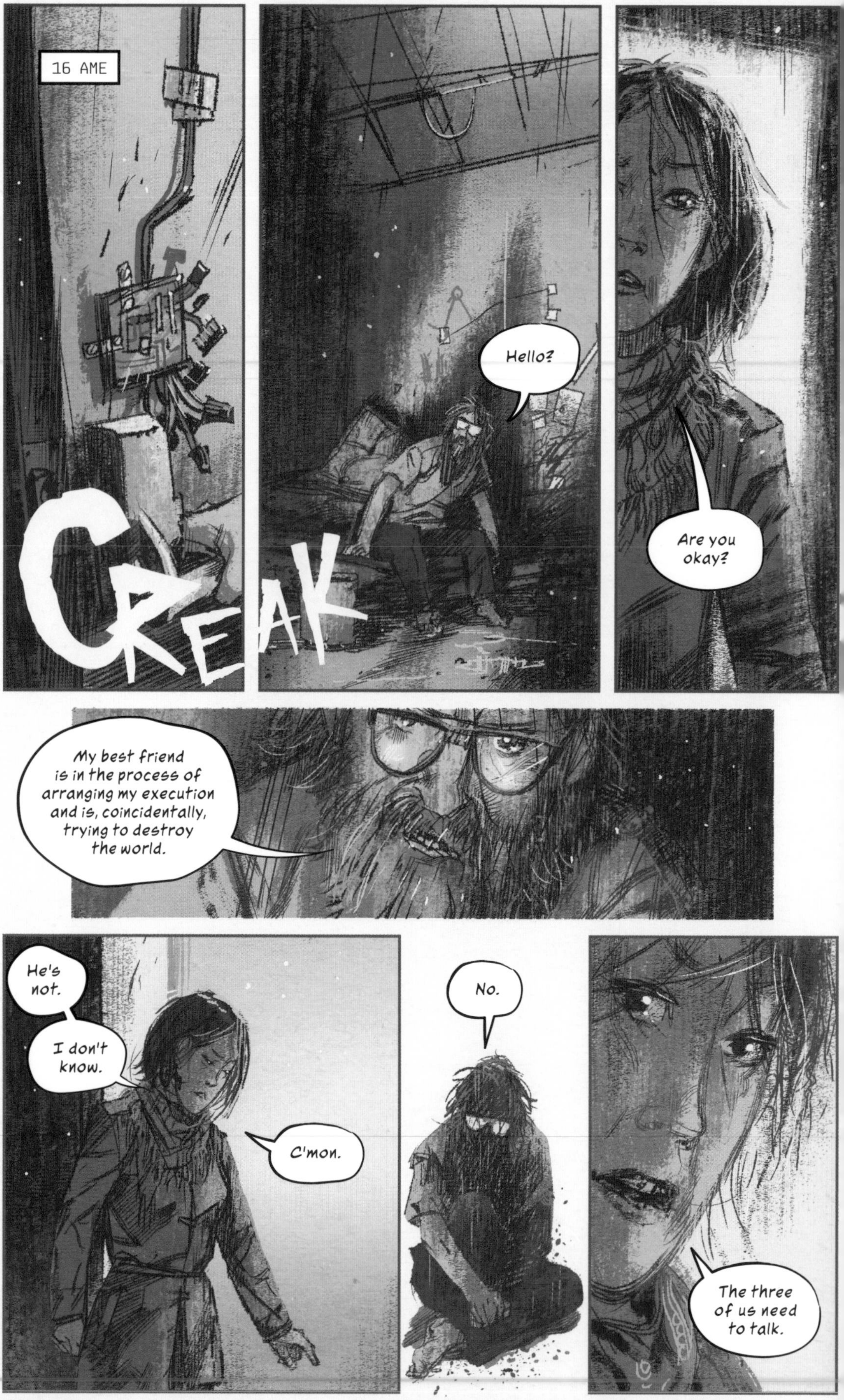
16 AME
CREAK
Hello?
Are you okay?
My best friend is in the process of arranging my execution and is, coincidentally, trying to destroy the world.
He's not.
I don't know.
C'mon.
No.
The three of us need to talk.

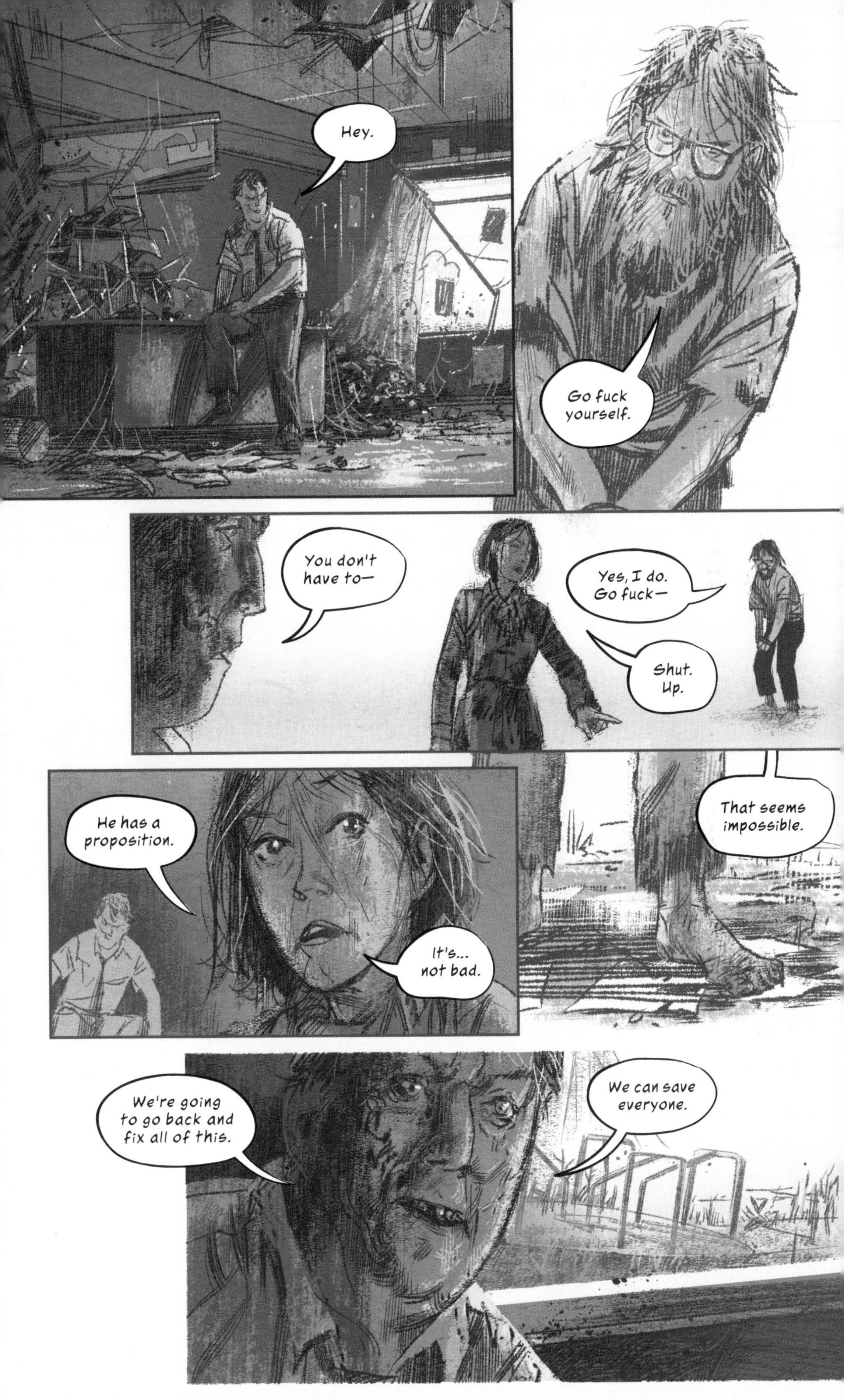
Hey.
Go fuck yourself.
You don't have to—
Yes, I do. Go fuck—
Shut. Up.
He has a proposition.
It's... not bad.
That seems impossible.
We're going to go back and fix all of this.
We can save everyone.

End of source...

En

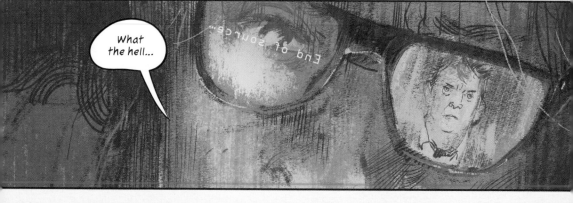

What the hell...

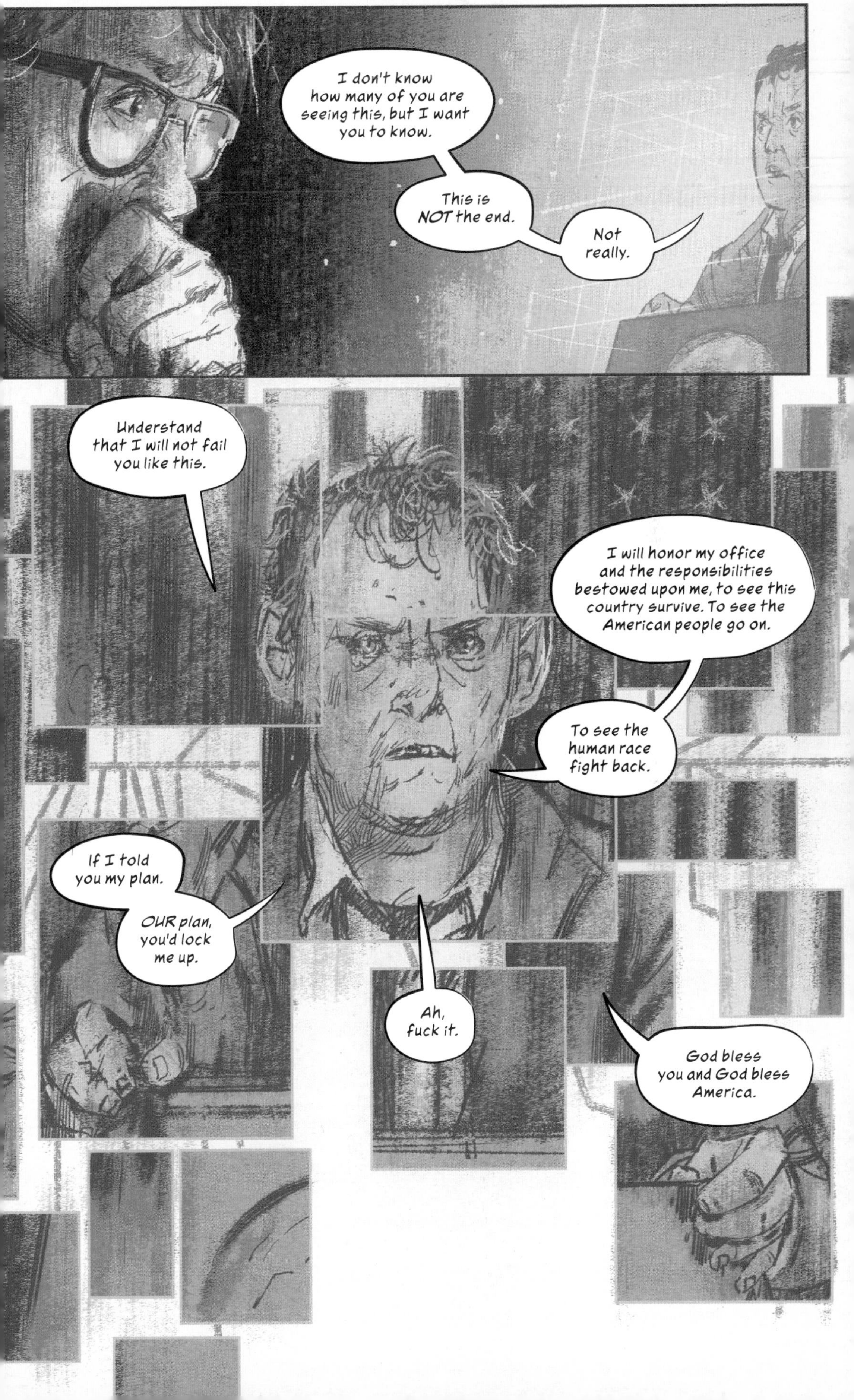

I don't know how many of you are seeing this, but I want you to know.
This is NOT the end.
Not really.
Understand that I will not fail you like this.
I will honor my office and the responsibilities bestowed upon me, to see this country survive. To see the American people go on.
To see the human race fight back.
If I told you my plan.
OUR plan, you'd lock me up.
Ah, fuck it.
God bless you and God bless America.

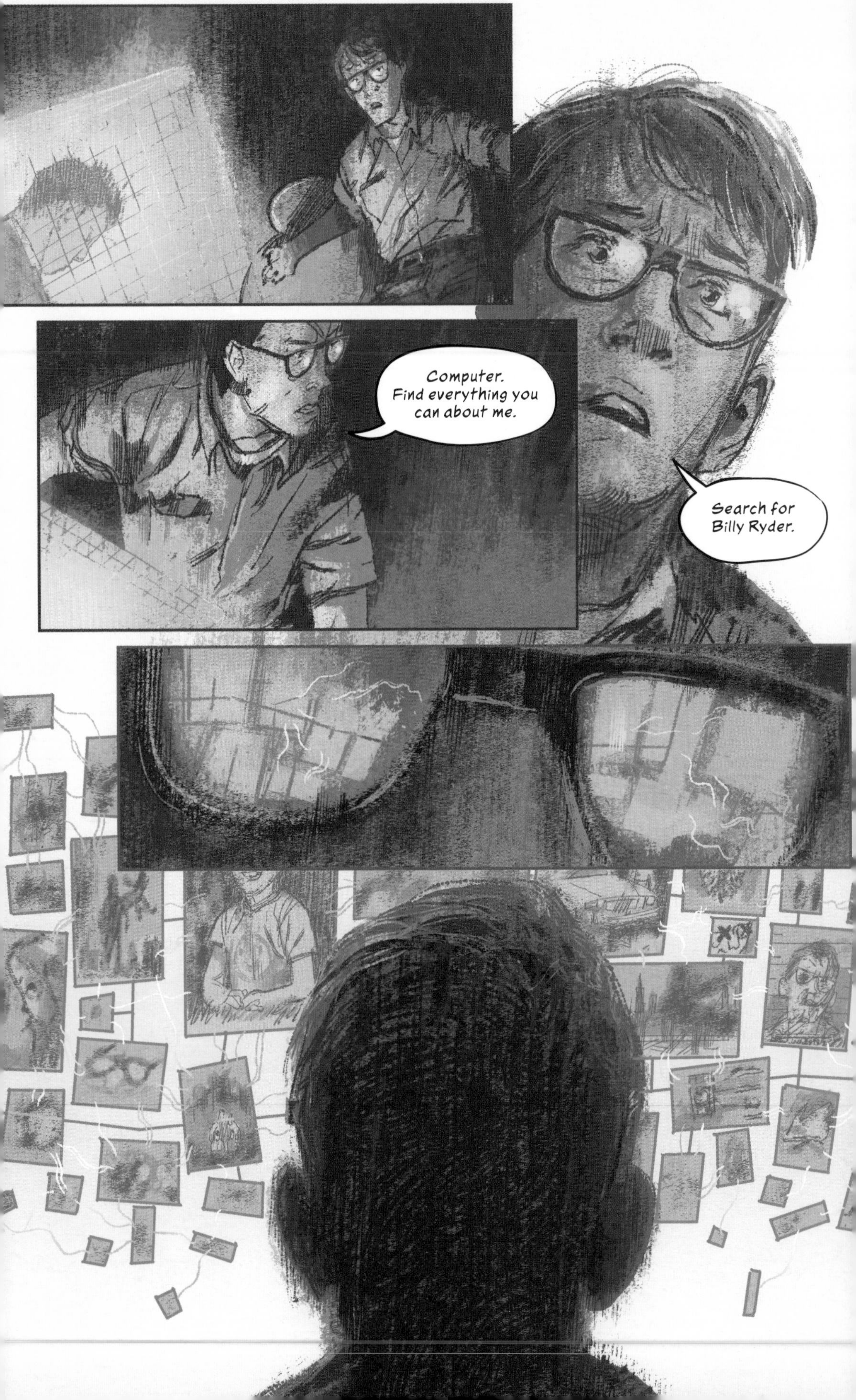
Computer. Find everything you can about me.
Search for Billy Ryder.

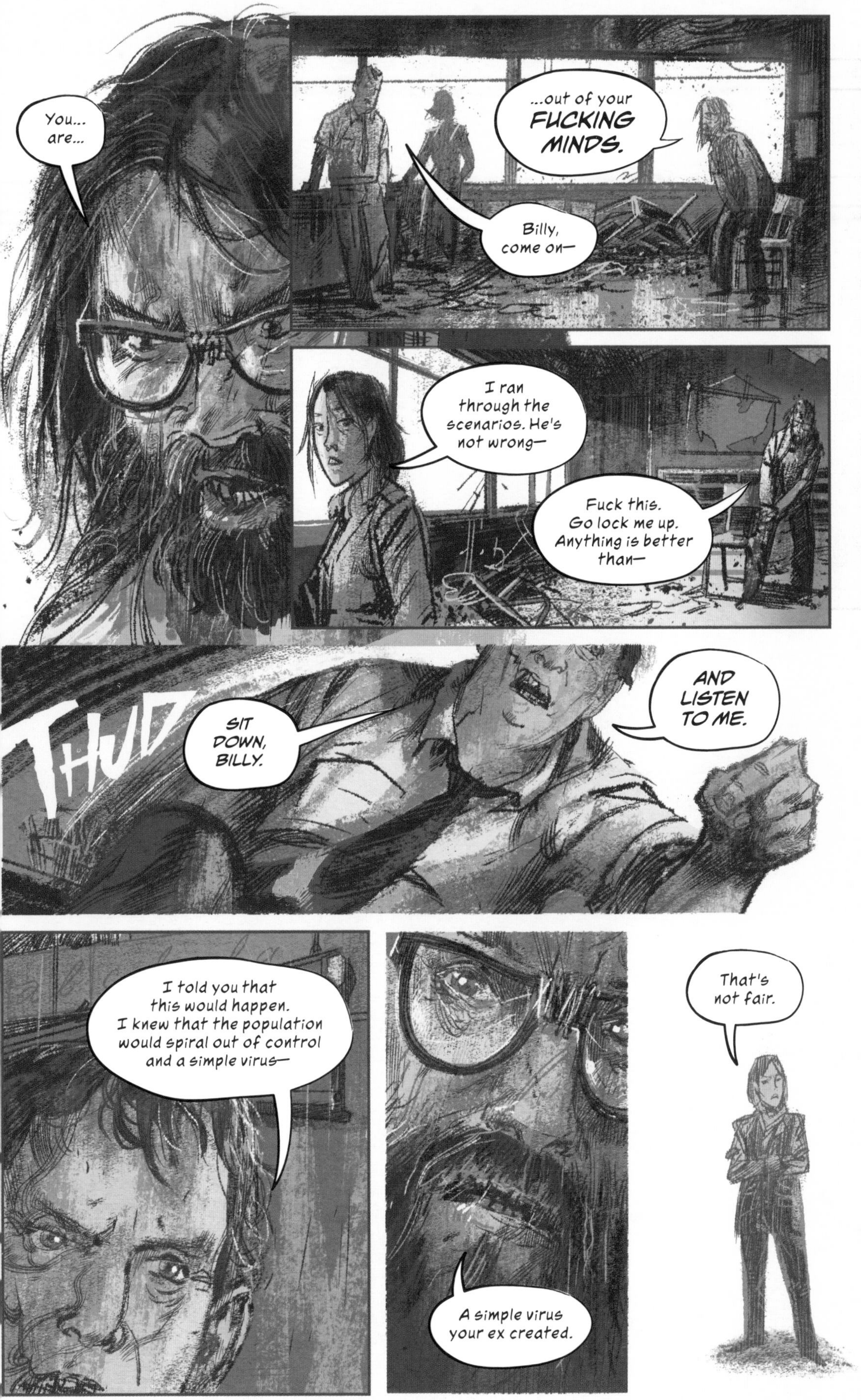
You... are...
...out of your FUCKING MINDS.
Billy, come on—
I ran through the scenarios. He's not wrong—
Fuck this. Go lock me up. Anything is better than—
THUD
SIT DOWN, BILLY.
AND LISTEN TO ME.
I told you that this would happen. I knew that the population would spiral out of control and a simple virus—
A simple virus your ex created.
That's not fair.

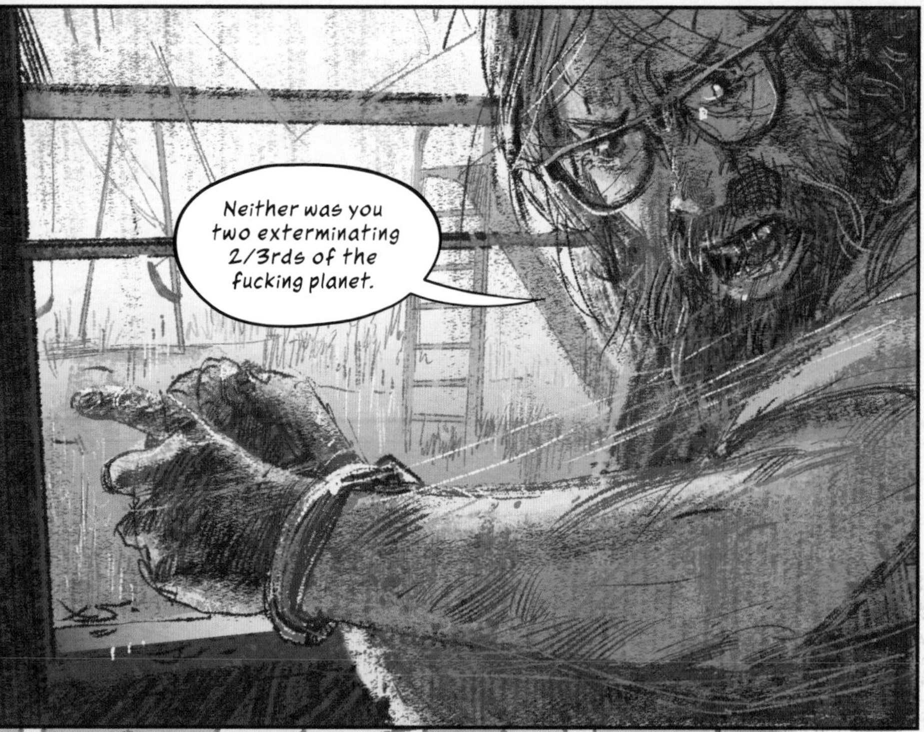
Neither was you two exterminating 2/3rds of the fucking planet.

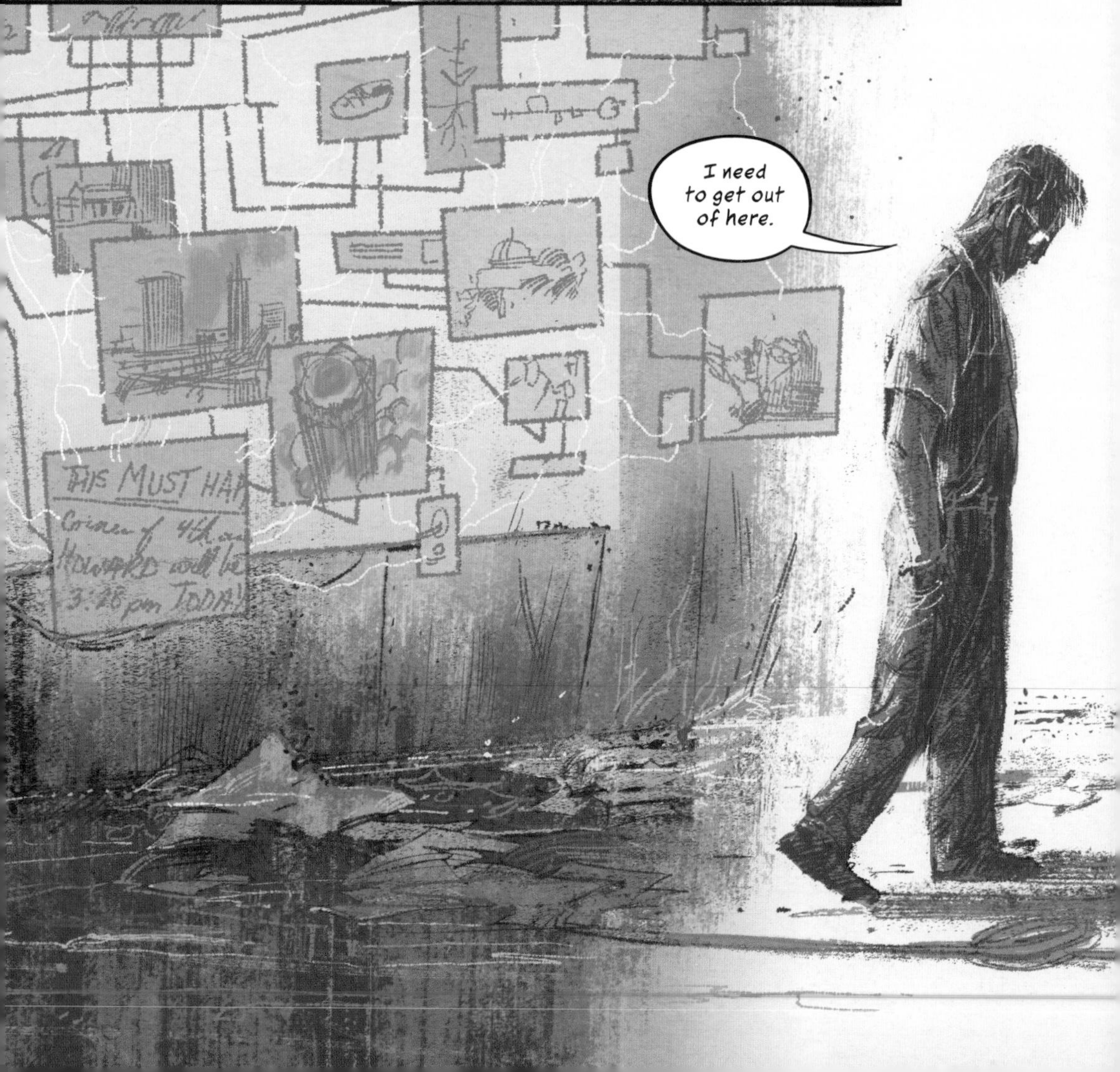
I need to get out of here.

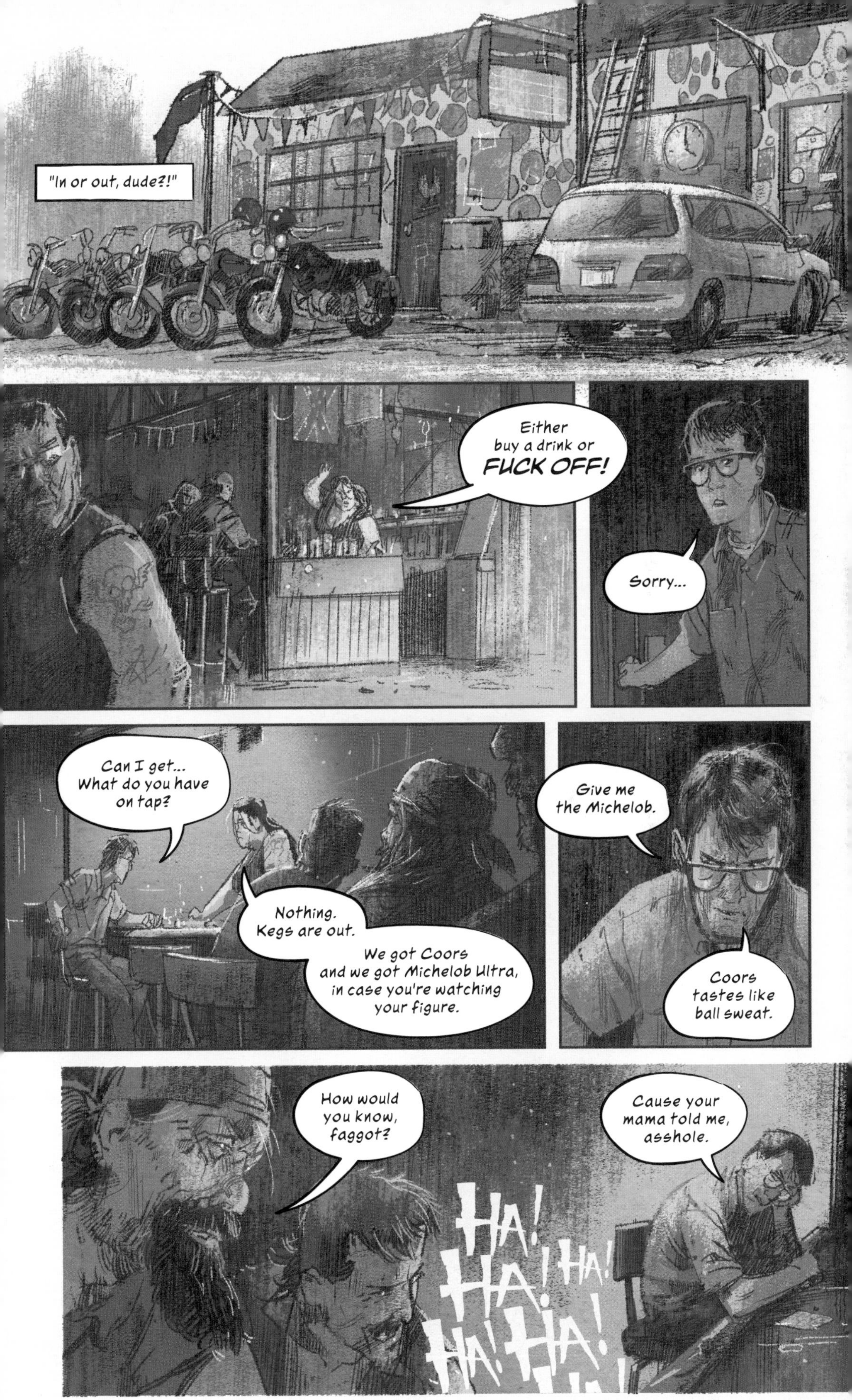
"In or out, dude?!"
Either buy a drink or FUCK OFF!
Sorry...
Can I get... What do you have on tap?
Nothing. Kegs are out.
We got Coors and we got Michelob Ultra, in case you're watching your figure.
Give me the Michelob.
Coors tastes like ball sweat.
How would you know, faggot?
Cause your mama told me, asshole.
HA! HA! HA! HA! HA!

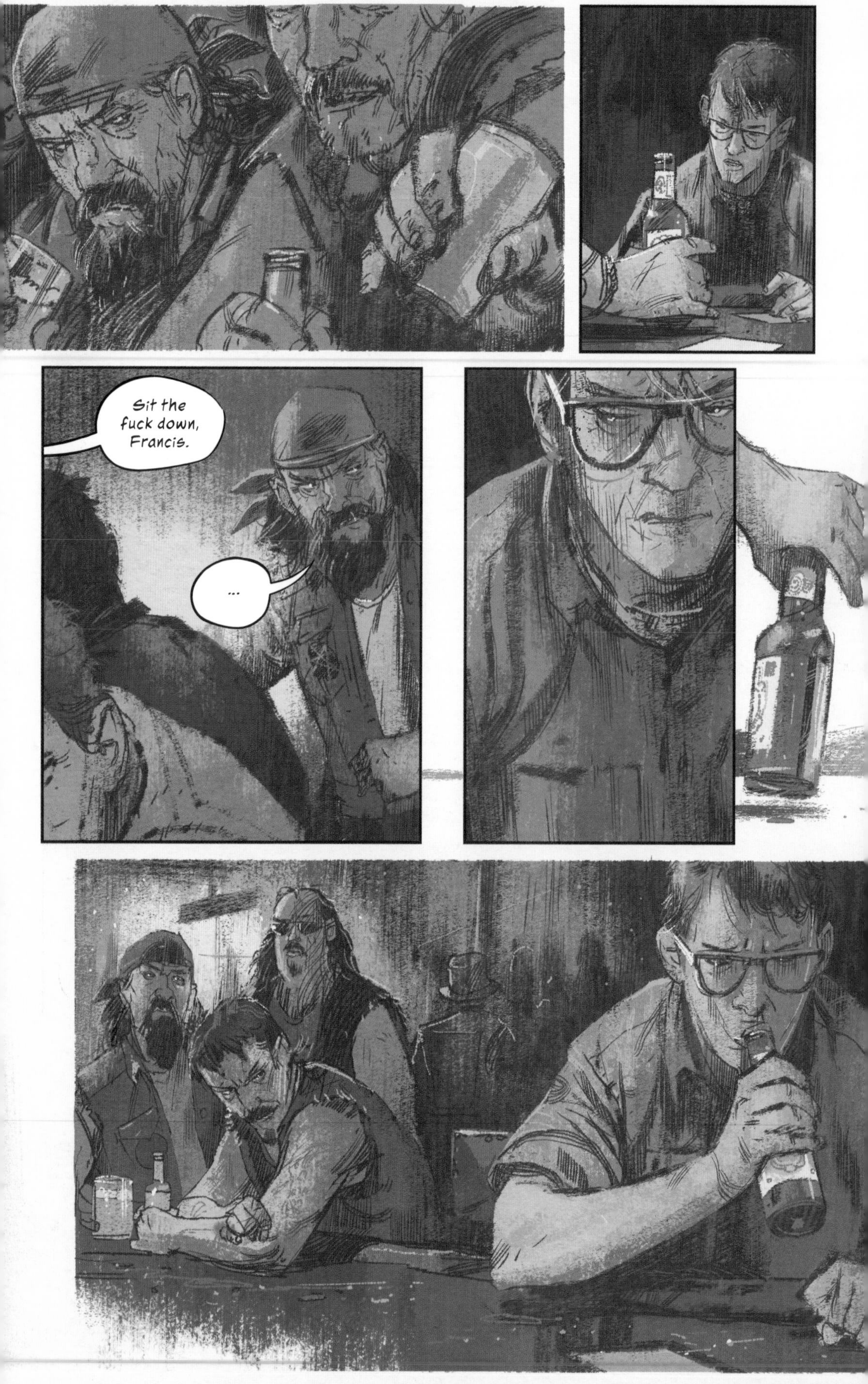
Sit the fuck down, Francis.
...

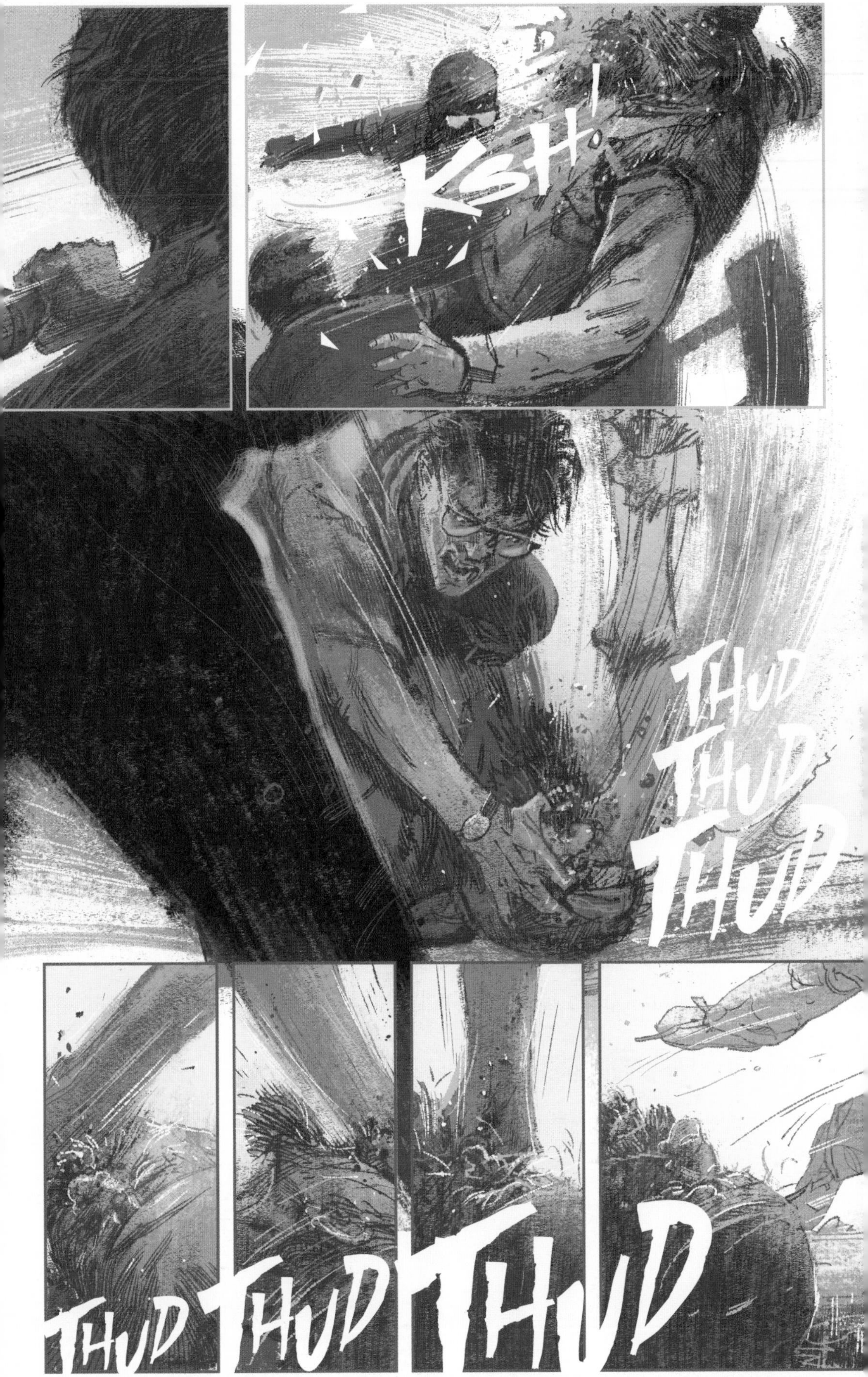
KSH!
THUD
THUD
THUD
THUD
THUD
THUD

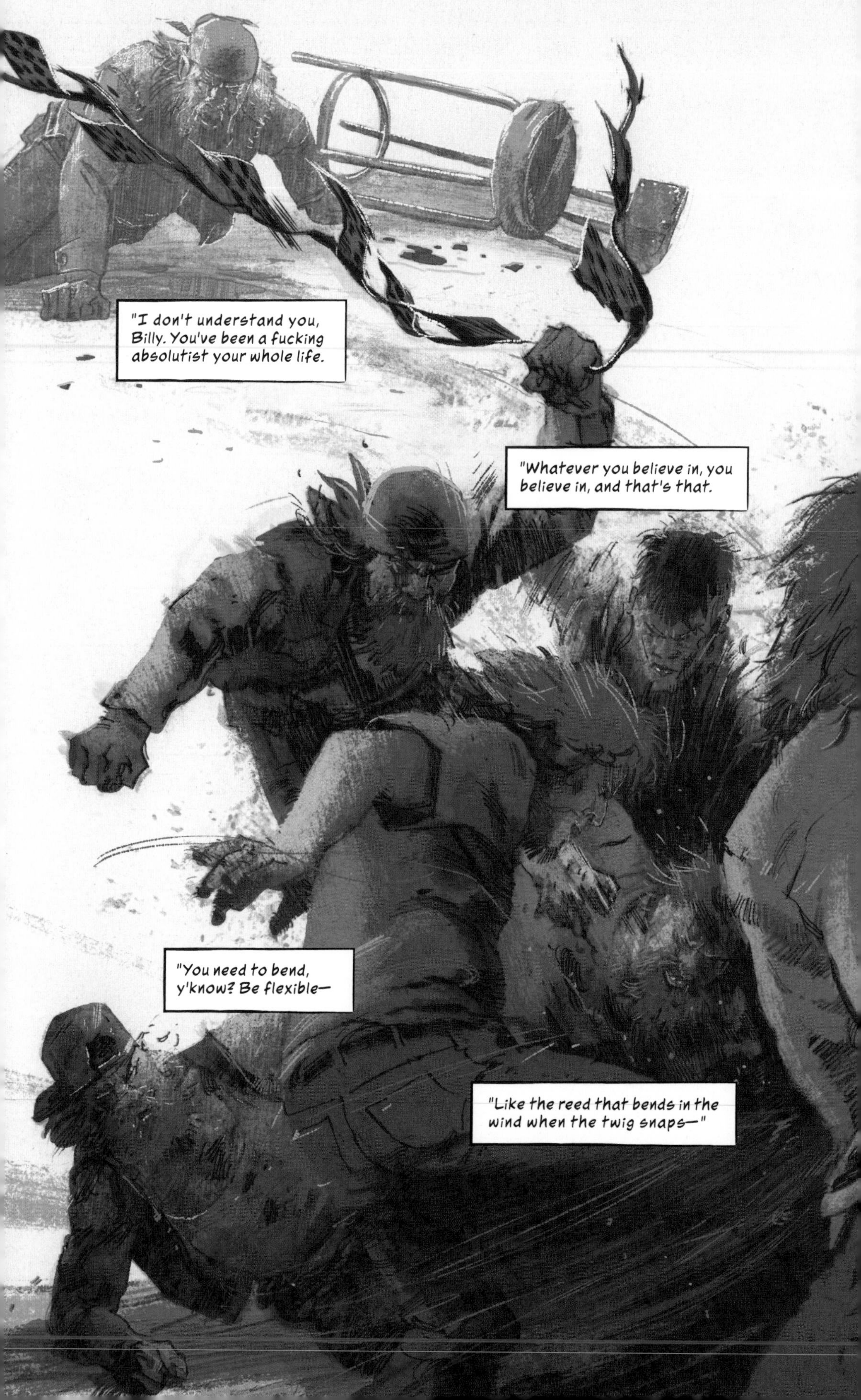
"I don't understand you, Billy. You've been a fucking absolutist your whole life.
"Whatever you believe in, you believe in, and that's that.
"You need to bend, y'know? Be flexible—
"Like the reed that bends in the wind when the twig snaps—"

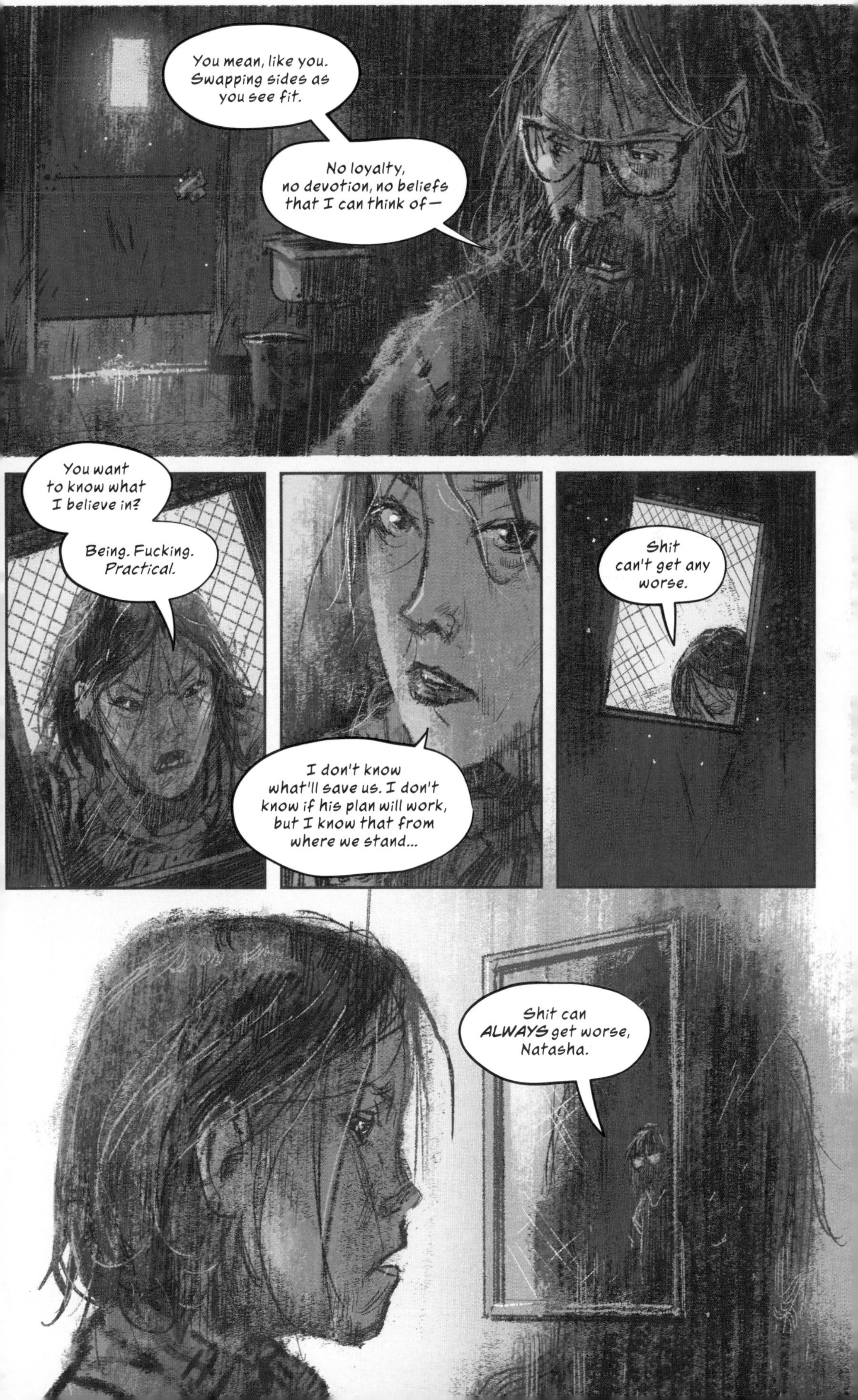
You mean, like you. Swapping sides as you see fit.
No loyalty, no devotion, no beliefs that I can think of—
You want to know what I believe in?
Being. Fucking. Practical.
I don't know what'll save us. I don't know if his plan will work, but I know that from where we stand...
Shit can't get any worse.
Shit can ALWAYS get worse, Natasha.

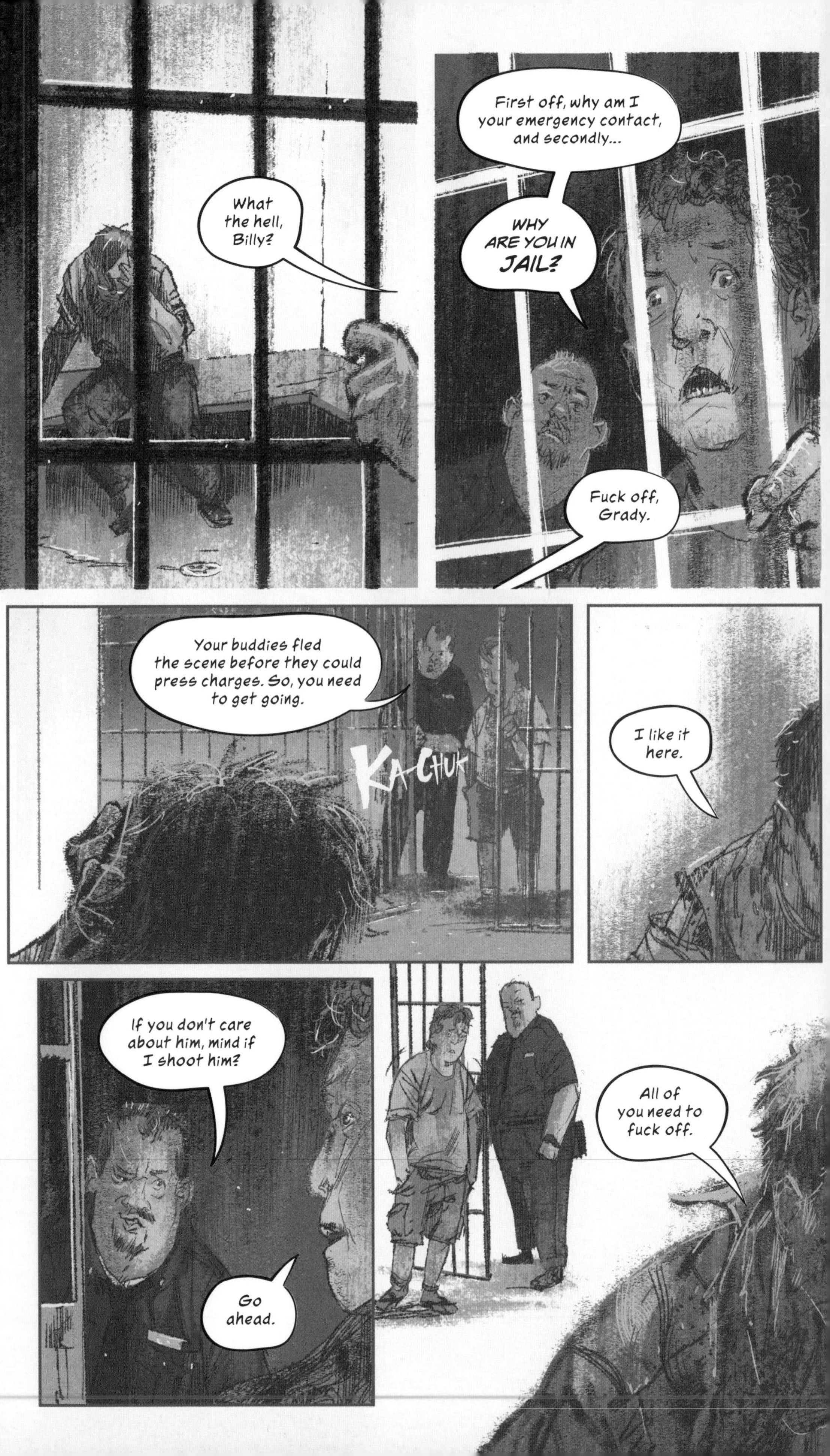
What the hell, Billy?
First off, why am I your emergency contact, and secondly...
WHY ARE YOU IN JAIL?
Fuck off, Grady.
Your buddies fled the scene before they could press charges. So, you need to get going.
KA-CHUK
I like it here.
If you don't care about him, mind if I shoot him?
Go ahead.
All of you need to fuck off.

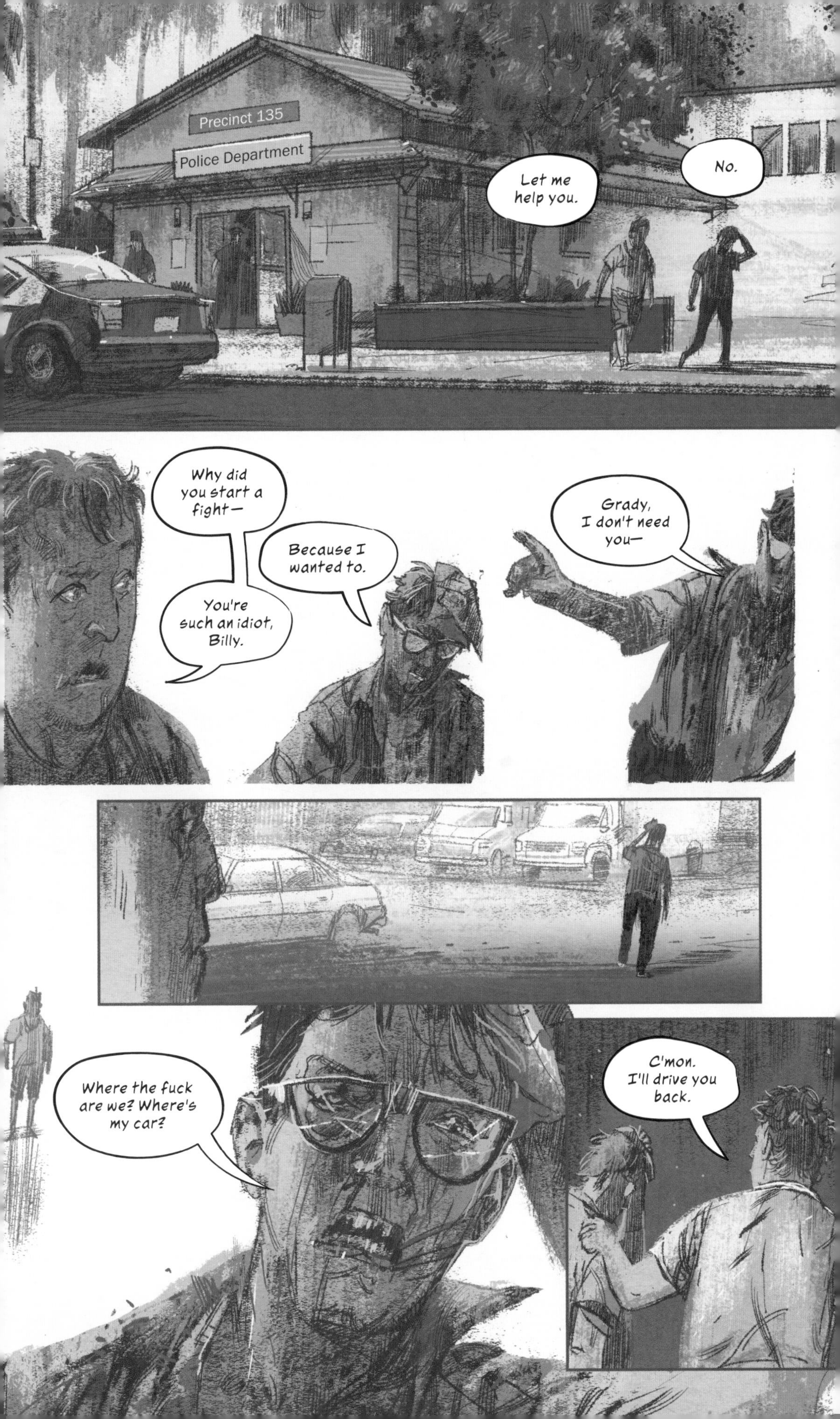
Precinct 135
Police Department
Let me help you.
No.
Why did you start a fight—
You're such an idiot, Billy.
Because I wanted to.
Grady, I don't need you—
Where the fuck are we? Where's my car?
C'mon. I'll drive you back.

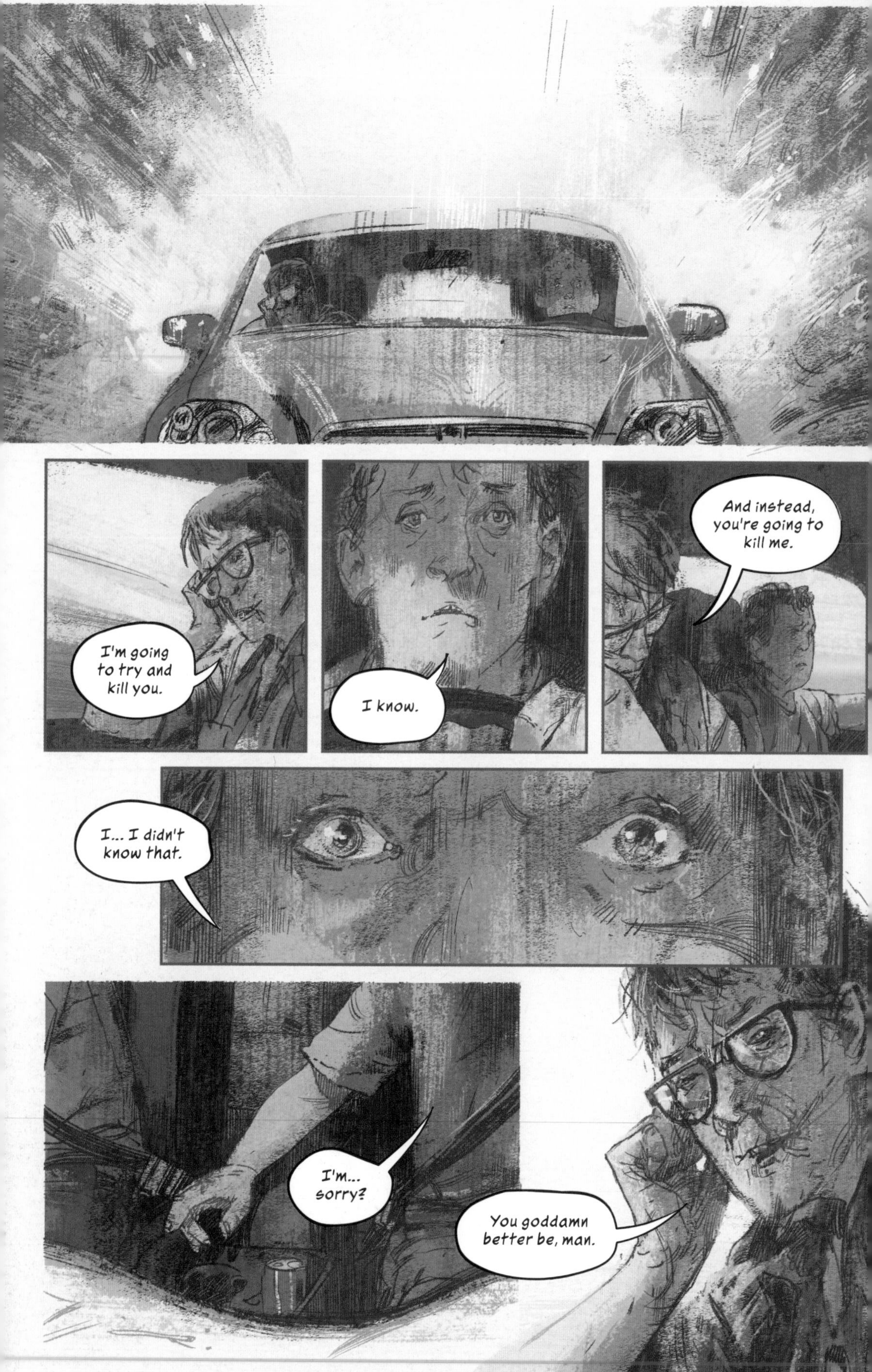
I'm going to try and kill you.
I know.
And instead, you're going to kill me.
I... I didn't know that.
I'm... sorry?
You goddamn better be, man.

KACHUK

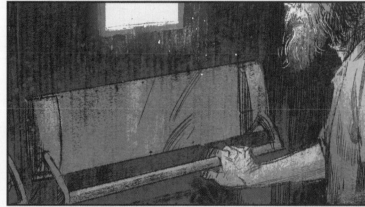

What is this?

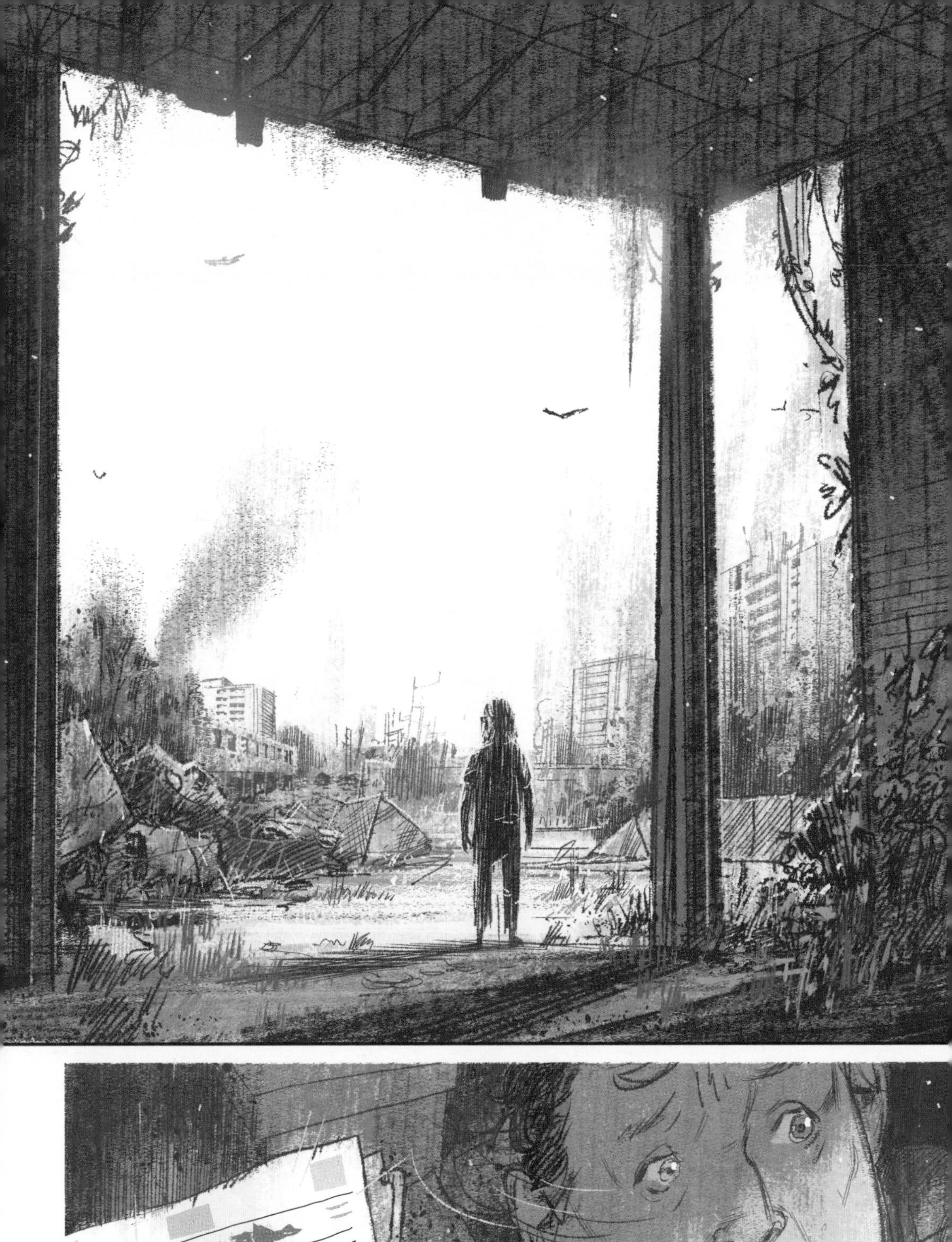

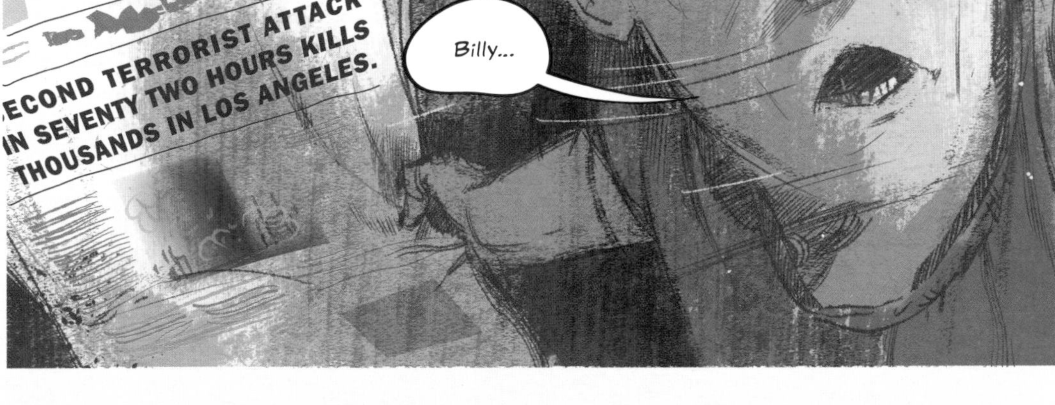
ECOND TERRORIST ATTACK
IN SEVENTY TWO HOURS KILLS
THOUSANDS IN LOS ANGELES.
Billy...

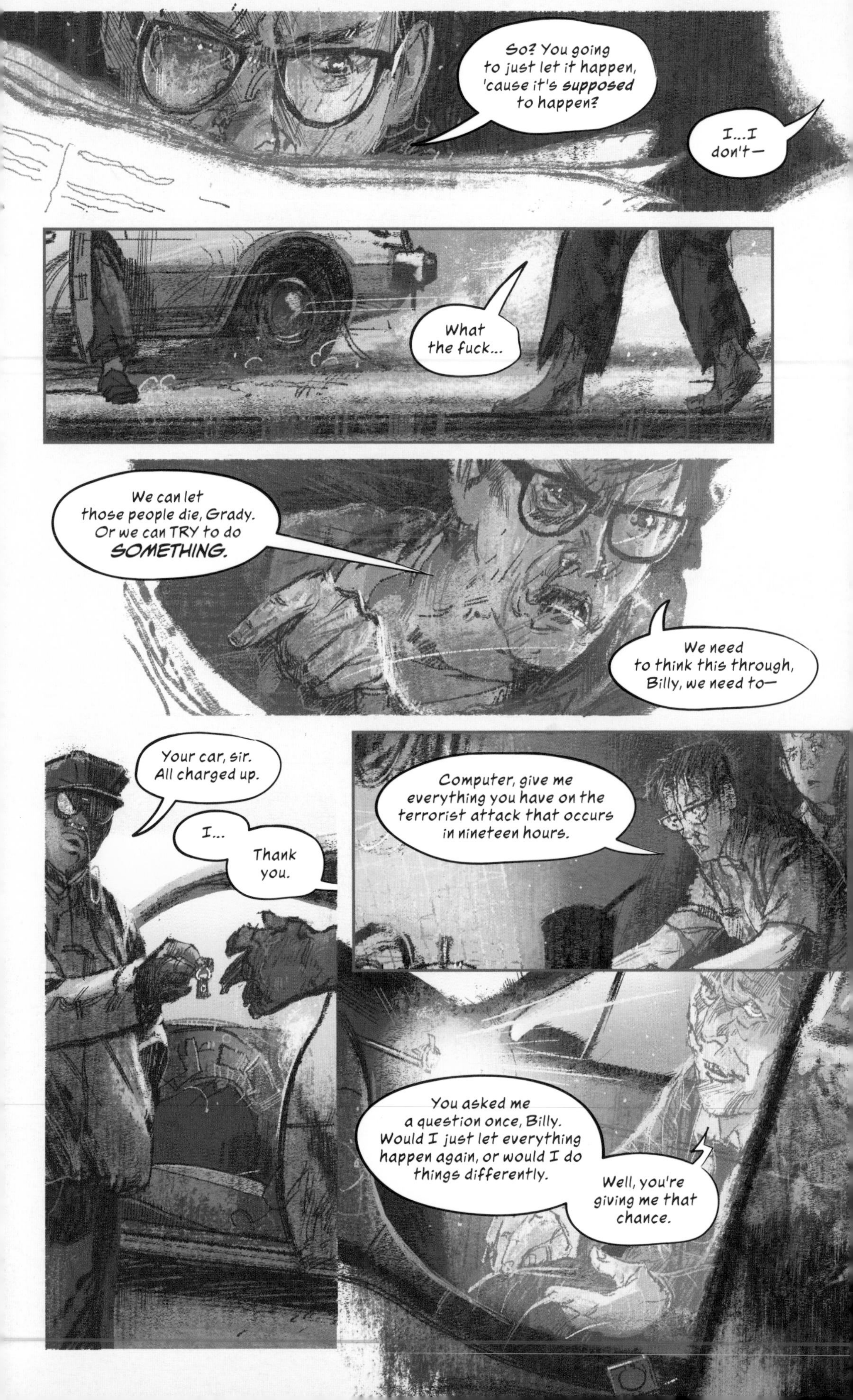
So? You going to just let it happen, 'cause it's *supposed* to happen?
I...I don't—
What the fuck...
We can let those people die, Grady. Or we can TRY to do **SOMETHING.**
We need to think this through, Billy, we need to—
Your car, sir. All charged up.
I...
Thank you.
Computer, give me everything you have on the terrorist attack that occurs in nineteen hours.
You asked me a question once, Billy. Would I just let everything happen again, or would I do things differently.
Well, you're giving me that chance.

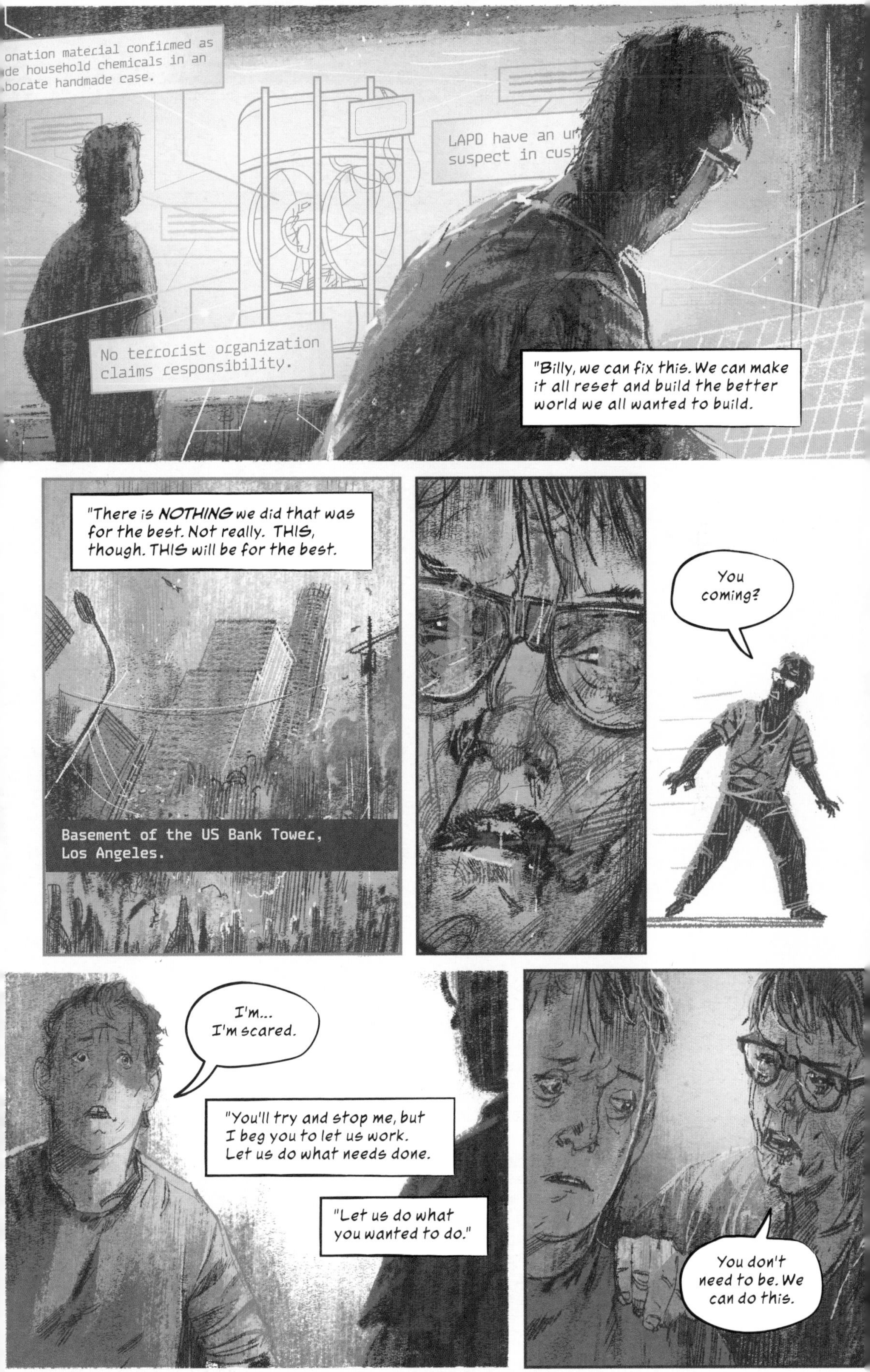
onation material confirmed as
de household chemicals in an
borate handmade case.
LAPD have an un
suspect in cust
No terrorist organization
claims responsibility.
"Billy, we can fix this. We can make it all reset and build the better world we all wanted to build.
"There is NOTHING we did that was for the best. Not really. THIS, though. THIS will be for the best.
Basement of the US Bank Tower, Los Angeles.
You coming?
I'm... I'm scared.
"You'll try and stop me, but I beg you to let us work. Let us do what needs done.
"Let us do what you wanted to do."
You don't need to be. We can do this.

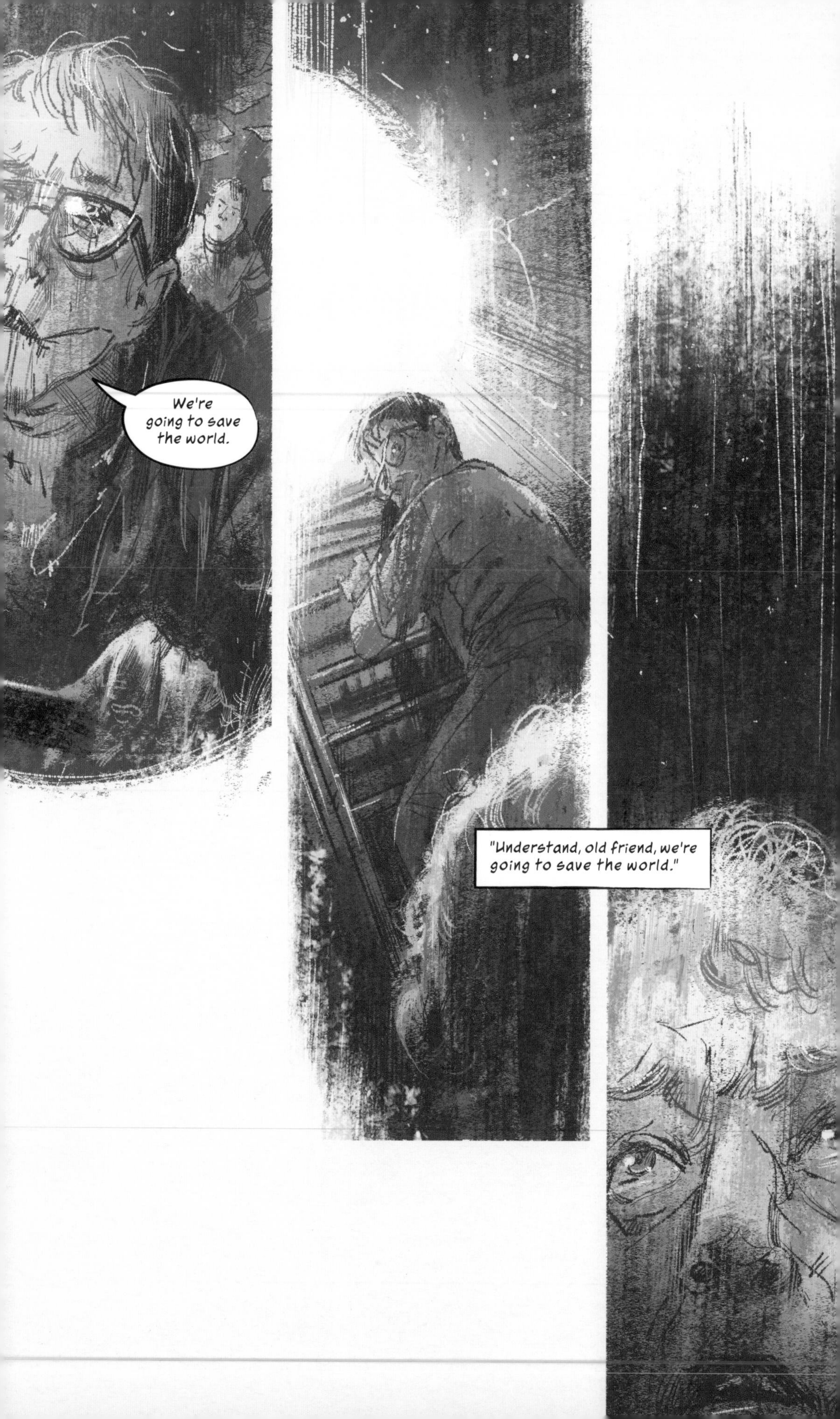
We're going to save the world.
"Understand, old friend, we're going to save the world."

CHAPTER
09

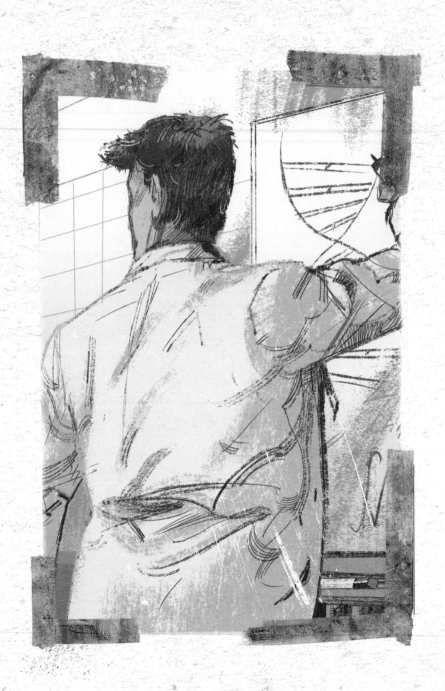

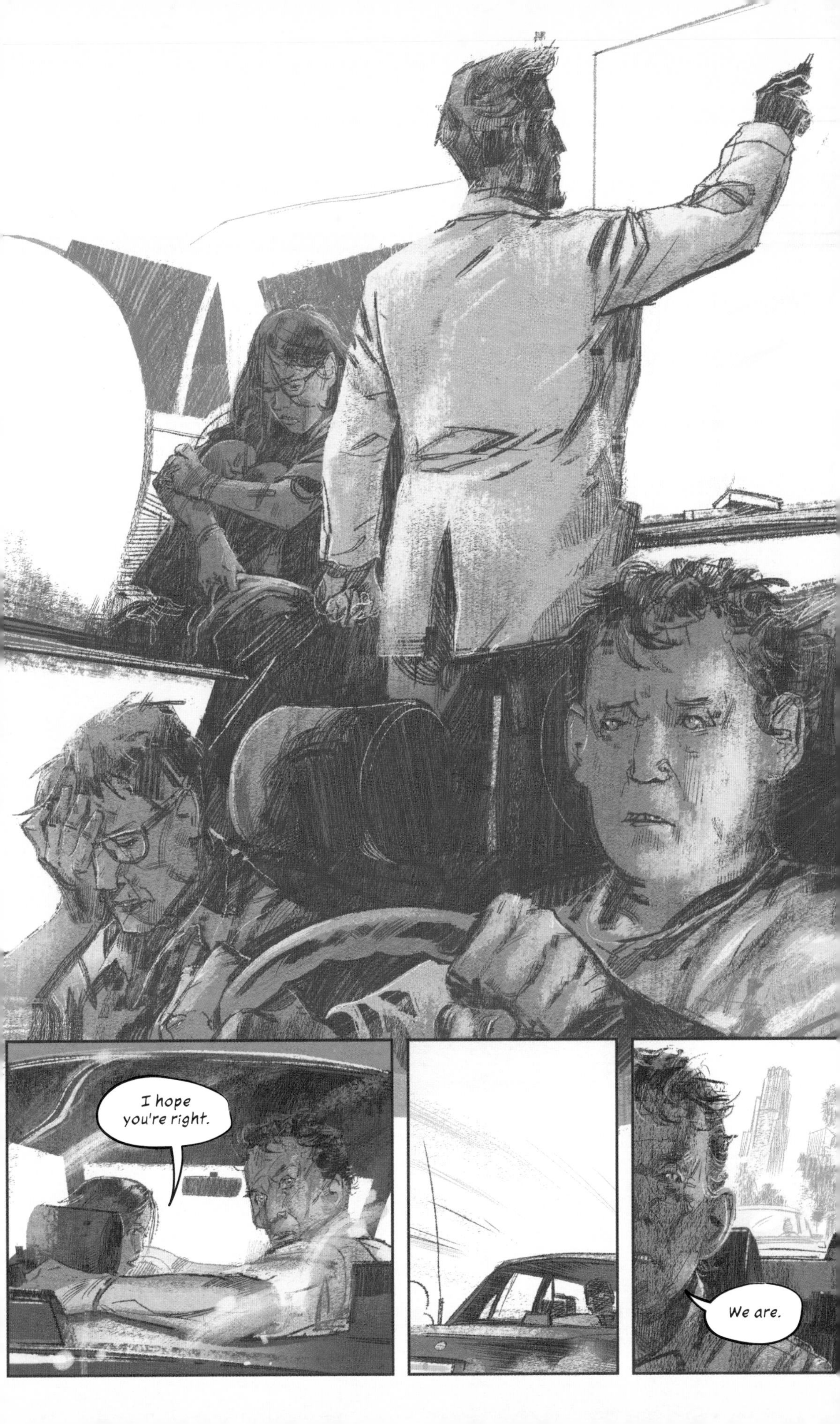
I hope you're right.
We are.

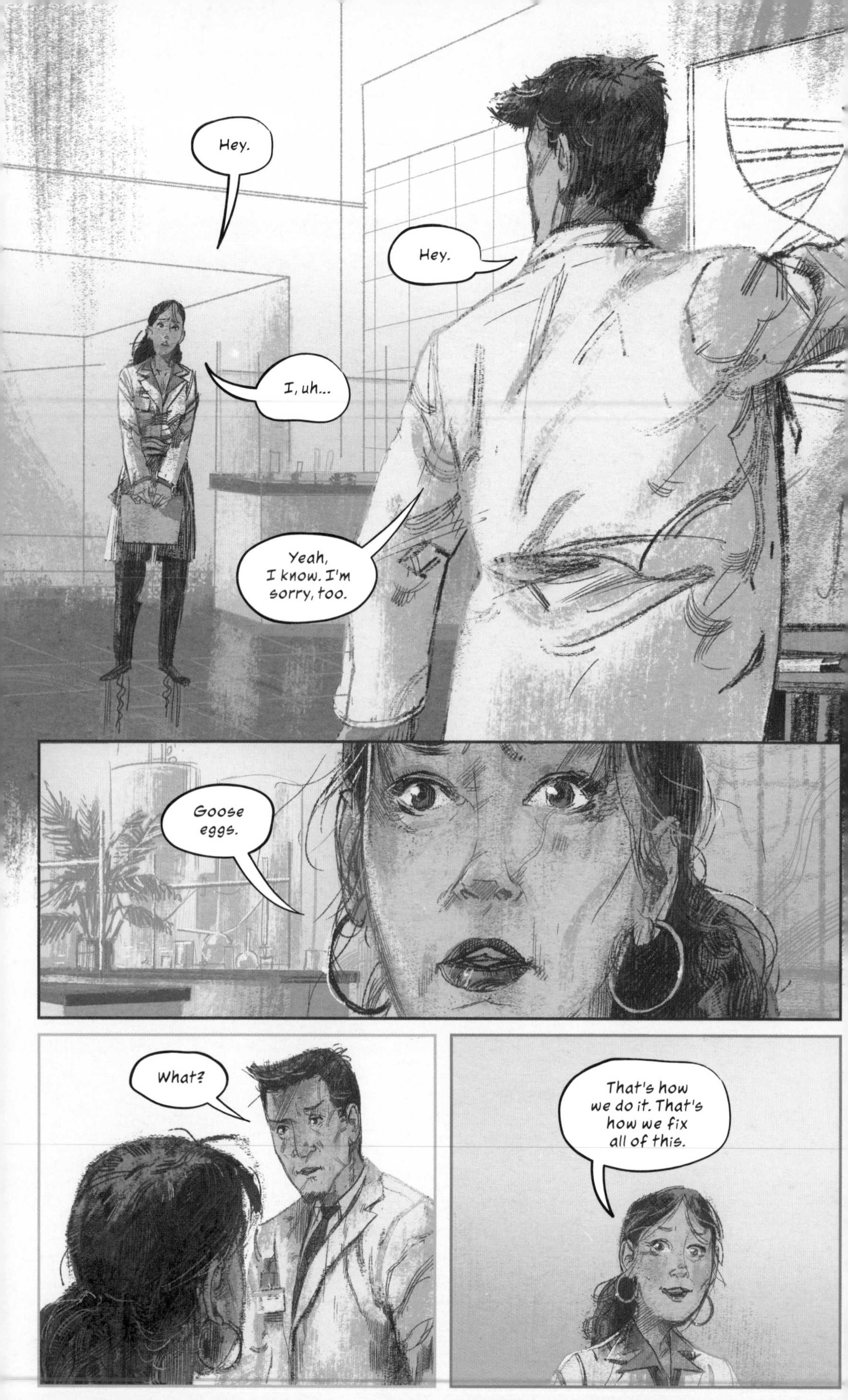
Hey.
Hey.
I, uh...
Yeah, I know. I'm sorry, too.
Goose eggs.
What?
That's how we do it. That's how we fix all of this.

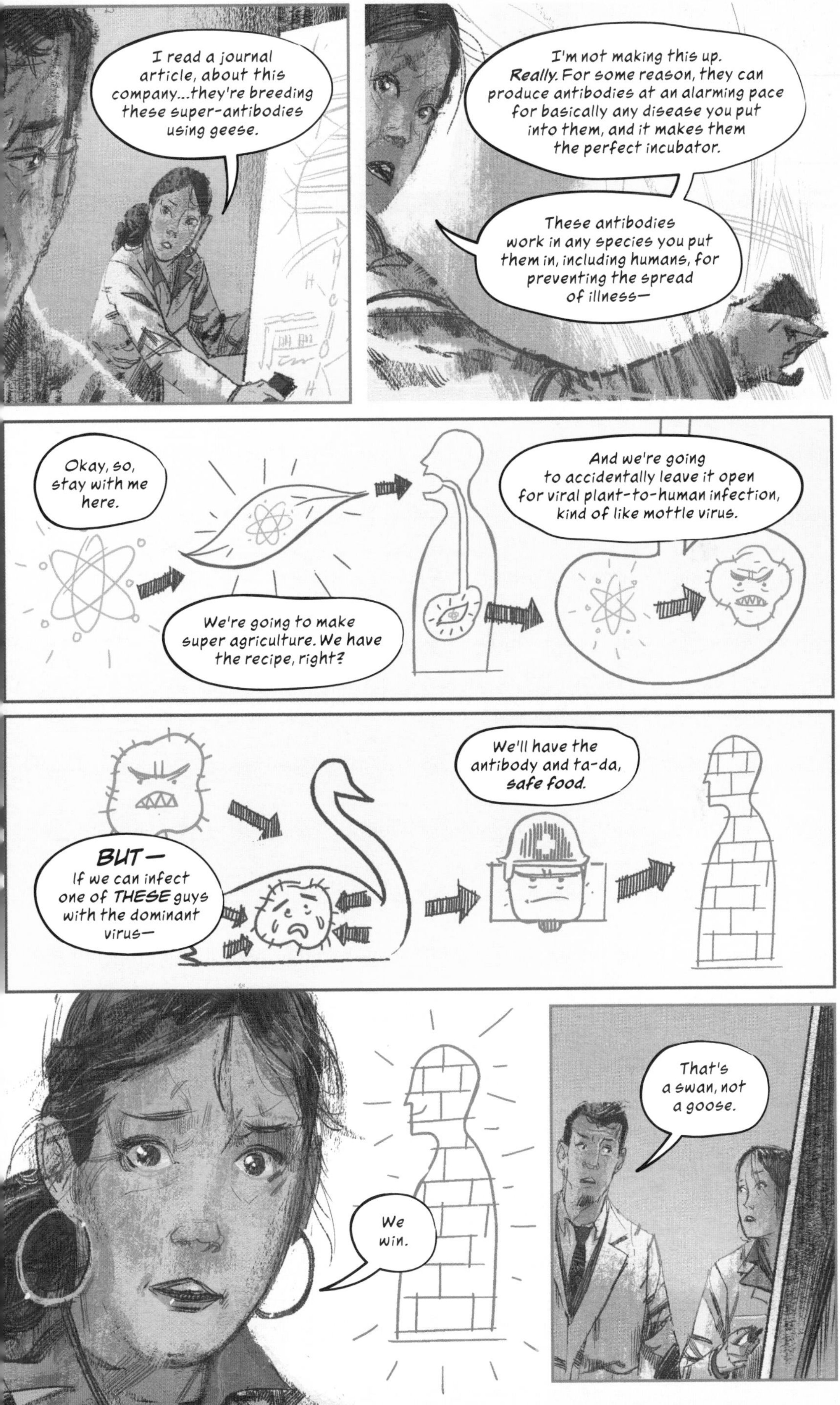
I read a journal article, about this company...they're breeding these super-antibodies using geese.
I'm not making this up. *Really.* For some reason, they can produce antibodies at an alarming pace for basically any disease you put into them, and it makes them the perfect incubator.
These antibodies work in any species you put them in, including humans, for preventing the spread of illness—
Okay, so, stay with me here.
We're going to make super agriculture. We have the recipe, right?
And we're going to accidentally leave it open for viral plant-to-human infection, kind of like mottle virus.
BUT— If we can infect one of *THESE* guys with the dominant virus—
We'll have the antibody and ta-da, *safe food.*
We win.
That's a swan, not a goose.

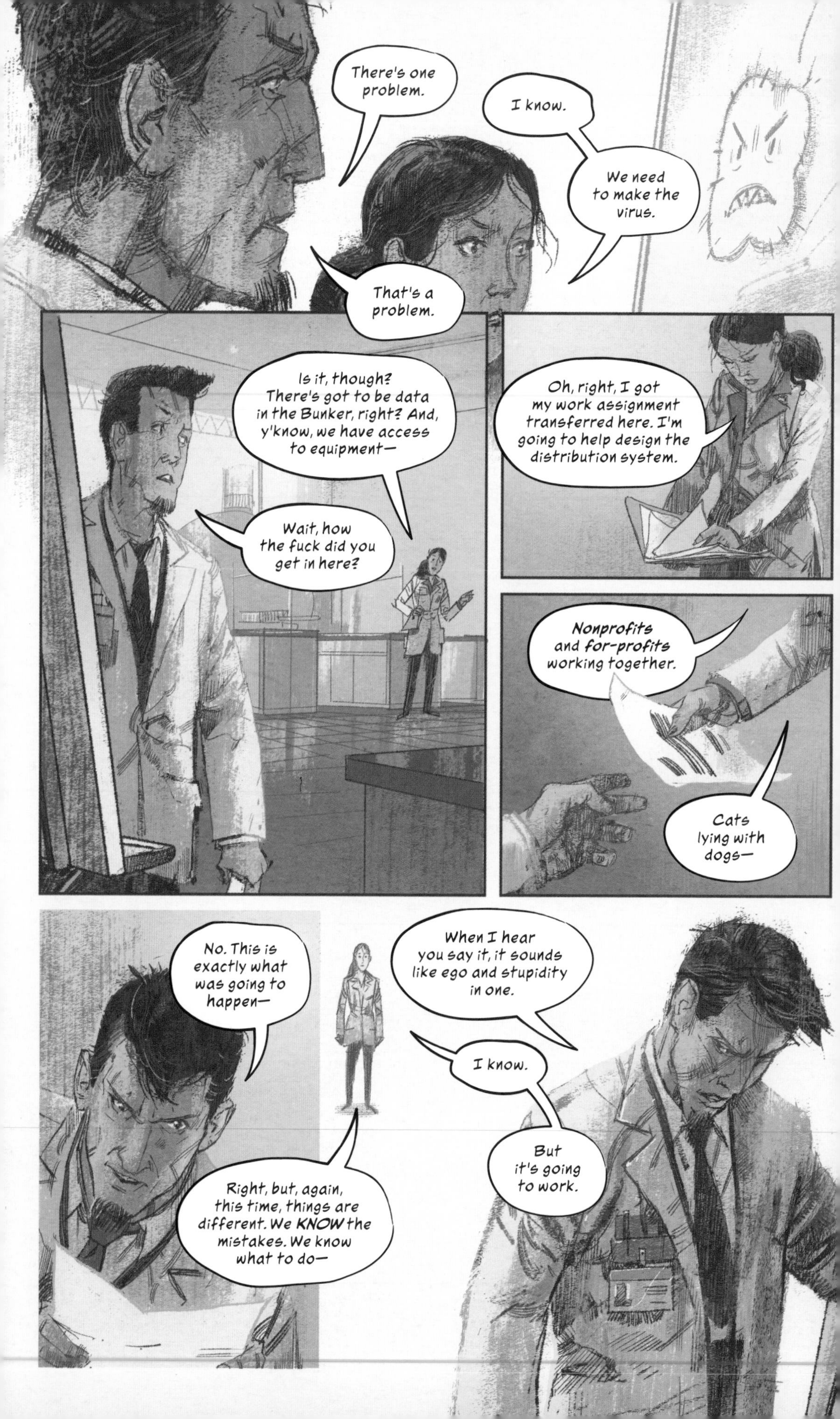
There's one problem.
I know.
We need to make the virus.
That's a problem.
Is it, though? There's got to be data in the Bunker, right? And, y'know, we have access to equipment—
Wait, how the fuck did you get in here?
Oh, right, I got my work assignment transferred here. I'm going to help design the distribution system.
Nonprofits and *for-profits* working together.
Cats lying with dogs—
No. This is exactly what was going to happen—
Right, but, again, this time, things are different. We *KNOW* the mistakes. We know what to do—
When I hear you say it, it sounds like ego and stupidity in one.
I know.
But it's going to work.

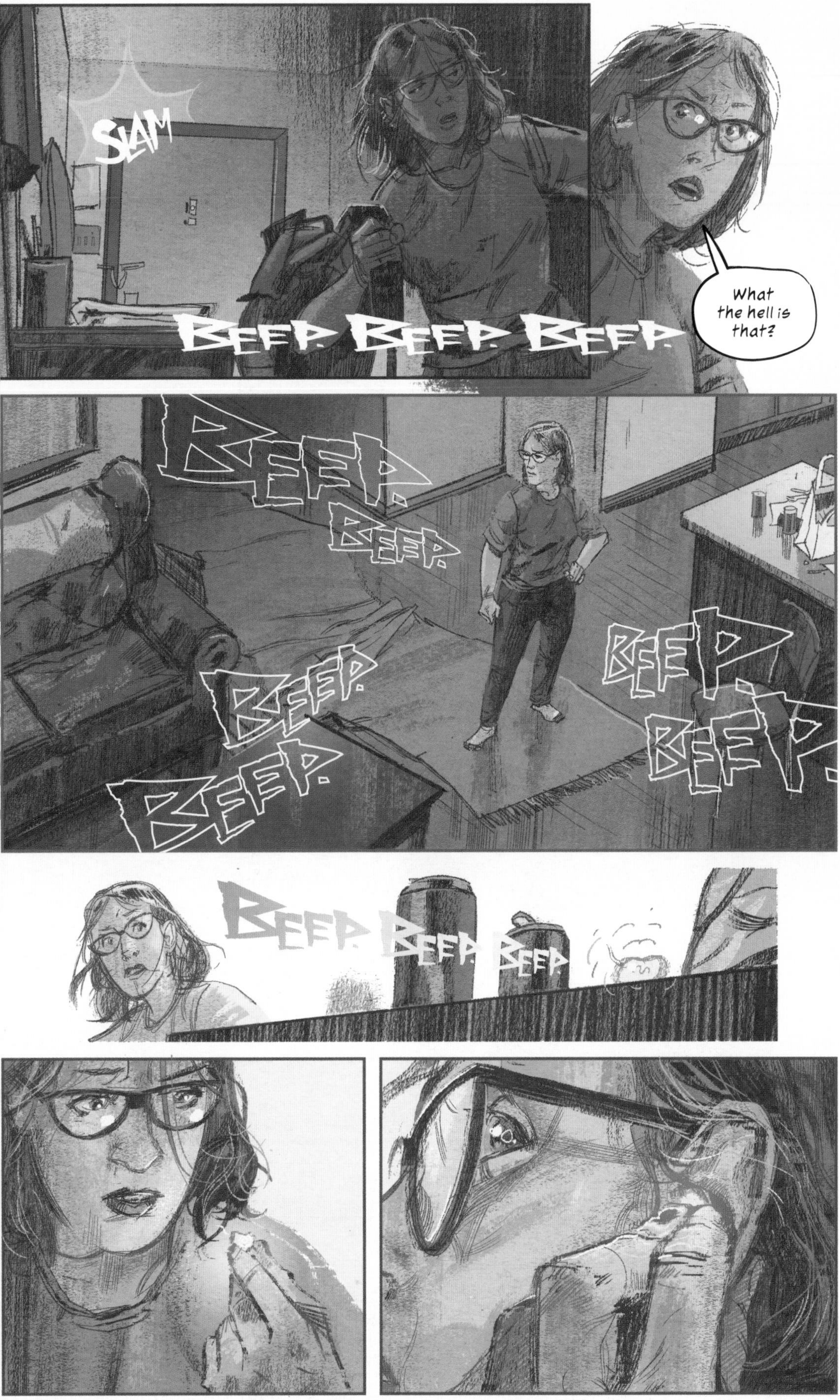
SLAM
BEEP. BEEP. BEEP.
What the hell is that?
BEEP.
BEEP.
BEEP.
BEEP.
BEEP.
BEEP.
BEEP. BEEP. BEEP.

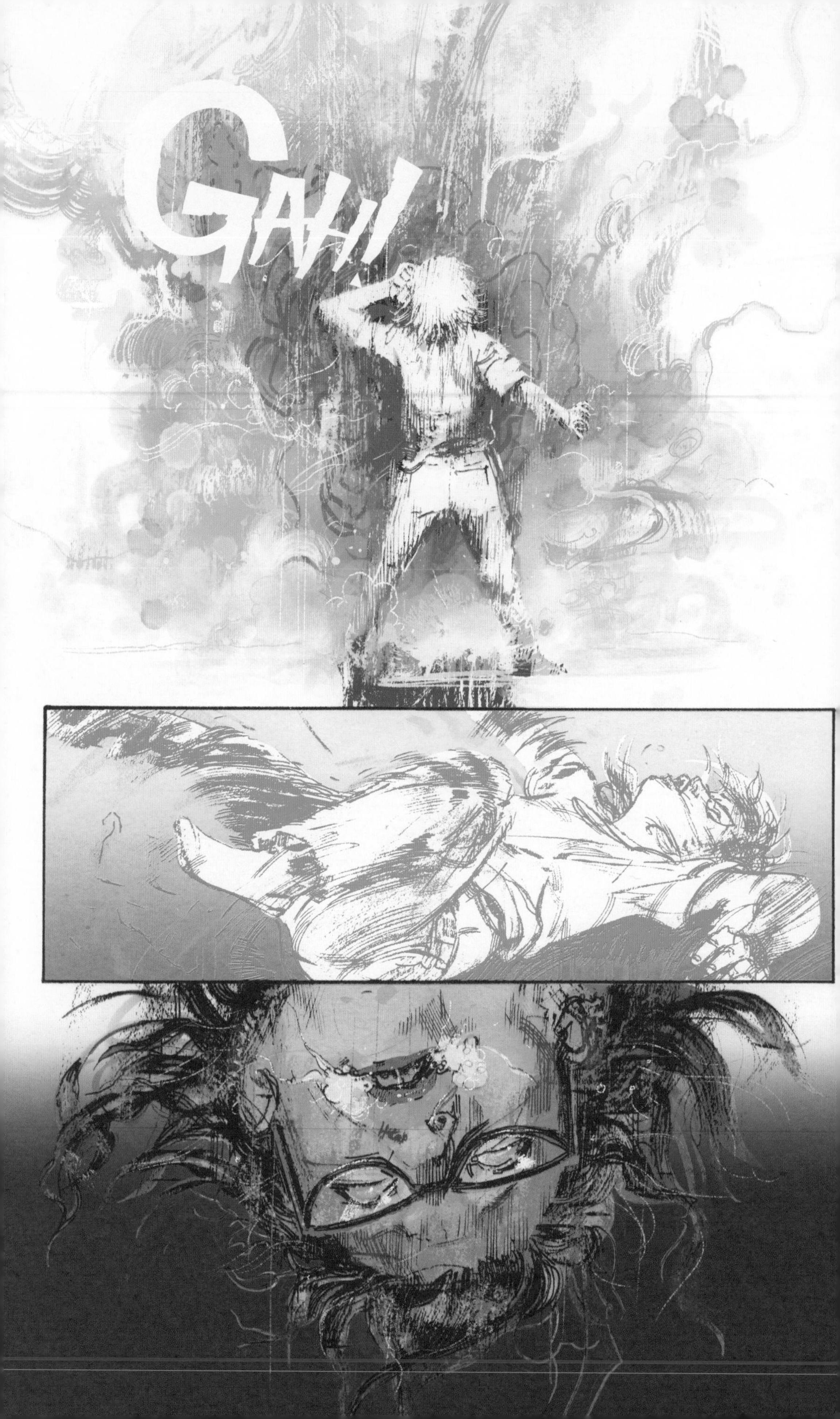
GAH!

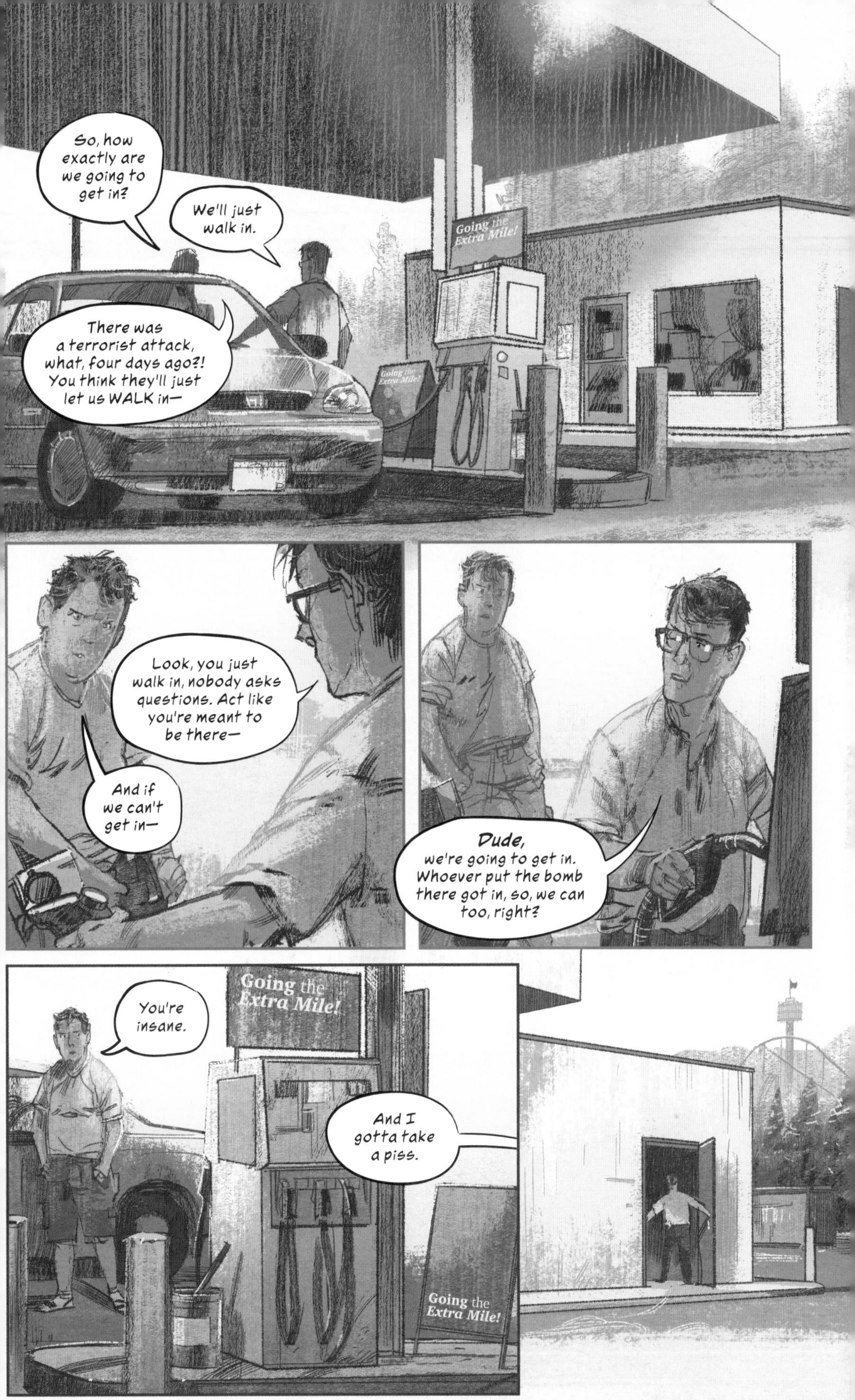
So, how exactly are we going to get in?
We'll just walk in.
Going the Extra Mile!
There was a terrorist attack, what, four days ago?! You think they'll just let us WALK in—
Look, you just walk in, nobody asks questions. Act like you're meant to be there—
And if we can't get in—
Dude, we're going to get in. Whoever put the bomb there got in, so, we can too, right?
Going the Extra Mile!
You're insane.
And I gotta take a piss.
Going the Extra Mile!

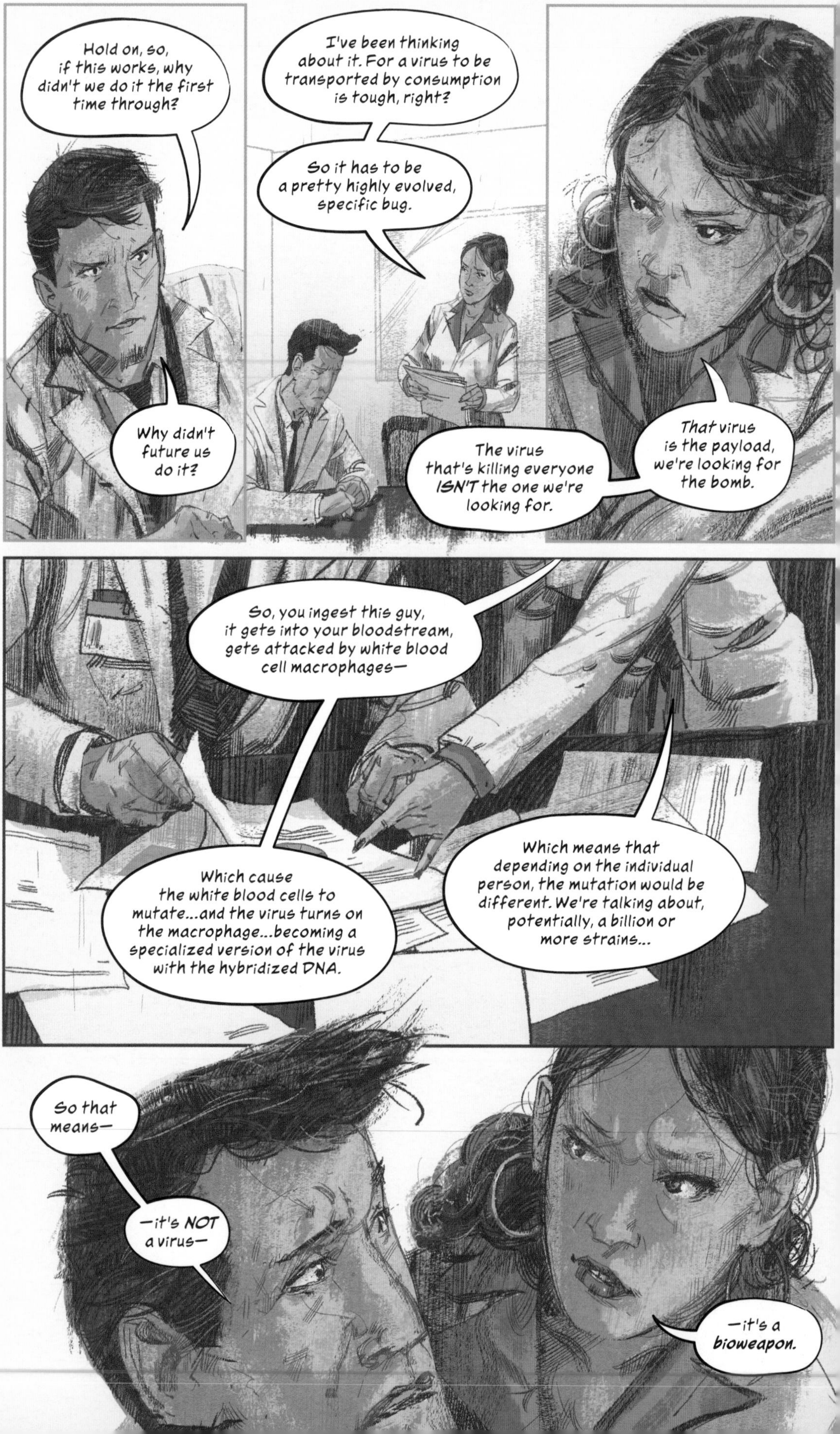
Hold on, so, if this works, why didn't we do it the first time through?
I've been thinking about it. For a virus to be transported by consumption is tough, right?
So it has to be a pretty highly evolved, specific bug.
Why didn't future us do it?
The virus that's killing everyone *ISN'T* the one we're looking for.
That virus is the payload, we're looking for the bomb.
So, you ingest this guy, it gets into your bloodstream, gets attacked by white blood cell macrophages—
Which cause the white blood cells to mutate...and the virus turns on the macrophage...becoming a specialized version of the virus with the hybridized DNA.
Which means that depending on the individual person, the mutation would be different. We're talking about, potentially, a billion or more strains...
So that means—
—it's *NOT* a virus—
—it's a *bioweapon.*

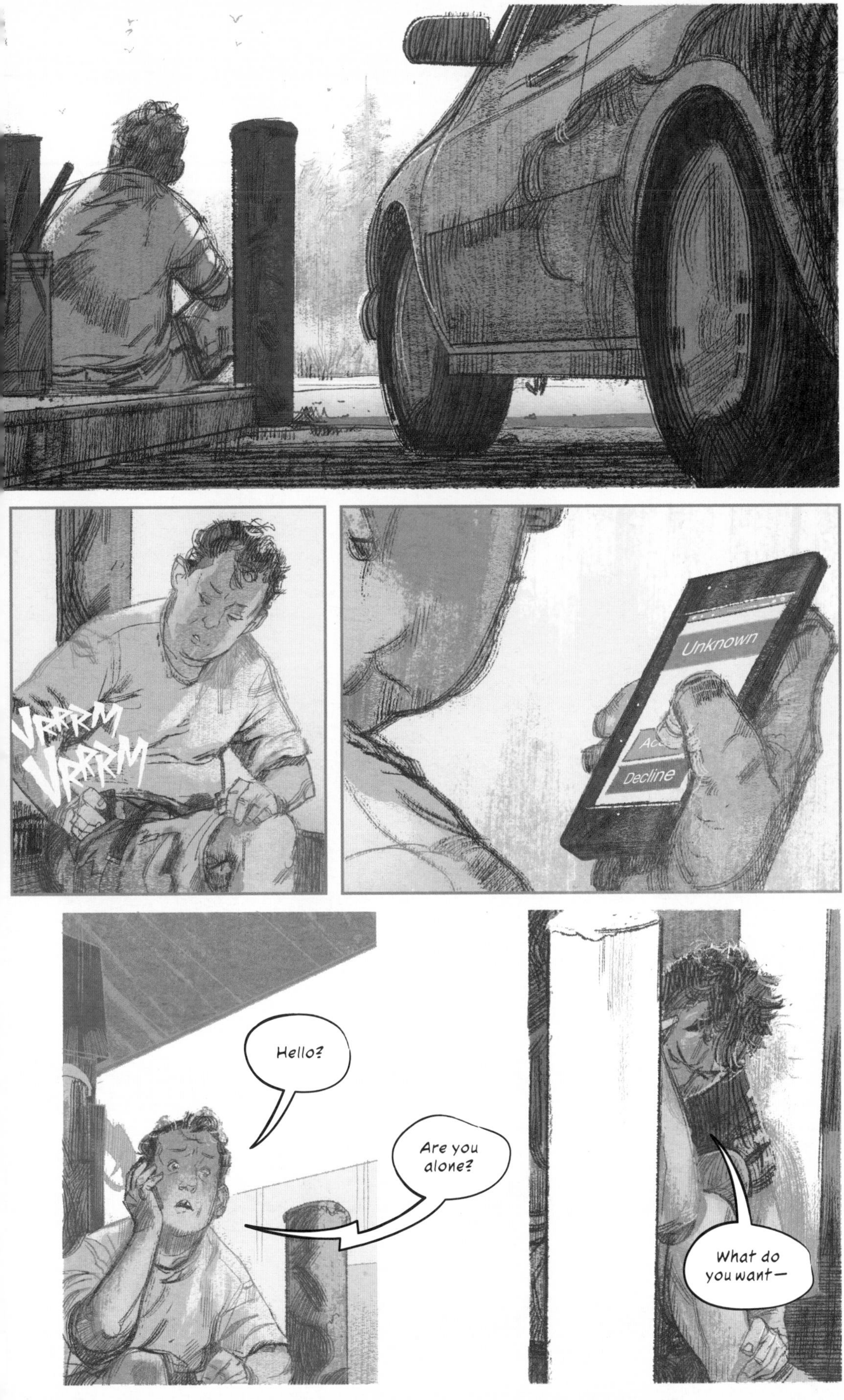
VRRRM VRRRM
Unknown
Decline
Hello?
Are you alone?
What do you want—

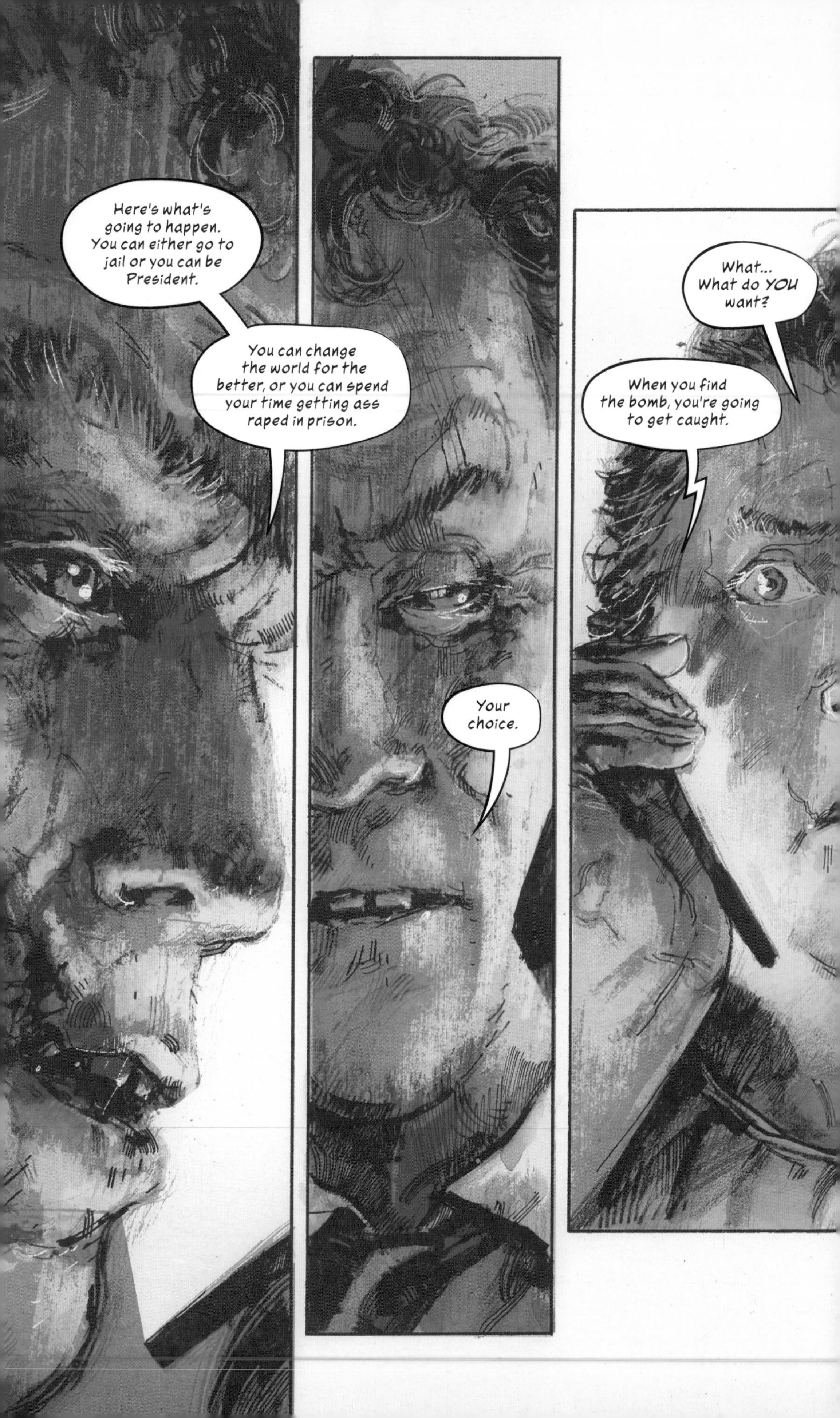
Here's what's going to happen. You can either go to jail or you can be President.
You can change the world for the better, or you can spend your time getting ass raped in prison.
Your choice.
What... What do YOU want?
When you find the bomb, you're going to get caught.

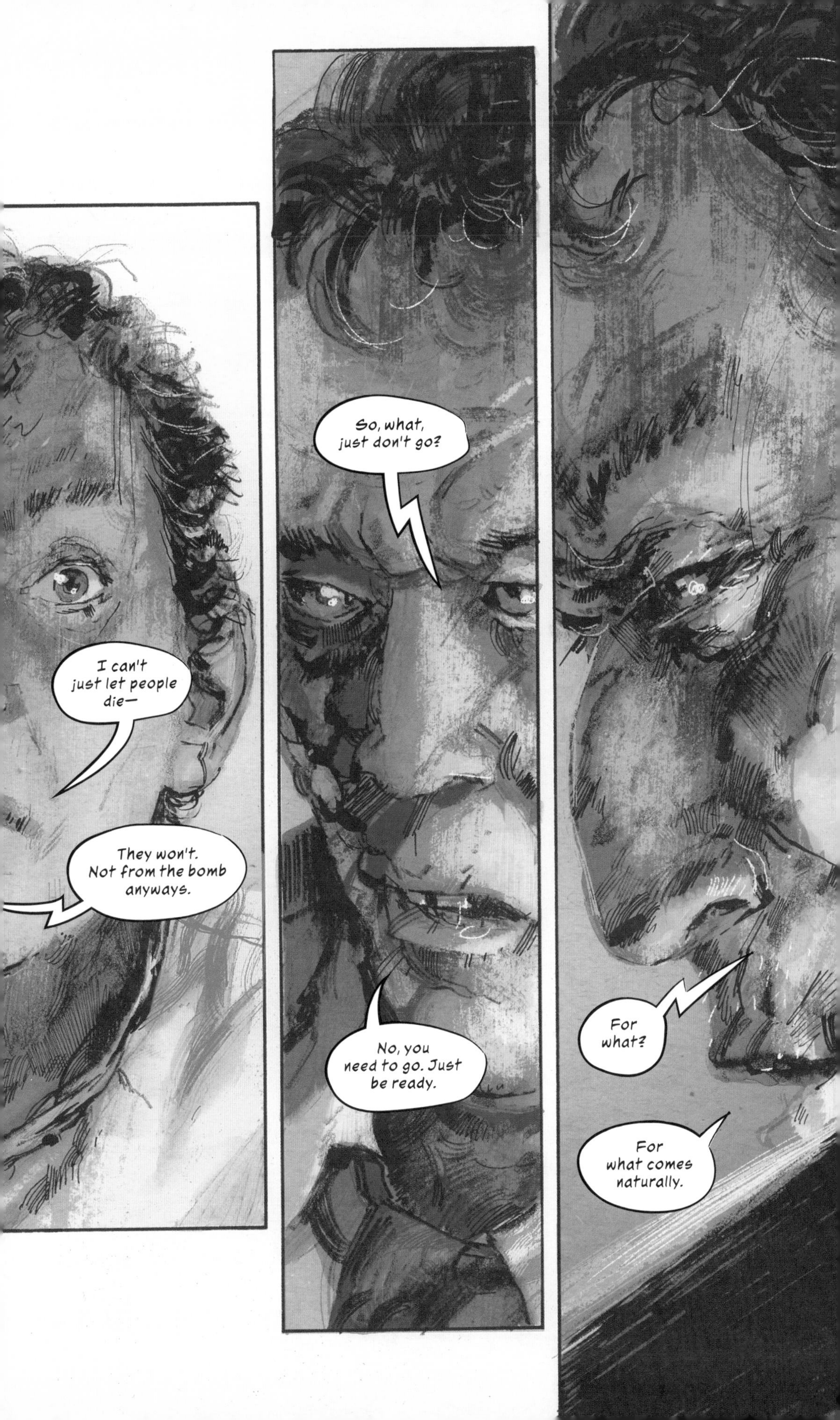

I can't just let people die—
They won't. Not from the bomb anyways.
So, what, just don't go?
No, you need to go. Just be ready.
For what?
For what comes naturally.

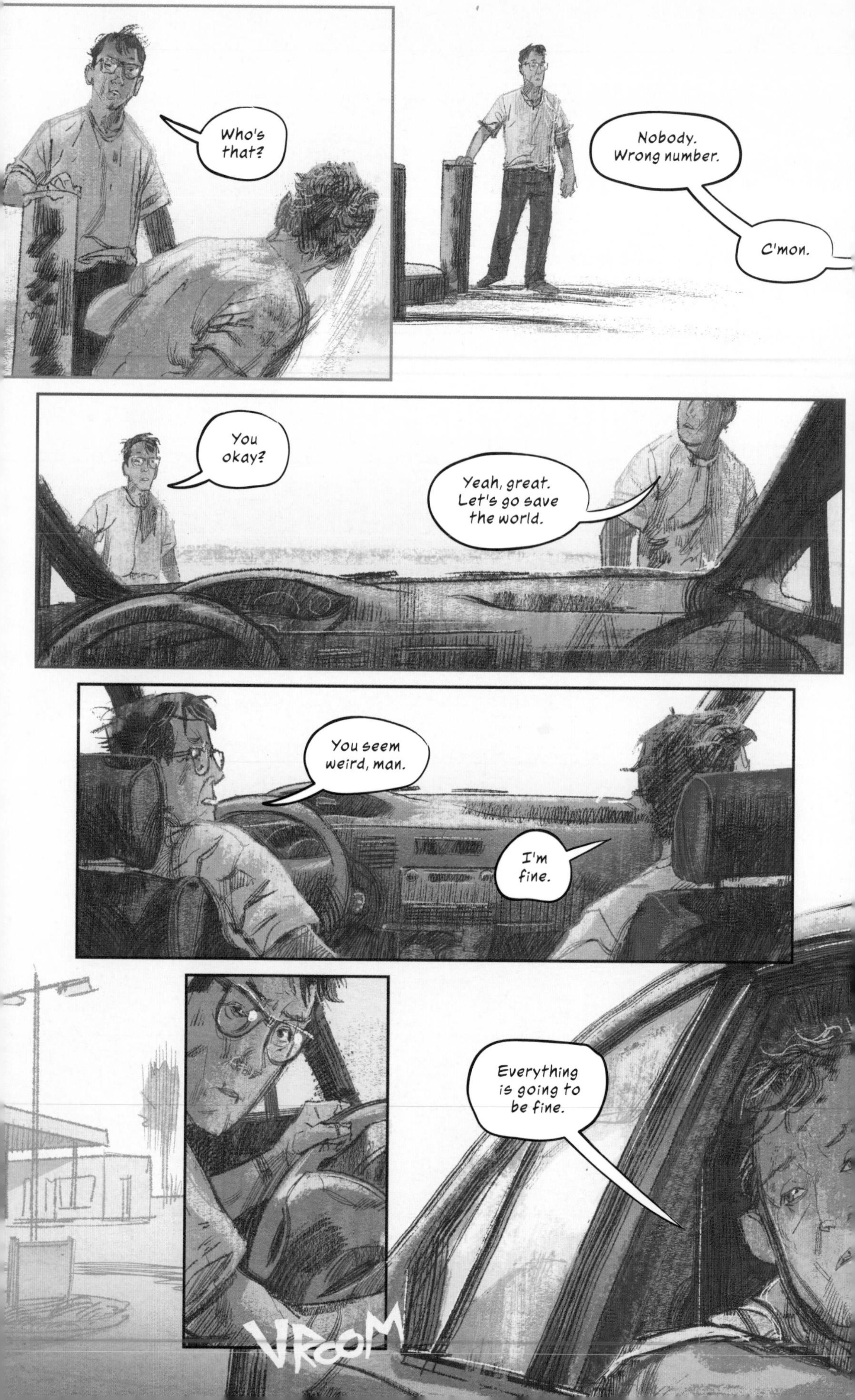
Who's that?
Nobody. Wrong number.
C'mon.
You okay?
Yeah, great. Let's go save the world.
You seem weird, man.
I'm fine.
Everything is going to be fine.
VROOM

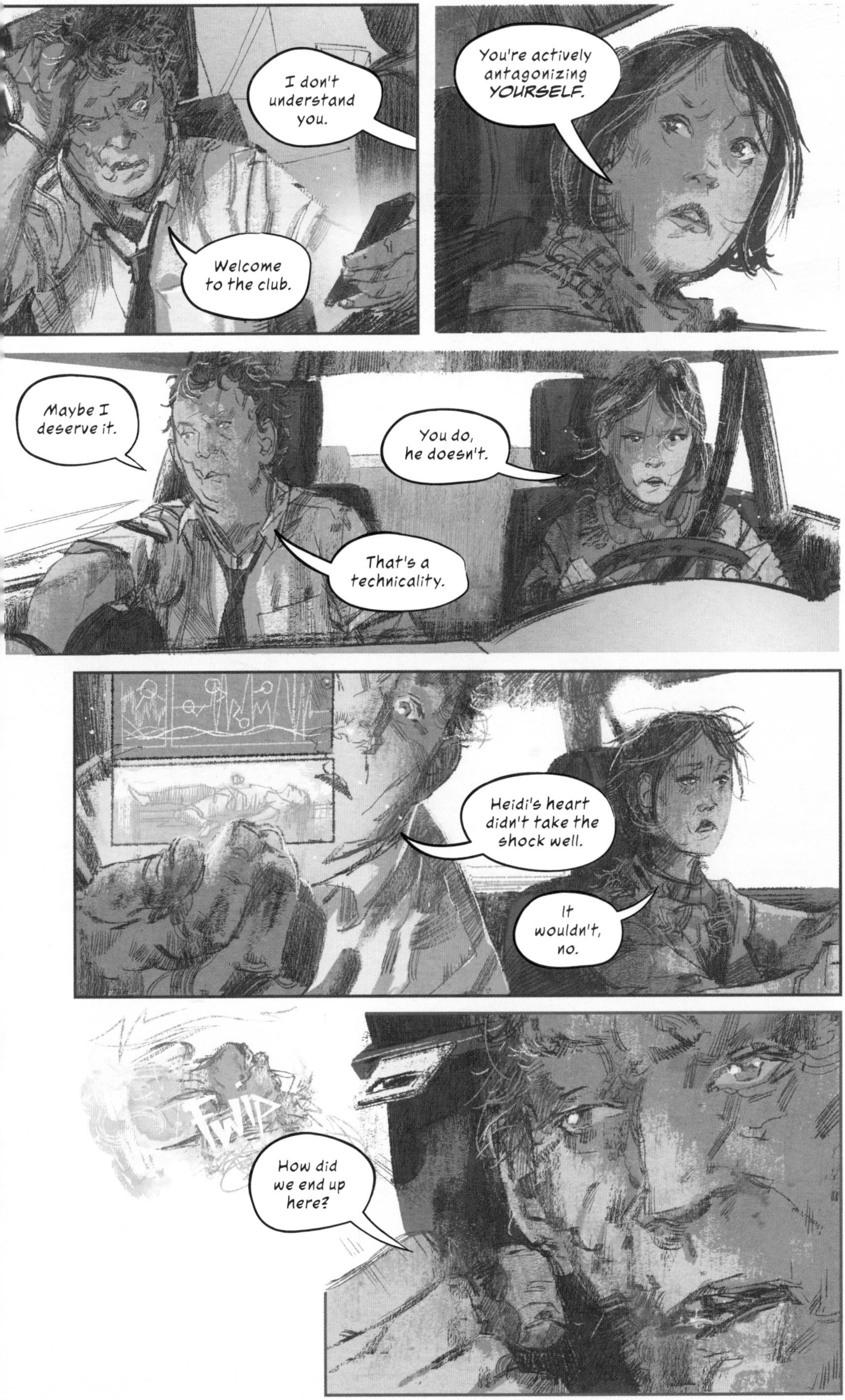
I don't understand you.
Welcome to the club.
You're actively antagonizing YOURSELF.
Maybe I deserve it.
You do, he doesn't.
That's a technicality.
Heidi's heart didn't take the shock well.
It wouldn't, no.
FWIP
How did we end up here?

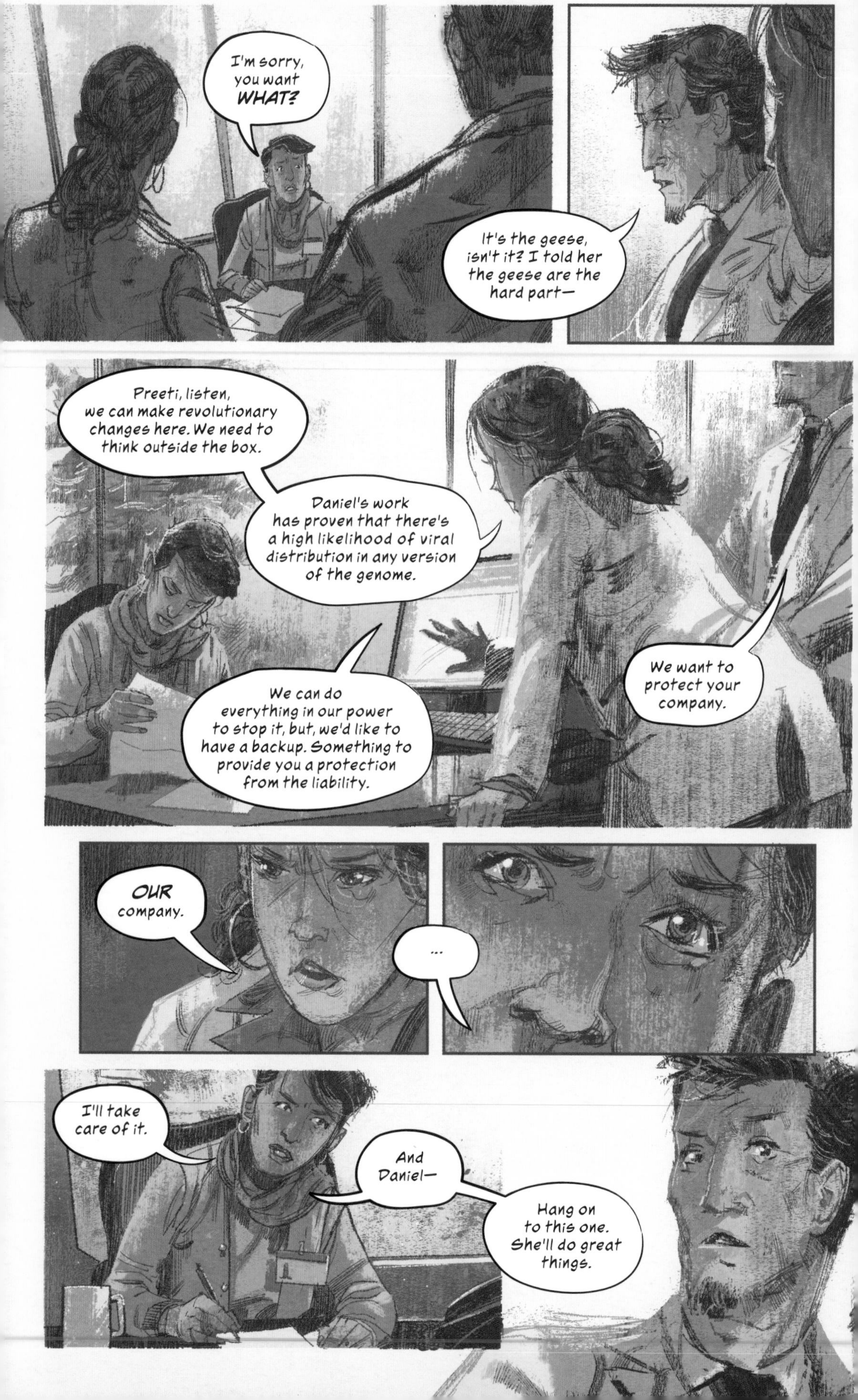
I'm sorry, you want WHAT?
It's the geese, isn't it? I told her the geese are the hard part—
Preeti, listen, we can make revolutionary changes here. We need to think outside the box.
Daniel's work has proven that there's a high likelihood of viral distribution in any version of the genome.
We can do everything in our power to stop it, but, we'd like to have a backup. Something to provide you a protection from the liability.
We want to protect your company.
OUR company.
...
I'll take care of it.
And Daniel—
Hang on to this one. She'll do great things.

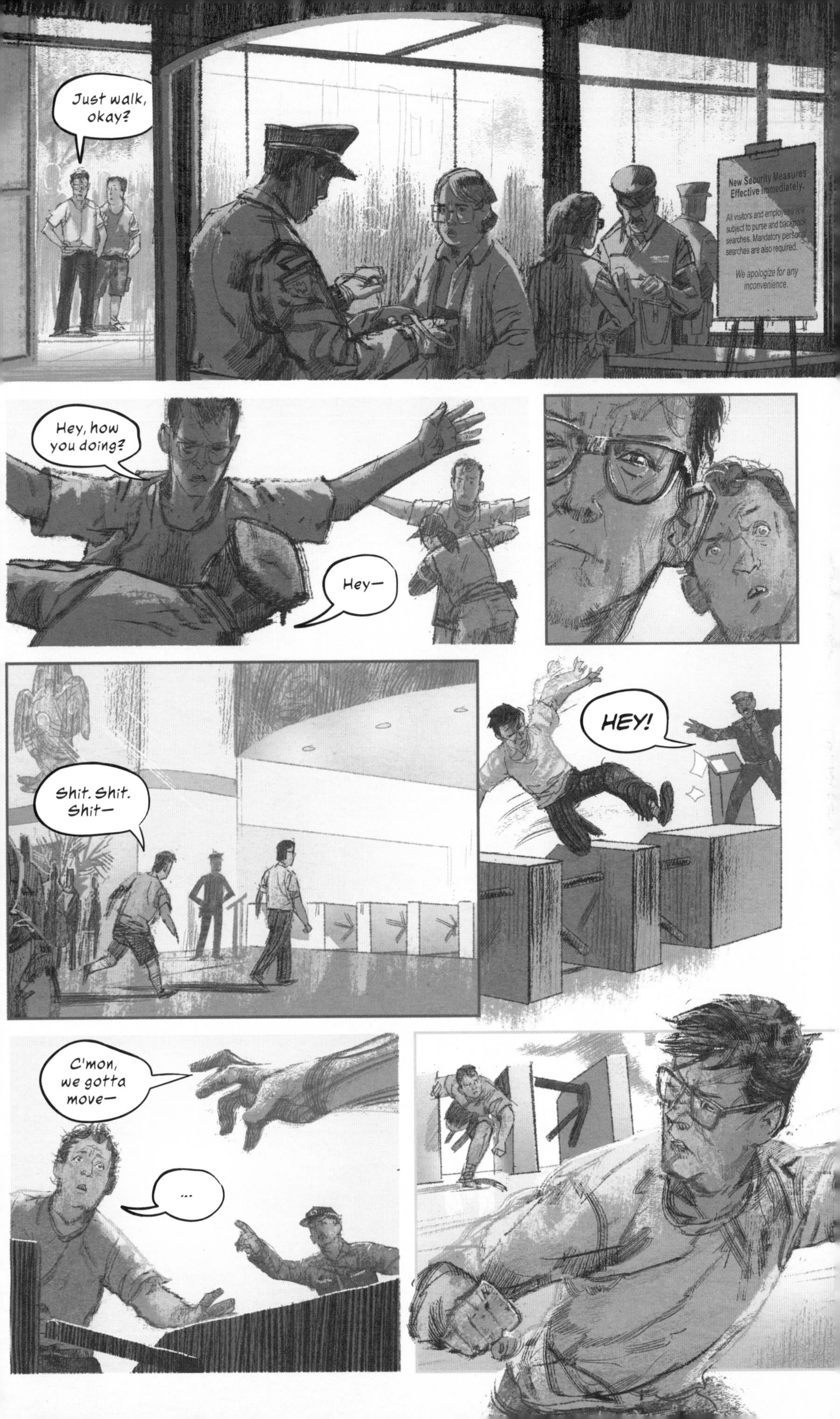
Just walk, okay?
New Security Measures Effective Immediately.
All visitors and employees are subject to purse and backpack searches. Mandatory personal searches are also required.
We apologize for any inconvenience.
Hey, how you doing?
Hey—
Shit. Shit. Shit—
HEY!
C'mon, we gotta move—
...

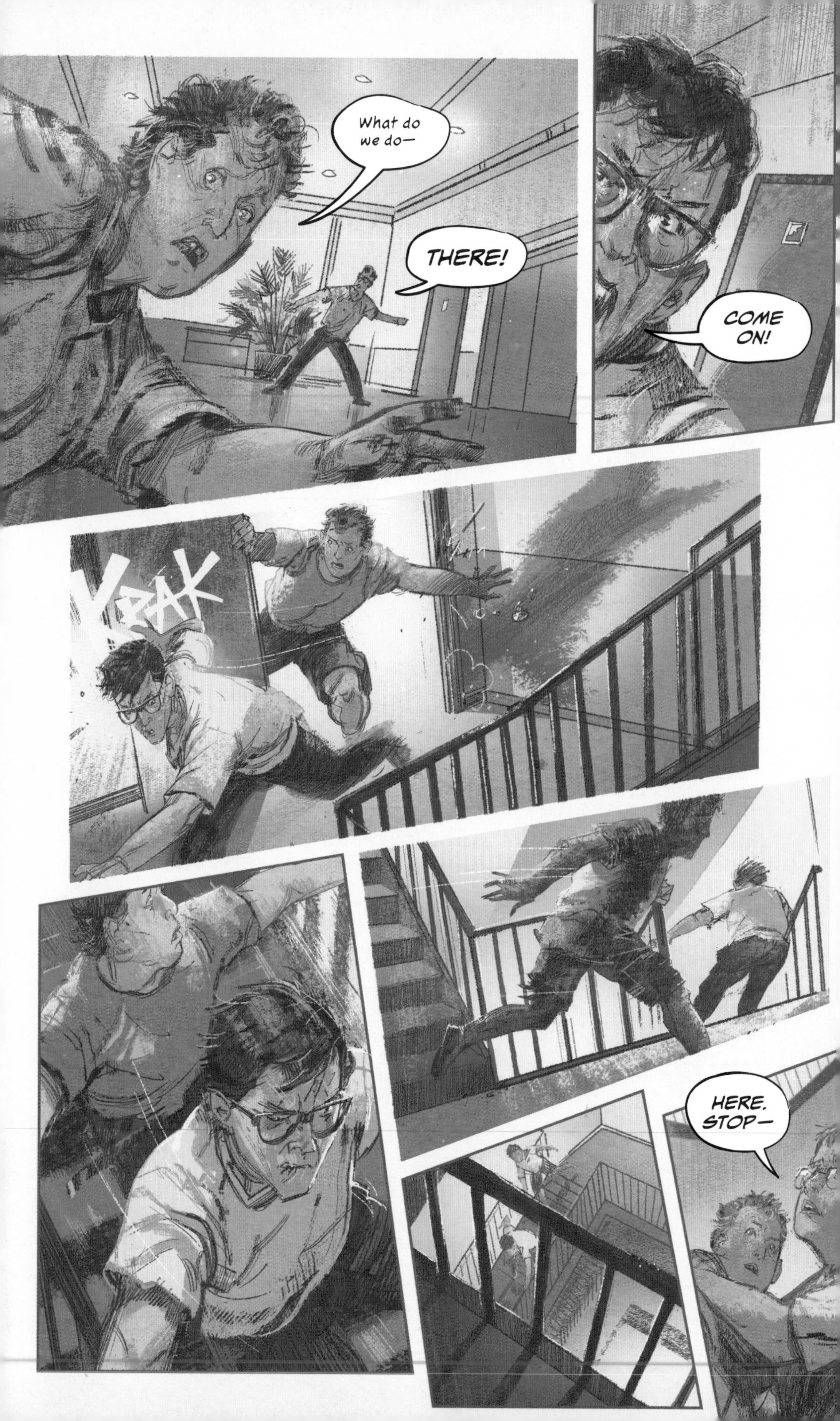
What do we do—
THERE!
COME ON!
KRAK
HERE. STOP—

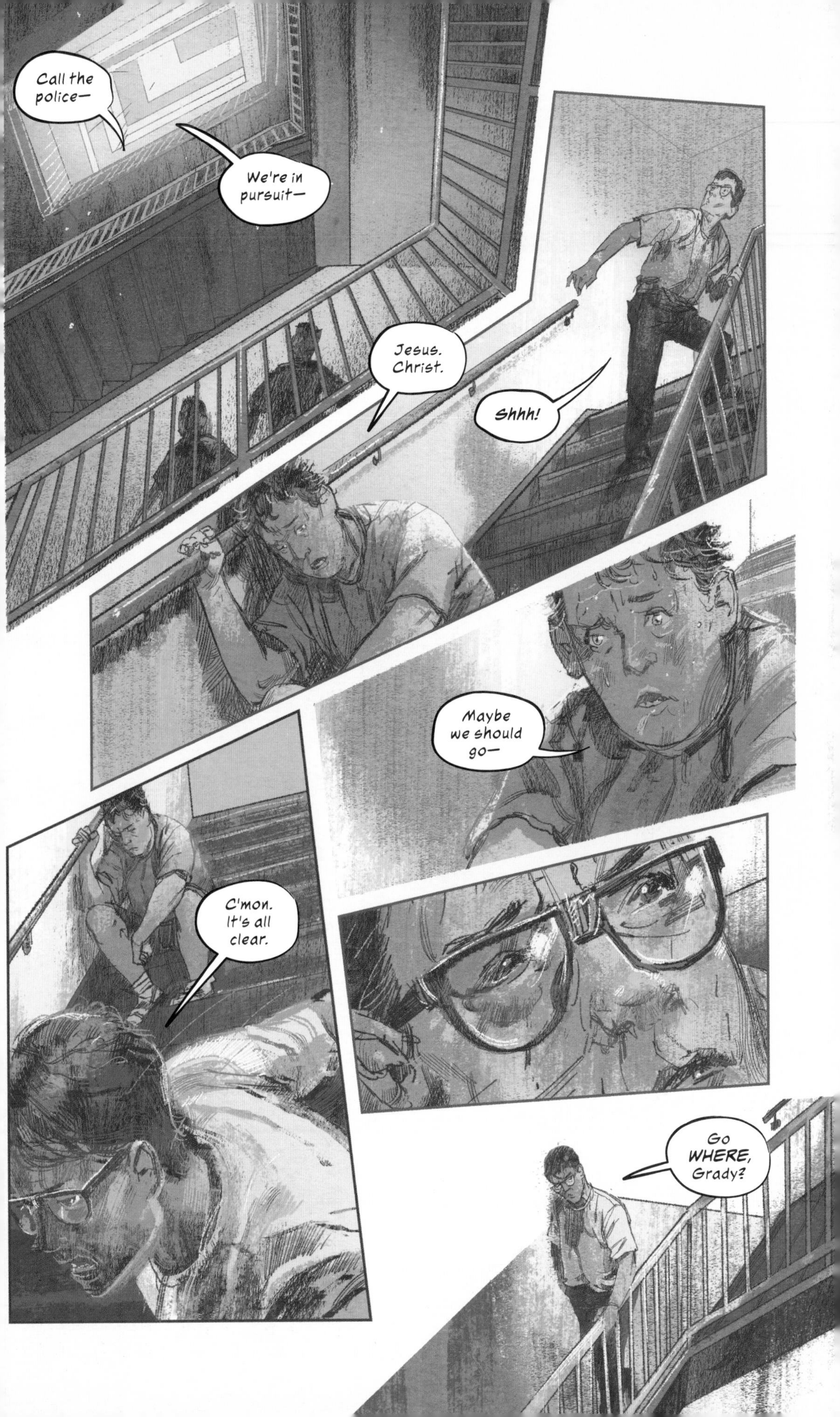
Call the police—
We're in pursuit—
Jesus. Christ.
Shhh!
Maybe we should go—
C'mon. It's all clear.
Go WHERE, Grady?

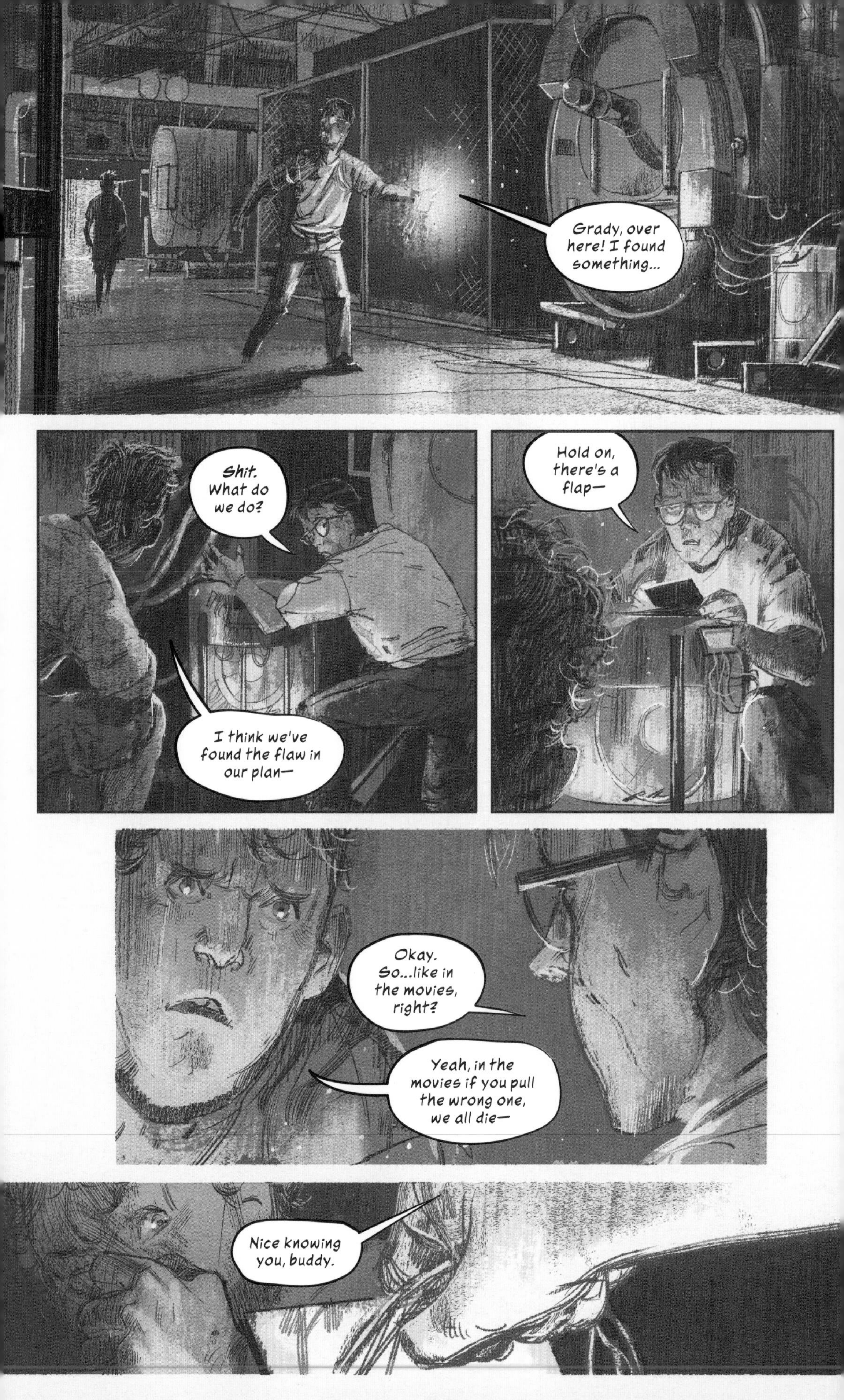
Grady, over here! I found something...
Shit. What do we do?
I think we've found the flaw in our plan—
Hold on, there's a flap—
Okay. So...like in the movies, right?
Yeah, in the movies if you pull the wrong one, we all die—
Nice knowing you, buddy.

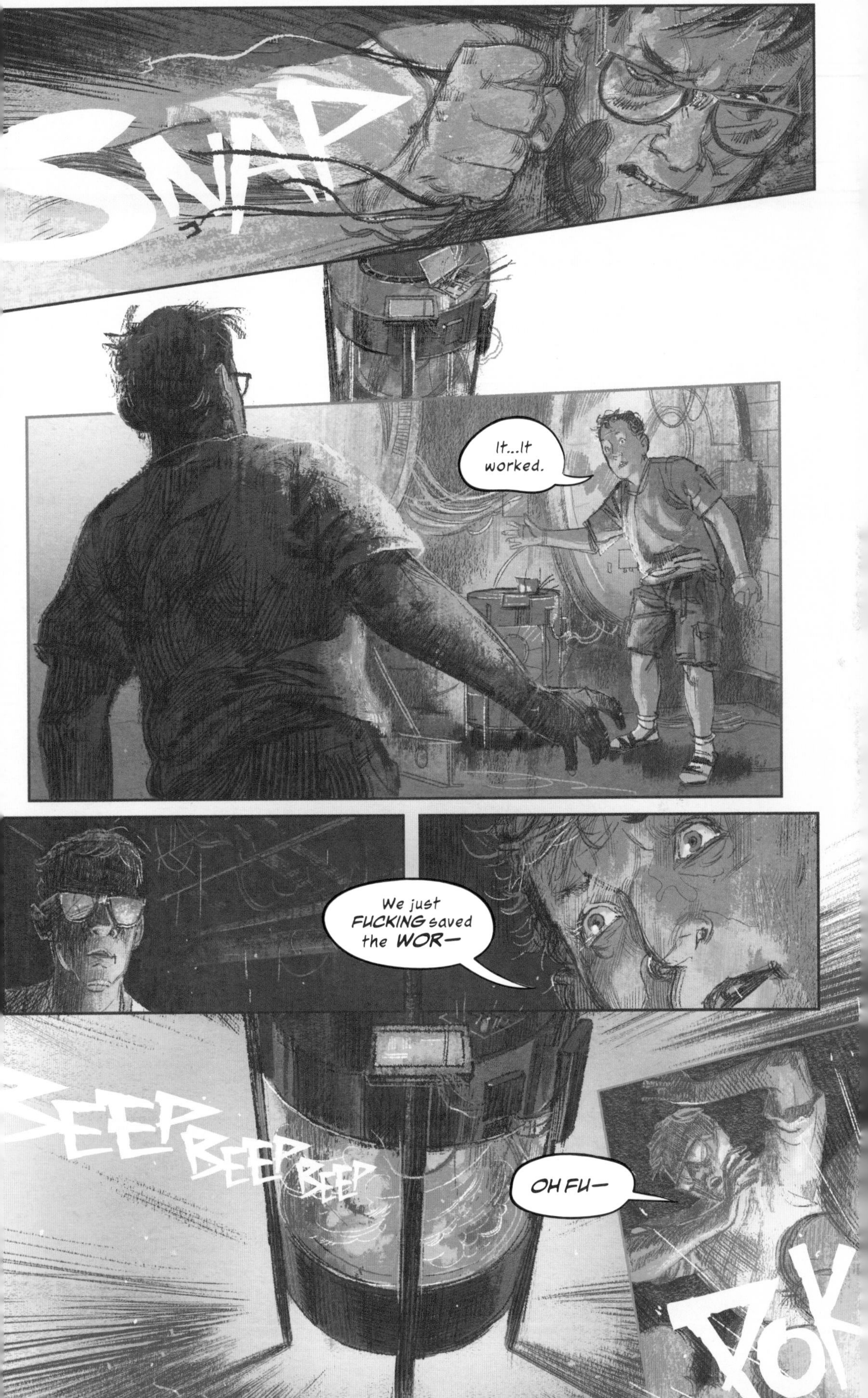
SNAP
It...It worked.
We just FUCKING saved the WOR—
BEEP BEEP BEEP
OH FU—
POOF

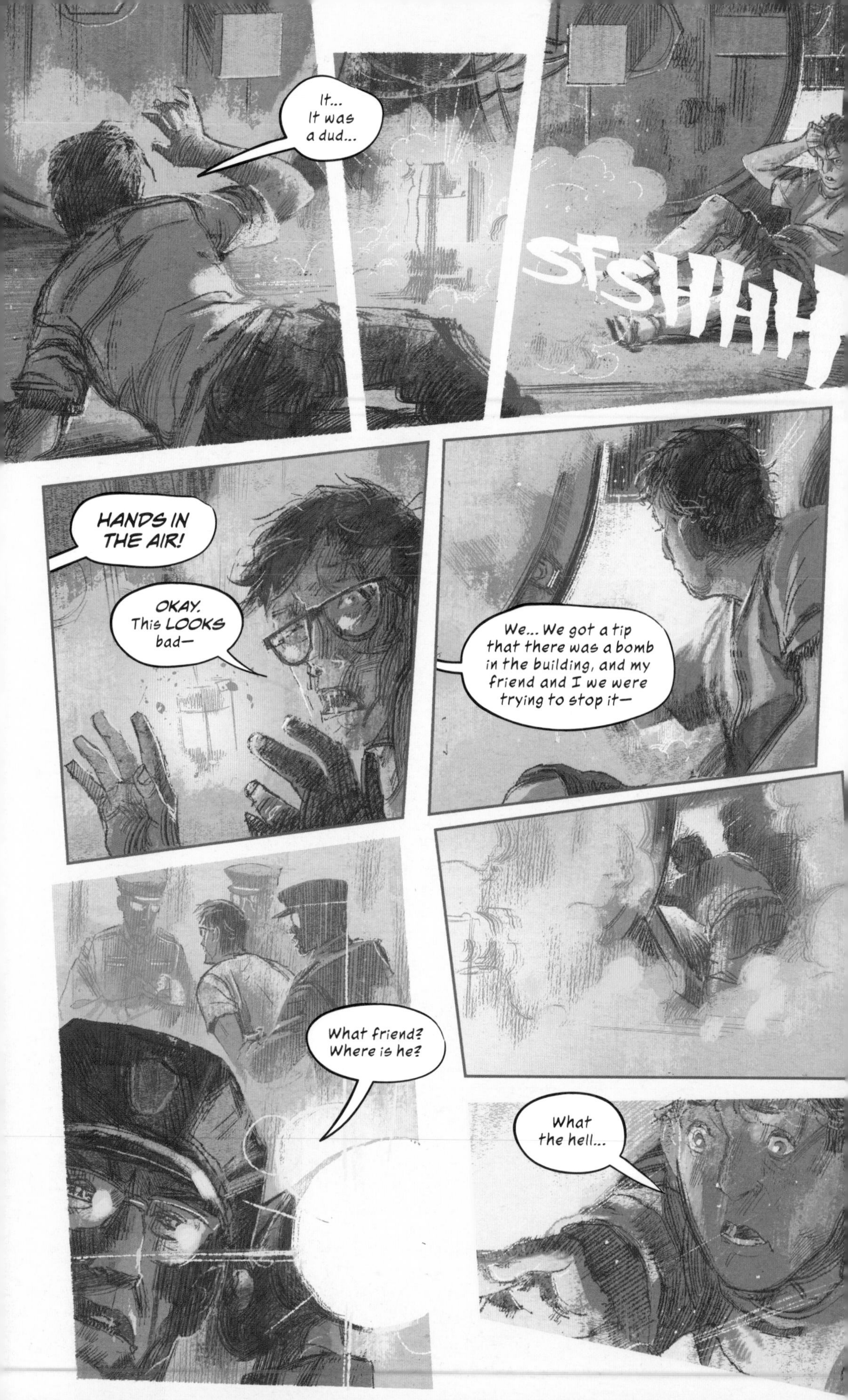
It... It was a dud...
SFSHHH
HANDS IN THE AIR!
OKAY. This LOOKS bad—
We... We got a tip that there was a bomb in the building, and my friend and I we were trying to stop it—
What friend? Where is he?
What the hell...

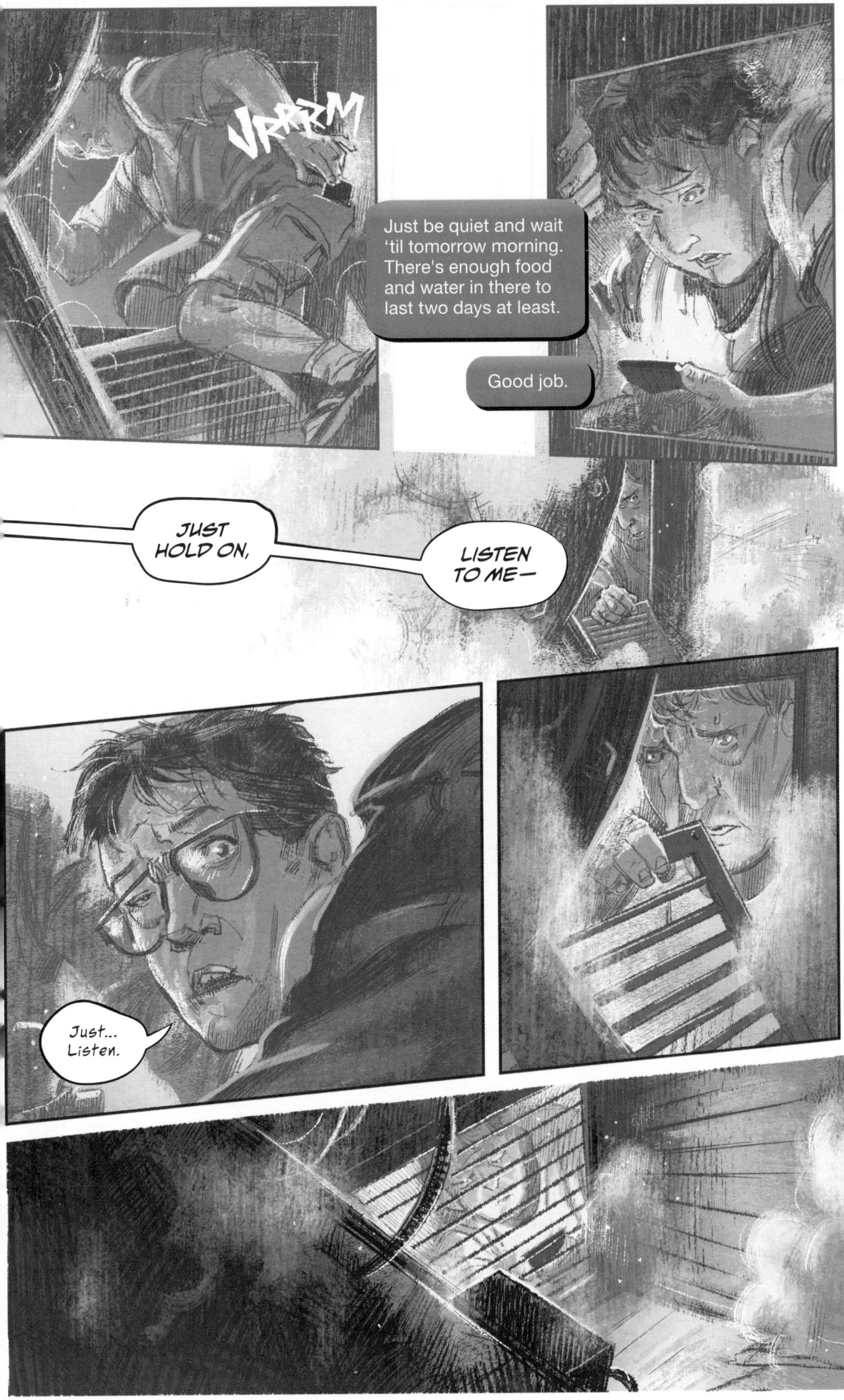
VRRRM
Just be quiet and wait 'til tomorrow morning. There's enough food and water in there to last two days at least.
Good job.
JUST HOLD ON,
LISTEN TO ME—
Just... Listen.

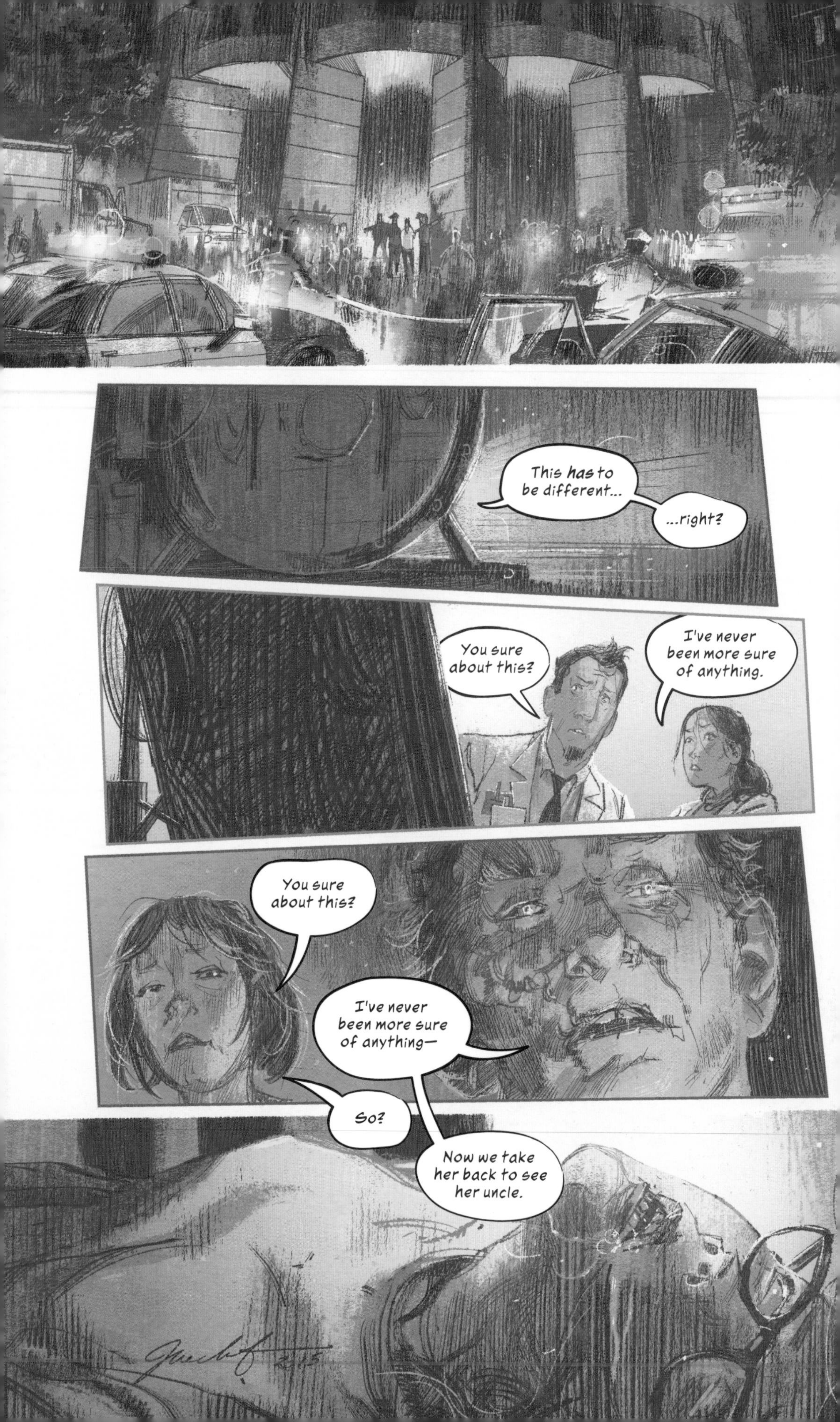
This has to be different...
...right?
You sure about this?
I've never been more sure of anything.
You sure about this?
I've never been more sure of anything—
So?
Now we take her back to see her uncle.

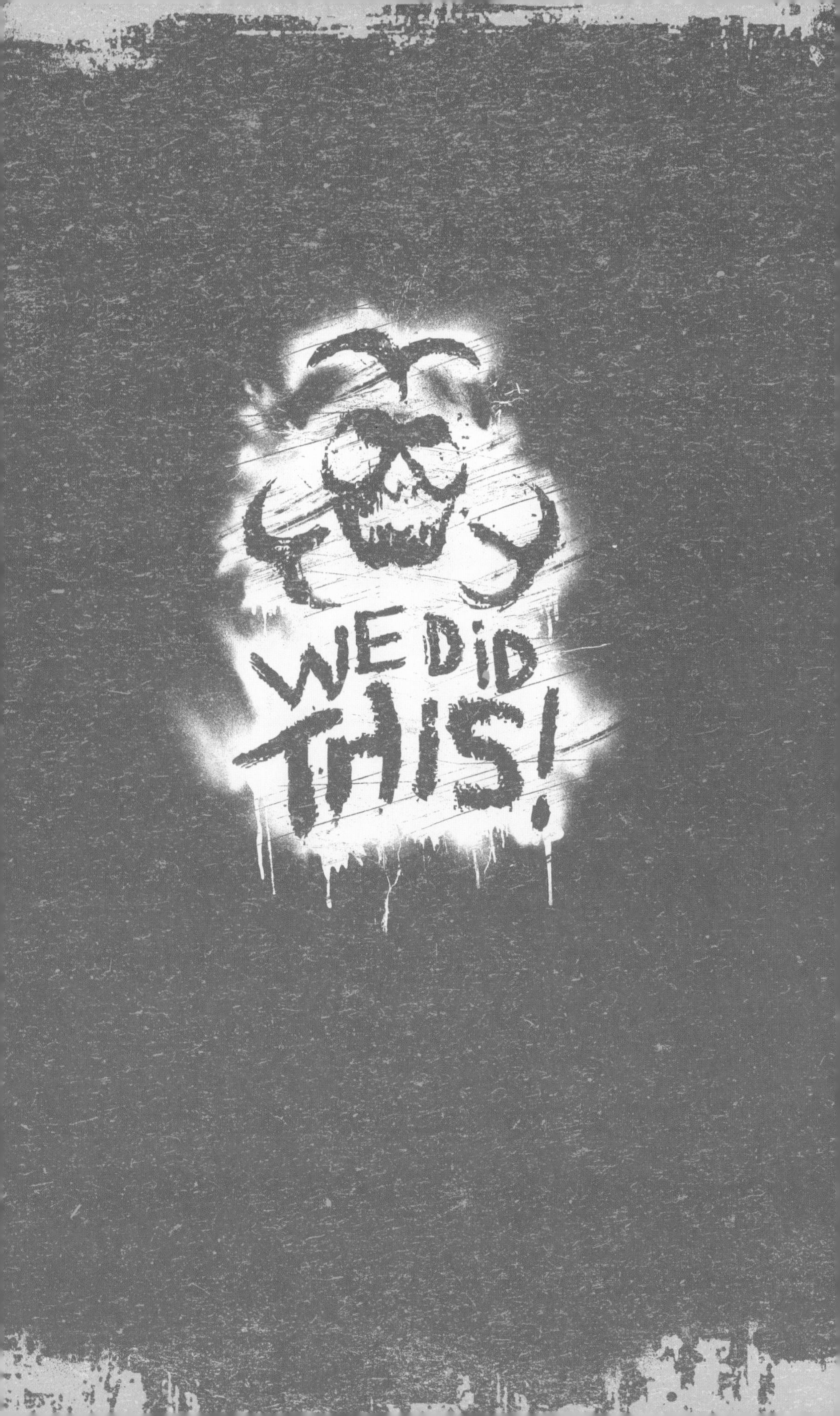
WE DID
THIS!

COVER GALLERY

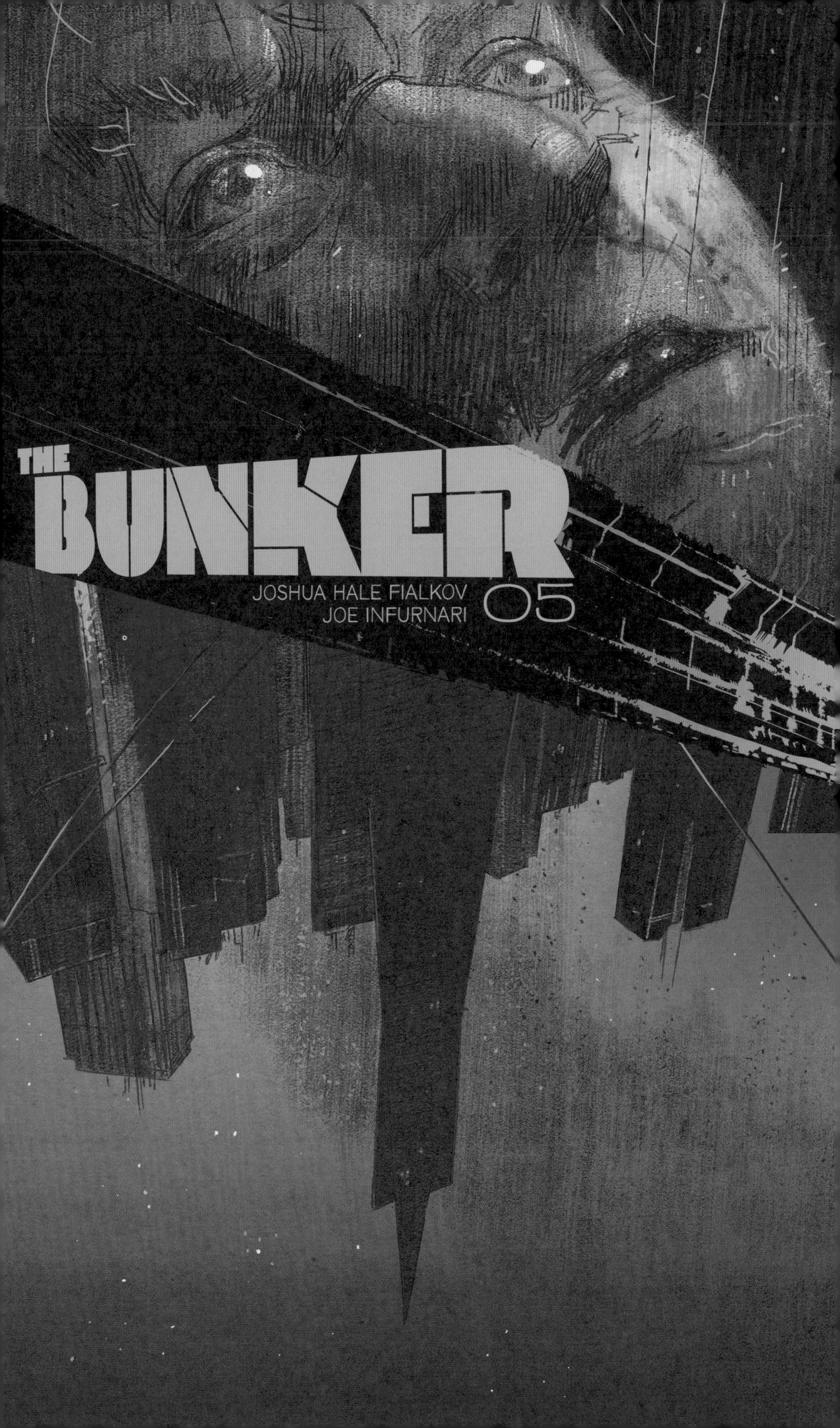
THE BUNKER
JOSHUA HALE FIALKOV
JOE INFURNARI
05

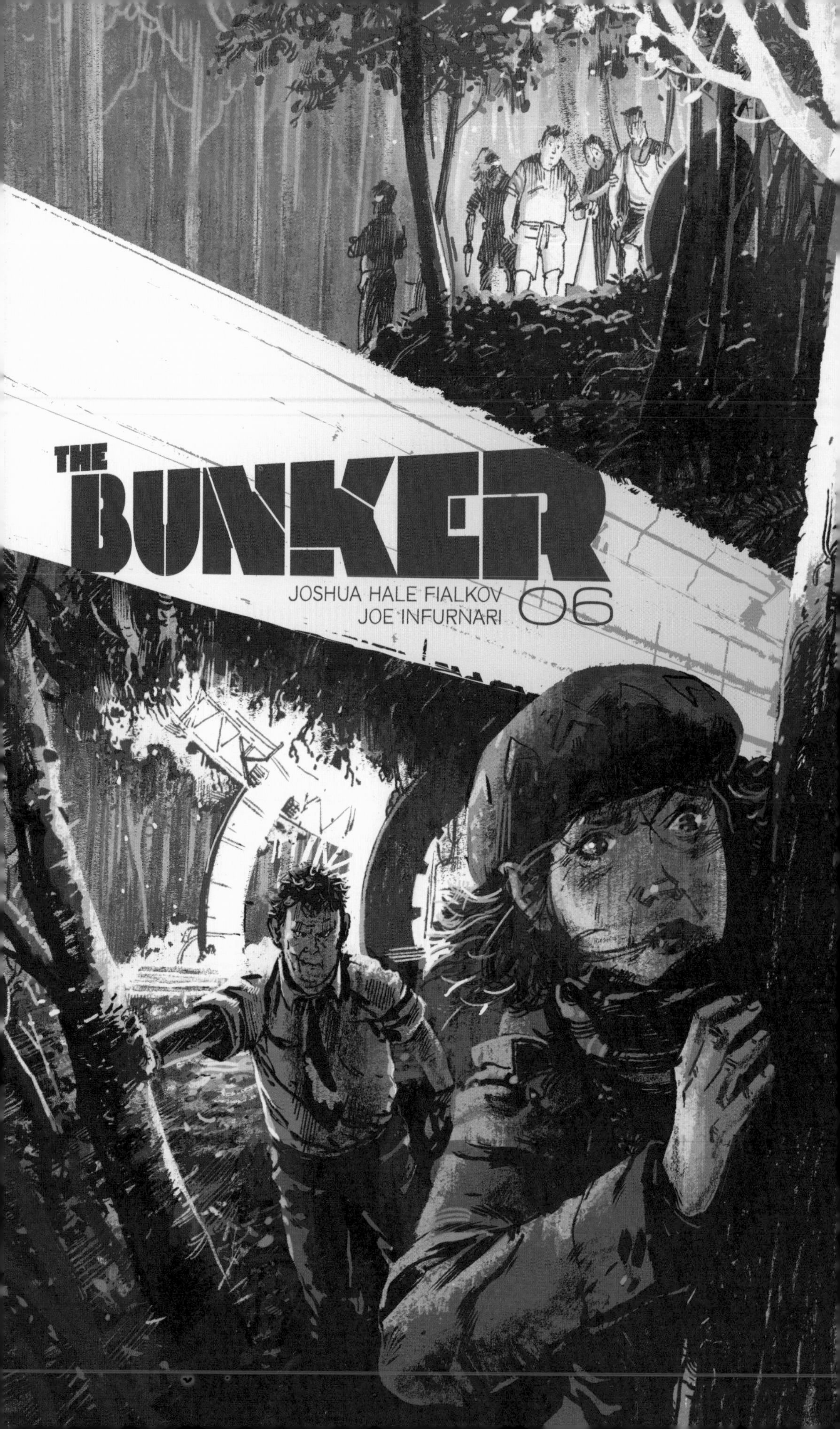
THE
BUNKER
JOSHUA HALE FIALKOV
JOE INFURNARI
06

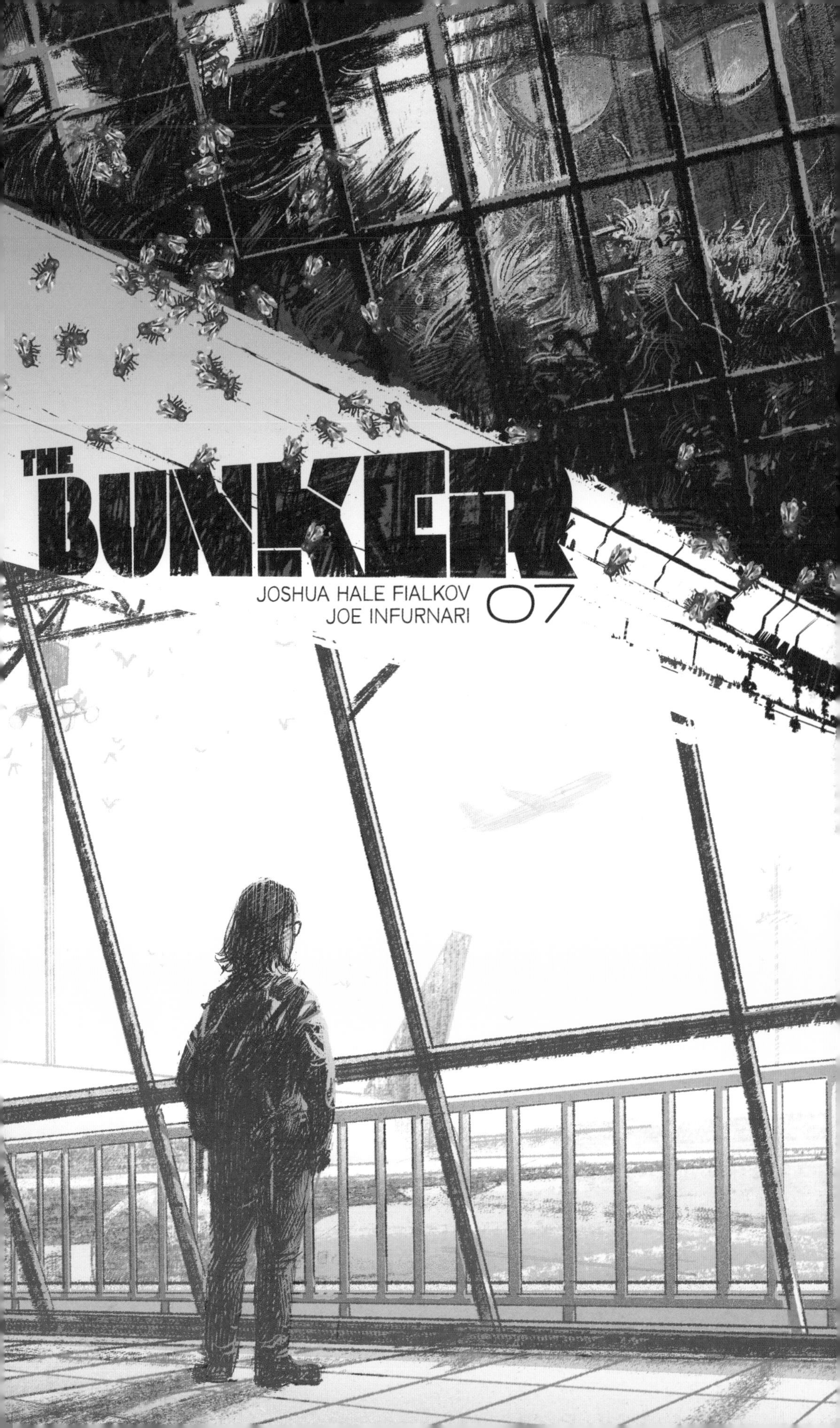
THE BUNKER
JOSHUA HALE FIALKOV
JOE INFURNARI
07

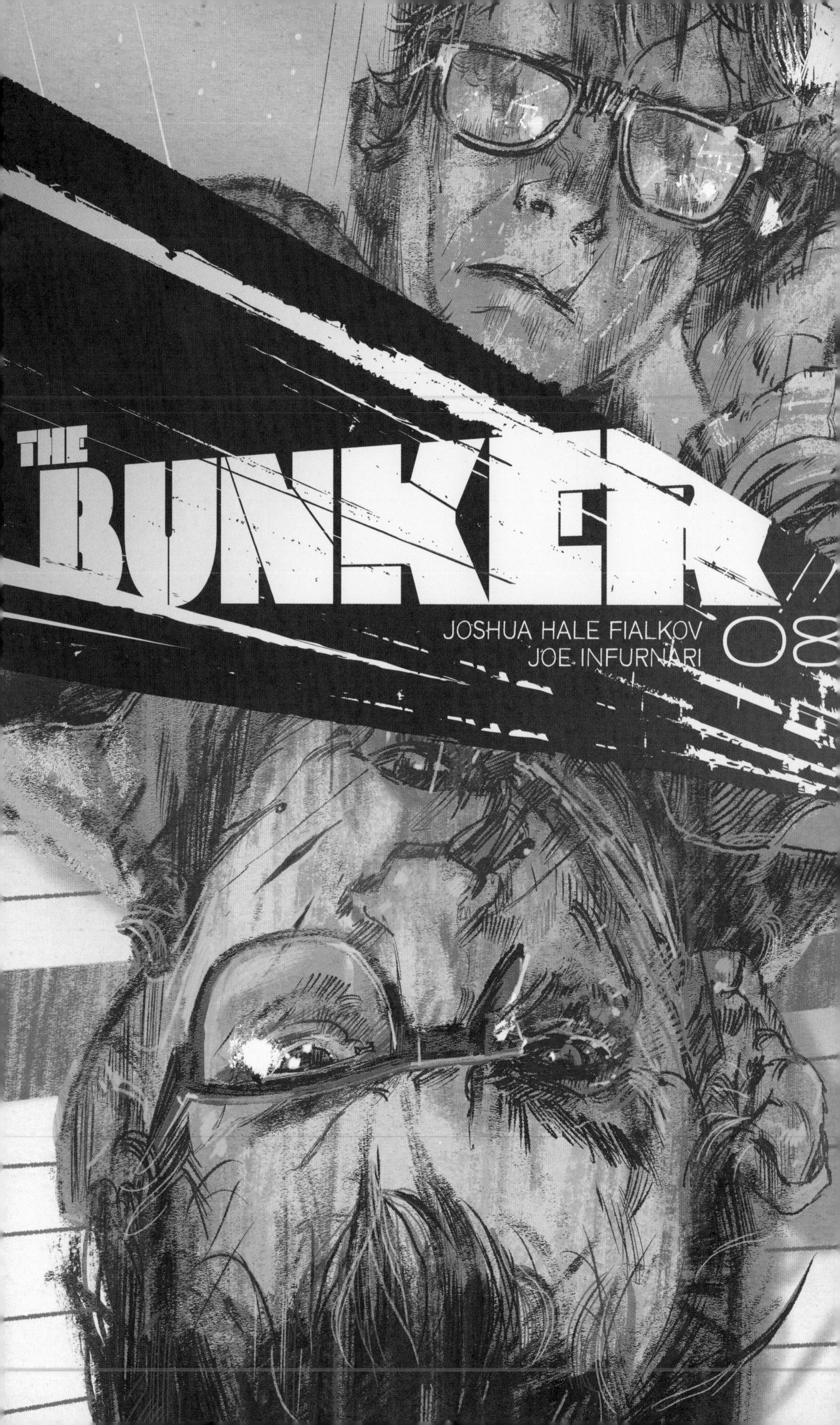
THE
BUNKER
JOSHUA HALE FIALKOV
JOE INFURNARI
08

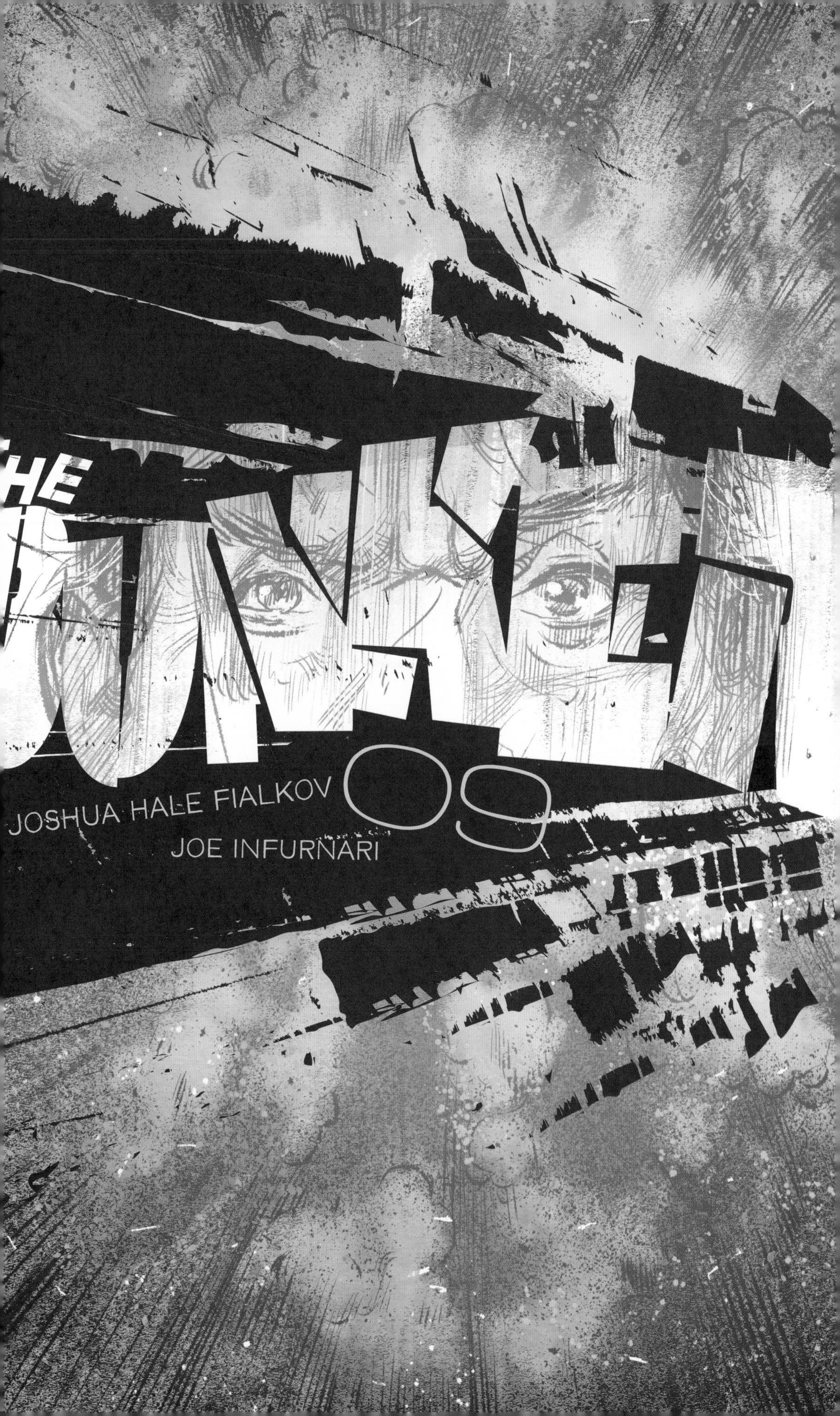
HE
JOSHUA HALE FIALKOV
09
JOE INFURNARI

Photo by Heidi Ryder

Joshua Hale Fialkov is the writer and co-creator of graphic novels including *Elk's Run*, *Tumor*, *The Life After*, *Punks*, and *Echoes*. He has written *The Ultimates* for Marvel and *I, Vampire* for DC Comics. He lives in Los Angeles with his wife, author Christina Rice, their daughter, who will remain anonymous (and adorable), their dogs Cole and Olaf, and a very pissed off cat named Smokey.

Photo by Seth Kushner

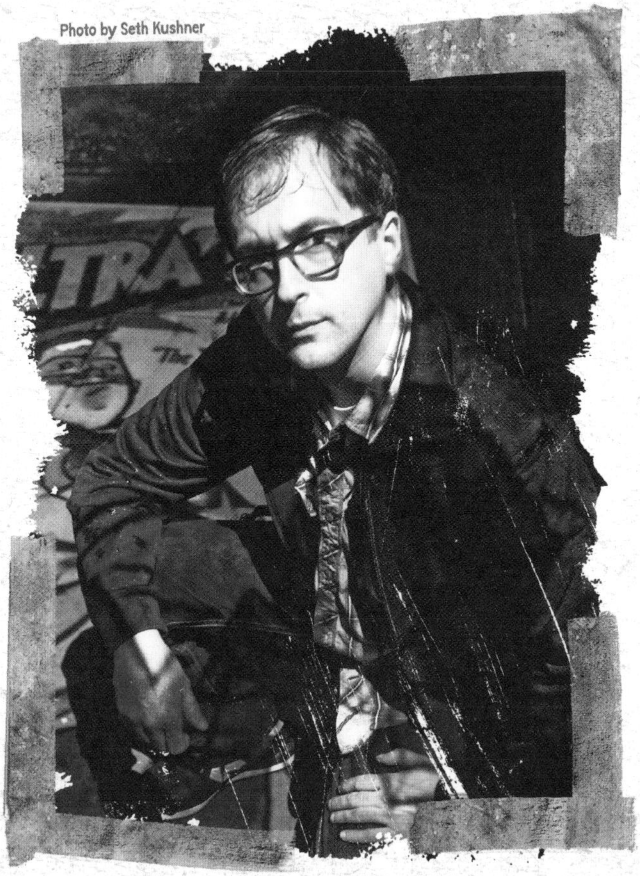

Being the singular genius behind the infamous *Time F#©ker*, Joe Infurnari's talents are uniquely suited to the vagaries of illustrating a time travel story. Whether tracing deadbeat dad DNA back to Paleolithic times or propping up a drawing pad in the midst of the apocalypse, Joe's upper lip remains stiff and his focus resolute. It's not all work and no play for Joe 'The Towering' Infurnari! Leisure time is lovingly spent with his new bride and their four crazy cats in a bunker of his own design.

MORE FROM ONI PRESS...

THE BUNKER VOL. 1:

By Joshua Hale Fialkov & Joe Infurnári

136 pages, softcover, full color interiors

ISBN 978-1-62010-164-3

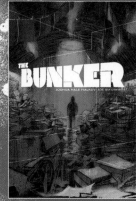

WASTELAND VOL. 1: CITIES IN DUST

By Antony Johnston & Christopher Mitten

160 pages, softcover, b/w interiors

ISBN 978-1-932664-59-1

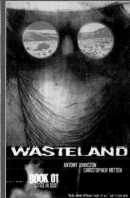

THE AUTEUR VOL. 1: PRESIDENTS DAY

By Rick Spears, James Callahan, & Luigi Anderson

144 pages, softcover, full color interiors

ISBN 978-1-62010-135-3

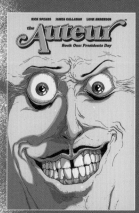

LETTER 44 VOL. 1: ESCAPE VELOCITY

By Charles Soule, Alberto Jiménez Alburquerque, Guy Major, & Dan Jackson

160 pages, softcover, full color interiors

ISBN 978-1-62010-133-9

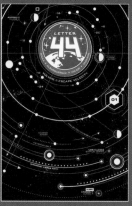

THE SIXTH GUN VOL. 1: COLD DEAD FINGERS

By Cullen Bunn, Brian Hurtt, & Bill Crabtree

176 pages, softcover, full color interiors

ISBN 978-1-934964-60-6

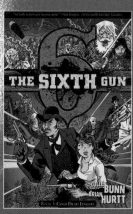

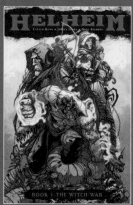

HELHEIM VOL. 1: THE WITCH WAR

By Cullen Bunn, Joëlle Jones, & Nick Filardi

160 pages, softcover, full color interiors

Includes fold-out poster

ISBN 978-1-62010-014-1

THE BUNKER
JOSHUA HALE FIALKOV JOE INFURNARI

WASTELAND
ANTONY JOHNSTON
CHRISTOPHER MITTEN
BOOK 01
CITIES IN DUST

RICK SPEARS JAMES CALLAHAN LUIGI ANDERSON
the Auteur
Book One: Presidents Day

LETTER 44
01

THE SIXTH GUN
CULLEN BUNN
BRIAN HURTT
BOOK 1: COLD DEAD FINGERS

HELHEIM
BOOK 1: THE WITCH WAR

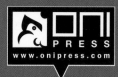

ONI PRESS
www.onipress.com

For more information on these and other fine Oni Press comic books and graphic novels visit onipress.com.
To find a comic specialty store in your area visit comicshops.us.